REDESIGNING Small-Group READING INSTRUCTION

STRUCTURED LITERACY PRACTICES FOR **DIFFERENTIATION**, **ACCELERATION**, AND **INTERVENTION**

JULIE A. TAYLOR

Solution Tree | Press

a division of
Solution Tree

555 North Morton Street
Bloomington, IN 47404
800.733.6786 (toll free) / 812.336.7700
FAX: 812.336.7790

email: info@SolutionTree.com
SolutionTree.com

Visit **go.SolutionTree.com/literacy** to download the free reproducibles in this book.

Printed in the United States of America

FSC
www.fsc.org
MIX
Paper | Supporting
responsible forestry
FSC® C008955

Library of Congress Cataloging-in-Publication Data
Names: Taylor, Julie A. (Educational consultant), author.
Title: Redesigning small-group reading instruction : structured literacy
    practices for differentiation, acceleration, and intervention / Julie A.
    Taylor.
Description: Bloomington, IN : Solution Tree Press, 2025. | Includes
    bibliographical references and index.
Identifiers: LCCN 2024041328 (print) | LCCN 2024041329 (ebook) | ISBN
    9781962188043 (paperback) | ISBN 9781962188050 (ebook)
Subjects: LCSH: Reading (Elementary) | Group reading. | Group work in
    education.
Classification: LCC LB1573 .T3484 2025 (print) | LCC LB1573 (ebook) | DDC
    372.4--dc23/eng/20241008
LC record available at https://lccn.loc.gov/2024041328
LC ebook record available at https://lccn.loc.gov/2024041329

Solution Tree
Jeffrey C. Jones, CEO
Edmund M. Ackerman, President

Solution Tree Press
President and Publisher: Douglas M. Rife
Associate Publishers: Todd Brakke and Kendra Slayton
Editorial Director: Laurel Hecker
Art Director: Rian Anderson
Copy Chief: Jessi Finn
Senior Production Editor: Suzanne Kraszewski
Copy Editor: Anne Marie Watkins
Proofreader: Elijah Oates
Text and Cover Designer: Rian Anderson
Acquisitions Editors: Carol Collins and Hilary Goff
Content Development Specialist: Amy Rubenstein
Associate Editors: Sarah Ludwig and Elijah Oates
Editorial Assistant: Madison Chartier

Acknowledgments

I would like to express my sincere gratitude to Douglas Rife, Todd Brakke, Kendra Slayton, Rian Anderson, and the entire Solution Tree Press team for their mentorship, support, and encouragement while writing this book. They truly are a family; I couldn't have asked to work with a better publishing company. This book wouldn't have been possible if associate editor Elijah Oates hadn't responded to my book proposal email, and for that, I am forever indebted. I am also grateful for Suzanne Kraszewski, my senior production editor. Her behind-the-scenes work was invaluable and very much appreciated. I owe special thanks to Amy Rubenstein, my content development specialist, for her guidance, honesty, and clear direction while navigating the writing process. Over the course of writing this book, she became not only an adviser and coach but someone who I now consider a dear friend.

Writing a book of this magnitude doesn't come without the support of loyal friends and colleagues and many years of experience working in the education field. I wouldn't have been successful without Ruth Harrison's guidance during my first few years of teaching. She's no longer with us, but her impact on my career in education was immeasurable. Few friends in this world are as precious to me as Connie Kepko. I spent my fondest teaching years being classroom neighbors with Connie at Holley-Navarre Intermediate School, and she remains one of my biggest cheerleaders to this day. Tammy Seals has not only been a colleague but also a mentor—she has given me invaluable insights and direction over the years we've worked together. I treasure her friendship; she's a true source of inspiration for me. Finally, I am ever appreciative of J. R. for allowing me to ride her coattails for the last decade—refining and improving the craft of powerful, efficient, and effective small-group instruction—while serving as my role model, mentor, and friend.

I'm especially grateful for the teachers and coaches I've worked with in Preston County, West Virginia, while writing this book, especially Amber Sponaugle, Caitlin Newton, Sophia Tichnor, Michelle Liga, and Amanda Rhodes. They've served as my sounding boards and listening ears, contributing ideas and perspectives that helped to enhance and enrich this book.

I wouldn't have been able to complete this book without the unwavering support of my husband and best friend, Scott. He and our five children, their spouses, and our grandchildren bring so much joy, love, and fulfillment into my life, and I'm so blessed to have every one of them.

In my heart, I still am—and always will be—a classroom teacher. I give my heartfelt thanks to the hundreds of teachers I've had the pleasure of working with over the past thirty years; this book is for each and every one of them.

Solution Tree Press would like to thank the following reviewers:

Becca Bouchard
Educator
Calgary, Alberta, Canada

Colleen Fleming
Literacy Specialist
Calgary Academy
Calgary, Alberta, Canada

Christie Shealy
Director of Testing and Accountability
Anderson School District One
Williamston, South Carolina

Rea Smith
Math Facilitator
Fairview Elementary
Rogers, Arkansas

Rachel Swearengin
Fifth-Grade Teacher
Manchester Park Elementary
Lenexa, Kansas

Kory Taylor
Reading Interventionist
Arkansas Virtual Academy
Little Rock, Arkansas

Jacqueline Yu
Doctoral Student; Student Services Coordinator
University of Calgary, The Centre for
Learning@HOME, Christ the Redeemer
Catholic Schools
Okotoks, Alberta, Canada

Visit **go.SolutionTree.com/literacy**
to download the free reproducibles in this book.

Table of Contents

Reproducible titles are in italics.

CHAPTER 4

Well on Their Way: The Full Alphabetic Phase

CHAPTER 5

Turning the Corner: The Consolidated Alphabetic Phase

CHAPTER 6

Reaching the Pinnacle: The Automatic Reading Phase

Conclusion

Glossary

APPENDIX A

Teacher Resources for the Pre-Alphabetic Phase

About the Author

Julie A. Taylor, PhD, is an education and curriculum consultant who provides professional development, training, and coaching to educators, administrators, and leaders in nonprofit organizations and state education agencies across the United States and worldwide. Dr. Taylor has been an educator since 1994, with a background as an elementary education teacher, a teacher of English learners, a special education inclusion teacher, a Spanish teacher, a reading interventionist, a literacy coach, and a staff developer. She has also served as a mentor teacher, a student teaching supervisor, and an instructor for teachers seeking their state reading endorsement.

Dr. Taylor is a member of the International Literacy Association and the International Dyslexia Association and has presented at numerous reading conferences across the United States since 2014. She is trained in LETRS (Language Essentials for Teachers of Reading and Spelling) and the Orton-Gillingham approach and is highly experienced in teaching practices that align with the science of reading. During her years as an education consultant, Dr. Taylor has written literacy curricula, reading intervention materials, and response to intervention manuals, and she has expert knowledge and experience in implementing literacy standards into everyday teaching practices.

Dr. Taylor specializes in transforming research into practical and effective instructional methods for teachers. She strives to implement systematic and supportive literacy frameworks in schools, a scaling-up model for large districts, and a train-the-trainer model for district literacy leaders—all while aligning with the most up-to-date reading research and evidence-based literacy programs.

Dr. Taylor earned bachelor's degrees in elementary education and Spanish from Keene State College, a master's degree in teaching English to speakers of other languages from Rhode Island College, and a doctoral degree in education with a specialization in curriculum and instructional leadership from Concordia University Chicago.

To learn more about Julie Taylor and to access numerous small-group literacy resources, visit redesigningreading.com.

To book Julie Taylor for professional development, contact pd@SolutionTree.com.

Introduction

Educational equity is not achieved when all children are treated "equally" by receiving the same instruction, the same resources, and the same allocation of time. Instead we support equity and best ensure student success when each learner receives the instruction they need when they need it.

—Linda Diamond

Of all the instruction that elementary educators have down pat, we certainly know how to teach students to read—don't we? The truth is, many reading teachers, according to *Education Week*'s Elizabeth Heubeck (2023), have "described being handed a mashup of literacy curriculums over the years. . . that left them feeling insecure about their instructional ability and uncomfortable about students who left their classrooms without a strong reading foundation." Perhaps you, too, have second-guessed your efficacy in this way, overwhelmed by a "landscape of literacy instruction" that feels just a bit messy (Heubeck, 2023).

Indeed, transforming reading research into instruction that meets the needs of *all* young learners has turned the teaching of reading into a job that can be quite challenging, let alone confusing. You may be unsure about what constitutes effective reading instruction or what it means to follow an instructional approach that aligns with the research-based *science of reading* (Heubeck, 2023). Moreover, when crunched for time, you may find yourself shifting toward mainly whole-group reading instruction. Yet, as researchers Wesley A. Hoover and William E. Tunmer (2020) note, solely using a whole-group approach to teaching beginning reading is neither efficient nor effective for many young learners.

According to data from educators M. Jufrianto and colleagues (2023), differentiated instruction produces superior outcomes in reading proficiency when compared to traditional whole-group instruction. And with student populations becoming increasingly diverse, as educator Sarah K. Clark (2020) confirms, it's crucial that teachers feel confident in their ability to differentiate their reading instruction. Researchers such as M. Meriyati and colleagues (2023) find that the more teachers optimize a differentiated framework for instruction, the more they develop students' potential.

This is the equity that educator Stavroula Valiandes (2015) captures in her work on differentiated instruction and literacy: *equity* in education is "the opportunity that all groups of students have in a mixed ability classroom to fulfill the curriculum's goals. . . according to their personal abilities and competences, ensuring thus equal access to knowledge for all" (p. 18). In this book, you'll find the resources you'll need to bring this type of classroom to life and set up all your students for continued success.

Whether you teach kindergarten or fifth-grade students; beginning, proficient, or advanced readers; English learners; students with unique education needs or individualized education programs; or students who require reading intervention through middle school—this book is for you. This book will help you design appropriate small-group reading lessons that accommodate your students' diverse needs; plan appropriate instruction in the five main skills of reading; scaffold learning so students master reading skills in a developmental progression; and feel confident about teaching small groups in a manner grounded in the soundest, most up-to-date reading research.

Before we dive into chapter 1, let's take a brief look at the science of reading, which gives us our baseline for understanding how people learn to read and thus, crucially, informs how to provide effective reading instruction. Then, we'll explore why students need small-group instruction in particular. Finally, we'll review the book's organization, which is structured around the five phases of reading development.

The Science of Reading

The term *science of reading* refers to a multidisciplinary body of research that helps us understand how the reading process occurs in the brain and what skills contribute to proficient reading. This understanding informs which methods and instructional techniques to use to ensure positive reading outcomes. Failure to use teaching methods that align with this research can have a negative impact on students' reading achievement. By grounding reading instruction in the science of reading, we ensure that we're activating all the areas of the brain that are involved in the reading process.

The *simple view of reading* refers to a depiction of the reading process that aligns with this body of scientific reading research (Hoover & Gough, 1990). According to the simple view of reading, reading comprehension is the product of decoding and language comprehension abilities, illustrated by the equation $D \times LC = RC$. That is, a student must be able to decode the words (D) and understand the language used in the text (LC) to produce reading comprehension (RC). The order of these processes is key. This research shows that the most effective and efficient way to build reading comprehension is to first explicitly and systematically teach students decoding skills, then teach them to determine what the words mean (language comprehension) within the context of what they're reading. This process leads to reading comprehension.

In 2001, psychologist and literacy expert Hollis S. Scarborough expanded on the simple view of reading and designed the reading rope to depict the discrete skills that make up each component of the simple view of reading. Scarborough's rope graphic shows how the distinct skills of language comprehension and word recognition—when implemented strategically and automatically—combine to create skilled reading. (Visit www.azed.gov/scienceofreading/scarbreadingrope to view the rope graphic.)

Decoding—or word recognition—requires that readers develop the alphabetic principle, phonological awareness, and the recognition of family words. Language comprehension—or the ability to understand the words in a text—requires that students have adequate background knowledge and vocabulary skills, are proficient with language structures and verbal reasoning, and have acquired literacy knowledge. Scarborough's reading rope, composed of concepts and skills we'll discuss in depth throughout the book, has shown educators that the process of becoming a proficient reader is an intricate one that requires us to deeply understand how to foster the development of these skills in a manner supported by reading research.

This teaching methodology is referred to as *structured literacy*, a term developed by the International Dyslexia Association that, according to researcher Louise Spear-Swerling (2019), describes an approach to teaching reading that's intentional, systematic, cumulative, and explicit. Structured literacy practices are distinguished from discovery-based instructional approaches, where the belief is that students learn to read naturally—similar to how people learn to talk.

Scientific research shows, however, that we don't learn to read in the same way that we learn to talk. A report from the Institute of Education Sciences (IES, 2016) confirms that direct, explicit, systematic, teacher-led instruction in the five main reading skills—(1) phonemic awareness, (2) phonics, (3) fluency, (4) vocabulary, and (5) comprehension—is the most beneficial method for most students (much more on these skills in chapter 1). In a discovery-based instructional reading model, phonemic awareness, phonics, fluency, vocabulary, and comprehension are considered to occur incidentally—they aren't necessarily planned and taught directly, intentionally, or systematically.

It's clear that teaching reading incidentally isn't enough to empower our youngest learners. The number of students who aren't able to read at a basic level by fourth grade exceeds 40 percent for students of color, those with learning difficulties, and those who are economically disadvantaged, and this statistic can largely be attributed to unequal access to highly effective reading instruction (National Council on Teacher Quality, 2024). In fact, most U.S. states have now passed legislation that requires educators to implement teaching practices that reflect science of reading-supported instruction (Council of Chief State School Officers, 2024a, 2024b). When education policies focus on ensuring a quality teacher workforce that's trained and supported to carry out instructional practices grounded in the science of reading, teachers are equipped to ameliorate these education inequities. The latest state education policies focus on preparing teachers in this effort and providing them with the resources to do so. Accordingly, all the instructional practices contained in this book are based on findings from the science of reading research, and this book will align with and fit seamlessly into curriculum for grades K–8.

The Benefits of Small-Group Instruction

There is a wealth of benefits to small-group instruction—and, as researchers Janice F. Almasi and Dongyang Yuan (2023) confirm, if you've shifted to more whole-group instruction, you may have overlooked some of those benefits. Your small-group reading instruction may have been a concrete, hour-long daily rotation, full of reading games and activities that you spent hours preparing. This process was probably extremely time-consuming, and perhaps ineffective. It may have left a lot of your students with very little instructional time and too much downtime—which didn't necessarily produce many reading gains. As a result, you may have reverted back to teaching mostly whole-group instruction throughout the school day. Yet, something about that format doesn't seem appropriate for meeting the needs of all your students.

According to researchers Elma M. Dijkstra, Amber Walraven, Ton Mooij, and Paul A. Kirschner (2016), when teachers emphasize whole-group instruction over a more individualized, differentiated approach, students' needs and abilities are misaligned, resulting in ineffective teaching techniques. Small-group differentiated reading lessons can create an equitable playing field for all your students. Effective small-group instruction is fluid, targeted, and flexible—where teachers meet all students' reading needs in a day of high-quality, evidence-based literacy instruction. After all, in a classroom of diverse learners, how can a one-size-fits-all approach to reading work for all students?

During small-group instructional time, you have the opportunity to listen to each student read and provide feedback that addresses their individual needs—whether that be phonemic awareness, phonics, fluency, vocabulary, or comprehension. Research shows that matching instruction to students' needs through small, differentiated reading groups produces greater reading growth over whole-group reading instruction—especially for students who experience difficulties with reading (Felts, 2019; Förster, Kawohl, & Souvignier, 2018; Jefferson, Grant, & Sander, 2017; Ruotsalainen, Pakarinen, Poikkeus, & Lerkkanen, 2022; Valiandes, 2015). If you don't meet with your students in small groups and aren't aware of their individual instructional needs, they could fall further behind or their reading progress could stagnate.

This continued research on differentiated and small-group instruction has resulted in enough data for a meta-analysis—one that makes a powerful case for the use of these instructional formats throughout the school day. Researchers Muh. Asriadi AM, Samsul Hadi, Edi Istiyono, and Heri Retnawati (2023) report that across sixty-three studies, implementing differentiated instruction positively affected achievement when compared to traditional whole-group learning. If you've abandoned small-group instruction, you must bring it back!

This guide will help you design small-group reading lessons that include the five main skills of reading in a structured, explicit, systematic, and evidence-based format. Using the resources herein, as well as the book's online resources, you'll have all the tools necessary to plan and teach each of your small-group lessons with targeted precision. Note that although you'll find general information in this book about managing small groups within a classroom, this book isn't about scheduling, classroom management, or whole-group instruction. You can visit the Reading Rockets website (www.readingrockets.org/classroom) for additional information about those topics pertaining to the literacy block specifically.

The Structure of This Book

This book is organized for educators who need to differentiate their reading instruction, teach advanced reading skills and strategies, or provide remedial reading lessons for students in any grade level. This book can help any reading teacher improve and elevate their students' literacy performance with its easy-to-follow scope and sequence and ability to meet students' needs, from beginning through advanced readers. Educators will also benefit from the systematic assessment and grouping recommendations for their students and the easy-to-use lesson plan templates. You'll find in chapter 1 the reading essentials— broadly, the content that will prime you for the book's main chapters and corresponding resources structured around the five phases of reading development: (1) pre-alphabetic, (2) partial alphabetic, (3) full alphabetic, (4) consolidated alphabetic, and (5) automatic. Chapter 1 first provides a general overview of the process of learning to read, its reciprocal relationship with writing, the means of transforming the five skills of reading into classroom instruction, and the steps for completing and teaching from the lesson plans. It presents the profiles of the five phases of reading development, how reading instruction can go wrong, and how to move forward with scientifically-based instructional practices for reading.

Chapters 2 through 6 each focus on a phase of reader based on Linnea C. Ehri's and Sandra McCormick's (1998) phase theory of reading development. Each of these chapters contains the following.

- Descriptions and characteristics of the given phase of reader and essential information about that phase

- Lesson plan templates you'll use to plan small-group instruction

- Step-by-step directions on how to complete the lesson plan templates

- Tools and resources to plan appropriate word-building activities that follow a systematic scope and sequence for teaching phonemic awareness, phonics, spelling, morphology, and vocabulary

- Samples of completed lesson plans and materials for your use

- QR codes that provide videos of teachers conducting lessons

At the end of the book, you'll find a glossary (page 195) that contains the reading terminology used throughout the text. The appendices, which each correspond to a chapter and reading development phase, contain student resources that you can use with your small groups. Finally, I note the online-only resources (exclusively available at **go.SolutionTree.com/literacy**) at different points in the book.

When educators face the challenge of ensuring equitable student learning, using a framework grounded in sound scientific research will help them provide students with high-quality instruction that targets individual strengths and areas for growth, thereby allowing them to make a major impact on student learning. This book will help classroom teachers do just that with all their students, who, throughout the process, will benefit from constructive feedback and strategies that promote active engagement. But other educators, too, will find value in this book, including administrators, curriculum specialists, instruction designers, literacy coaches, reading interventionists, and district leaders. Additionally, educators can use this book as an intervention tool within the response to intervention and multitiered system of supports frameworks through the eighth grade. Regardless of where learners are in their reading development, this book will support you in redesigning small-group instruction and equipping all students with the skills and confidence they'll need for long-term success in the classroom and beyond. Now, let's dive in!

CHAPTER 1

Reading Essentials

The whole world opened to me when I learned to read!

—Mary McLeod Bethune

Although the process of learning to read seems to come easier to some students than others, no one is actually born with the brain circuitry for reading. Research shows that the vast majority of people can learn how to read, but doing so involves adapting how we use existing brain regions to convert written words into language that our brains recognize (Goswami & Bryant, 2016; Socol, 2024; Valiandes, 2015). This can be a challenge for some students, while for others, it seems to occur naturally and seamlessly. But the way in which we teach students to read also plays a pivotal role in how well they learn to read. Accordingly, in the following pages, we'll take a much closer look at the five main skills of reading; the phase model of reading development; how to apply reading research to small-group instruction and fine-tune your reading instruction; and, critically, the nuts and bolts of planning and teaching the small-group lessons outlined in the subsequent phase chapters. Note that the latter section is one you'll return to throughout the book, as it provides the *general* instructions common among phases that will supplement the *unique* instructions and features you'll encounter within the phase chapters.

Targeting the Five Skills of Reading

As I mentioned in the book's introduction, becoming a skilled reader involves five main skills: (1) phonemic awareness, (2) phonics, (3) fluency, (4) vocabulary, and (5) comprehension. It's important to note that these skills aren't their own teaching topics. They also aren't separated by grade level; we don't teach phonemic awareness in kindergarten, phonics in first grade, fluency in second grade, vocabulary in third grade, and so on.

These skills do, however, fall into a hierarchy based on having the foundational skills necessary to ultimately achieve comprehension—the goal of reading instruction. We integrate most, if not all, of these skills across every phase of reading. But across different phases in students' reading development, we must adjust the *focus* and *intensity* of each skill that we teach. At every point in a students' reading development, the stronger they become in one skill area, each other area is then strengthened—so none of these skills can be ignored in reading instruction. As shown in figure 1.1, this cycle of strengthening these reading skills can continue endlessly as your students' reading proficiency advances.

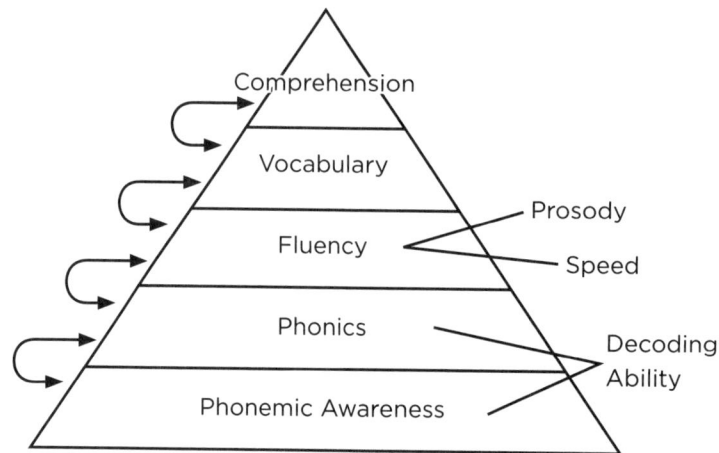

FIGURE 1.1: Hierarchy of reading skills.

Let's take a closer look at each of these five skills we'll be attending to in our small-group lessons, as well as how the concepts on the right-hand side of the figure—decoding ability, speed, and prosody—operate within this hierarchy.

Phonemic Awareness

Phonemic awareness is a skill that falls under the umbrella of phonological awareness. *Phonological awareness* is the ability to recognize and manipulate the larger spoken parts of words—such as syllables, onsets and rimes, and compound words—and words themselves in the context of sentences, such as rhyming and alliteration. *Phonemic awareness* is the ability to recognize the individual sounds, or *phonemes*, in spoken words—the smallest units of sound that fall under the umbrella of phonological awareness.

Phonemic awareness includes the ability to isolate, blend, segment, add, delete, and substitute phonemes. This ability to notice and think about the individual sounds in words becomes critical when we teach readers about the relationship between the sounds and letters (*graphemes*) in words. Phonemic awareness also involves understanding the position of sounds in words—for example, the initial sounds, final sounds, and medial sounds (the sound heard in the middle of a word). Developing these skills aids in the reading process because readers learn to analyze words at the individual phoneme level, which allows them to learn hundreds or thousands of new words that may differ by only one, two, or three phonemes. Figure 1.2 shows the relationship between phonological awareness skills and phonemic awareness skills.

Readers who have stronger phonological awareness skills tend to have better spelling and writing skills, as those skills have a strong reciprocal relationship with decoding and vocabulary skills. For this reason, psychologist David A. Kilpatrick (2015) explains, stronger readers are typically more highly skilled in overall phonological awareness, while students who have difficulty with reading tend to exhibit weaker phonological awareness skills. Reading intervention studies—where students are trained in advanced phonological awareness skills—have produced the best results. According to a meta-analysis by developmental psychologist Sebastian P. Suggate (2016), training in these skills closes learning gaps and catches readers up to their grade-level peers. Therefore, placing a strong emphasis on phonological awareness skills for beginning readers will minimize the probability of later reading difficulties and will maximize their potential for reading success.

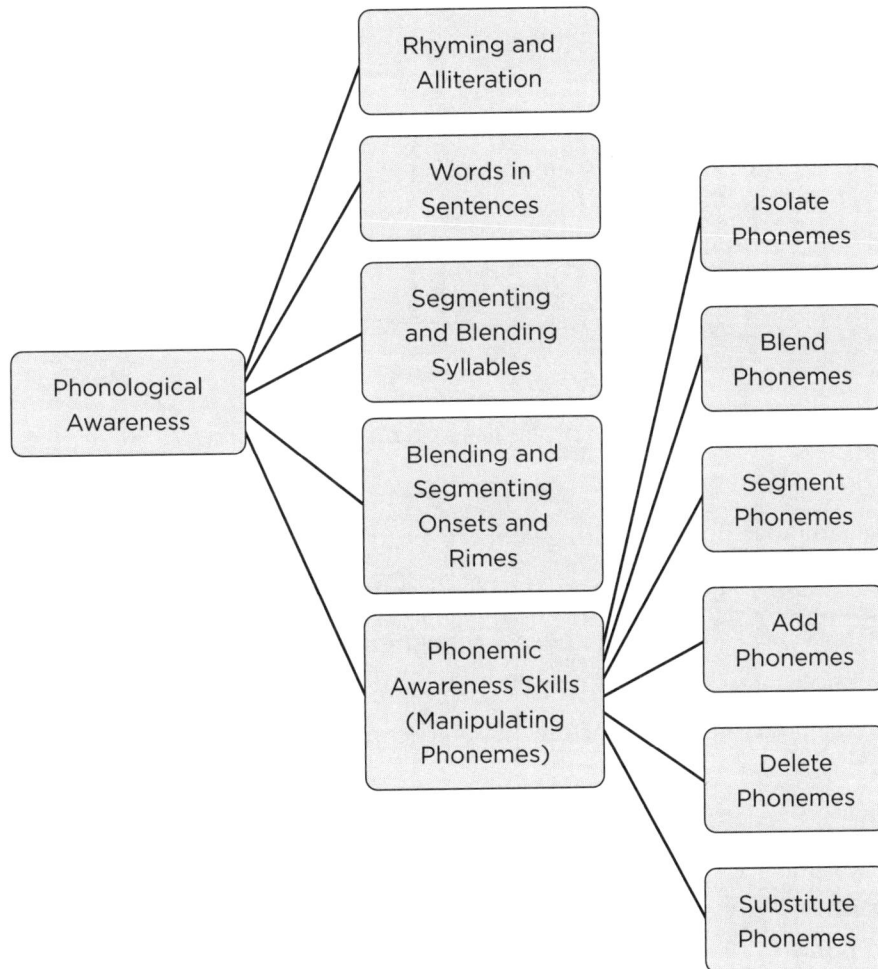

FIGURE 1.2: Phonological and phonemic awareness skills.

Building a strong prereading foundation of phonological awareness skills will strengthen not only students' decoding abilities but also their encoding—or writing and spelling—skills. *Encoding* involves writing the letters that represent sounds, which requires associating sounds with letters. This is the inverse and reciprocal relationship of *decoding*, which involves associating letters with sounds. Encoding is a more difficult skill to develop than decoding. Because of this, instruction for pre-alphabetic readers should strongly emphasize phonological awareness. This will establish the sound system for phonics instruction to build on.

Phonics

Having well-developed phonemic awareness skills creates a firm foundation for readers to then establish the phonics skills necessary to use when reading words. *Phonics* is the inverse of phonemic awareness: It's the skill that allows a reader to associate the letters in words to the sounds they represent. When combined, the skills of phonemic awareness and phonics can be referred to as *decoding ability*. The decoding process, or applying phonemic awareness and phonics skills, allows readers to turn printed words into spoken words. This involves using the two phonemic awareness skills of segmenting and blending sounds. When readers encounter an unknown word, they must do three things to decode it.

1. Identify and then segment each letter.
2. Identify the phoneme each letter represents (for example, the word *map* represents the phonemes /m/, /a/, and /p/).
3. Blend the phonemes together to read the word.

For most students to become successful with phonetic decoding skills, they need to practice this process regularly and consistently and in an instructional sequence that's explicit and systematic. The amount of practice students need can vary depending on their cognitive abilities, language and vocabulary skills, and prior knowledge. Some general guidelines for the teaching of phonics include the following.

- Short, frequent practice sessions
- Repetition to encounter particular phonics patterns multiple times
- Instruction tailored to students' level of proficiency
- Practice within reading and writing-connected text
- Multiple learning opportunities that involve listening, speaking, and writing
- Regular assessments to identify students' strengths and instructional needs

It's essential to be flexible and responsive to students' progress with phonics instruction, adjusting the degree, amount, and intensity of instruction and practice as needed.

Fluency

Fluency is a two-pronged skill set made up of (1) speed and (2) prosody. *Speed* is being able to accurately decode words at a sufficient pace to free up working memory in the brain to focus on the meaning of the words in print. *Working memory* is the brain's ability to use the current information it's concentrating on. The amount of information being used in working memory for one reading skill influences the brain's ability to focus on the skills that are higher up on the hierarchy. Fluency speed is the result of proficiency with phonemic awareness and phonics (decoding)—the skills at the base of the triangle.

Prosody refers to being able to read with expression and intonation. This fluency skill is connected to vocabulary and comprehension—the skills at the top of the triangle. The reader must understand the meaning of the printed words and how they're being used in the context of sentences to read them with expression and intonation. Having good prosody indicates proficiency with vocabulary and comprehension.

Even though reading comprehension is at the top of the triangle, fluency in terms of adequate speed and prosody is an early indicator of proficient comprehension. The inverse of this is also true: Slow or inadequate reading speed and a lack of prosody—or poor fluency—indicate difficulties with phonetic decoding. These challenges could be in phonemic awareness, phonics, or both skill areas.

Vocabulary

Vocabulary is a component of language comprehension, the skill that most impacts overall reading comprehension. It's composed of all the words that readers need to recognize and understand when reading—whether they're basic, complex, or content specific. Educator Marcos Benevides (2015) states that comprehension is ultimately knowing what 98 percent of the words in a text mean. Although there are additional language comprehension skills that also influence proficient reading comprehension, vocabulary skills encompass a large majority of what underpins strong reading comprehension.

A rich vocabulary is essential for understanding the meaning of texts. Readers with a strong vocabulary can comprehend the nuances and subtleties of written language more effectively, leading to improved understanding. Knowing a wide range of words aids in quickly recognizing and understanding words while reading. This contributes to fluent reading, allowing readers to focus on comprehension rather than struggling with decoding and determining the meaning of many words.

A robust vocabulary enables readers to make inferences and draw conclusions about the author's intent or the meaning of a text. It supports critical thinking by allowing readers to analyze and evaluate information. Vocabulary is not only a fundamental reading skill but also a key component of overall literacy. It plays a vital role in critical thinking, communication, and overall academic success.

Comprehension

Comprehension is not only the ability to understand what we've read but the ability to interpret it—a complex critical-thinking process that involves the following.

- **Literal comprehension:** The ability to identify basic, surface-level details such as *who, what, when,* and *where*

- **Inferential comprehension:** The ability to infer and explain *how* and *why*, as well as understand how elements and concepts within the text influence each other

- **Evaluative comprehension:** The ability to support opinions and existing knowledge with evidence from the text, as well as transfer and integrate new knowledge into new learning constructs

Comprehension is the end goal of reading, but it involves the application of well-developed sets of discrete skills that contribute to each of the other skills involved in reading. Before readers can proficiently comprehend written text, they must first be able to decode the words at an efficient speed, understand the tone and vocabulary of what they've read, and then connect to what they've read by interpreting, analyzing, and evaluating it.

Understanding the Phase Model of Reading Development

Linnea C. Ehri (1995) proposes phases of development in learning to read, commonly known as *Ehri's phases of reading model*. This model describes the characteristics and cognitive processes that students move through in phases as they learn to read. The phases are sequential and emphasize the importance of phonemic awareness, phonics, and the gradual development of orthographic mapping skills. The first four phases are the pre-alphabetic, partial alphabetic, full alphabetic, and consolidated alphabetic phases.

In 1998, Ehri and McKormick expanded on these phases to include the automatic phase, which they adapted from Jeanne S. Chall's (1983) stages of reading development. Students progress through the phases of reading development at different rates; therefore, this model provides a framework for understanding the development of reading skills and can be used to guide teachers in tailoring instruction to support students at each phase.

The most influential process involved in decoding and understanding words is orthographic mapping. *Orthographic mapping* is a mental process used for storing and remembering words that involves being able to easily decode words. This ability requires proficiency with the foundational skills of phonemic awareness and phonics, which are at the base of the triangle in figure 1.1 (page 8). Orthographic mapping occurs when neural connections between different areas of the brain are formed over and over when readers decode words in connected text.

As you might guess, orthographic mapping, then, isn't a skill or teaching activity you can simply *do* with students; it's a strategic process that develops when readers repeatedly employ the following three skills at once (Ehri, 2020).

1.   Keen phonemic awareness
2.   Automatic letter-sound correspondence
3.   Accurate and quick decoding of a word through segmenting and blending its letters and sounds

To complete the process of orthographically mapping a word, the reader must utilize parts of the brain that aren't naturally connected—the visual and language processing areas. The visual area of the brain stores the letters, or graphemes, that represent the sounds of letters. The oral language processing area of the brain determines the pronunciations and meanings of the decoded words. Once a word is decoded, pathways are formed from the visual to the language processing part of the brain, where the correct pronunciation and meaning of the word are confirmed. When this process has been completed over and over, the brain is able to store and remember a word.

Defining the Phases of Reading Development

As I mentioned, Ehri's and McCormick's (1998) model of reading development comprises five phases: (1) pre-alphabetic, (2) partial alphabetic, (3) full alphabetic, (4) consolidated alphabetic, and (5) automatic.

Pre-Alphabetic

In the first phase, pre-alphabetic readers are still learning their letters and sounds and need to develop the alphabetic principle. The *alphabetic principle* is the understanding that written words are based on sets of letters that represent individual sounds in spoken language. Establishing the alphabetic principle allows readers to match oral language they know with unfamiliar words on the page to translate print into meaning.

Pre-alphabetic readers aren't quite ready to decode words or sentences or to learn high-frequency or sight words—they're still building the foundational skills that underpin proficient phonetic decoding processes: phonemic awareness (the ability to recognize the individual sounds in spoken words) and phonics (the skill of associating the letters in words to the sounds they represent). These students must also develop beginning reading skills, such as the ability to blend and segment the sounds of oral language.

Partial Alphabetic

The second phase of learning to read is the partial alphabetic phase—the reading phase when students first begin to decode written words. Partial alphabetic readers have developed the alphabetic principle—they understand that the words we say can be written down using letters and we can then read those words back to ourselves by associating them with the sounds they represent. They segment and blend the letters and sounds in short words and discover that those phonemes—when combined—form a word that they can recognize as they hear themselves blend those sounds together.

Longitudinal studies confirm that early letter and sound knowledge is the strongest predictor in beginning reading success (Kjeldsen, Kärnä, Niemi, Olofsson, & Witting, 2014; Moll et al., 2014). The more efficiently students can associate letters to the sounds they represent, the more working memory becomes available in the brain, which enables readers to quickly and easily blend those sounds together, decode, and then pronounce a word. Efficient decoding leads to increased fluency and, later, vocabulary and comprehension development; therefore, teachers should introduce letter and sound associations to students as early as possible (IES, 2016). The partial alphabetic phase is a stepping stone. Readers in this phase begin to use letter-sound relationships to independently decode and read simple, unfamiliar words and sentences.

Full Alphabetic

When readers have reached the full alphabetic phase of reading development, they're able to make complete letter-to-sound connections and can decode simple, new words independently; in this phase, students appear to take off in their reading. Full alphabetic readers have internalized the ability to use the decoding strategy as the first course of action when reading new words. Due to their many opportunities to read simple words, students in this phase are now able to read short words automatically without having to segment and blend the letter sounds to read them each time. This is a signal that students' orthographic memory is being established. When students begin to map and retain the letter and sound (spelling) patterns in words, they're building an orthographic memory. This memory system enables them to decode more complex words containing short vowels, digraphs, consonant blends, and long vowels. Since readers have established a secure foundation of reading, the focus during the full alphabetic reading phase shifts to phonics and fluency, opening the gateway for acquiring higher-level vocabulary and comprehension skills.

Consolidated Alphabetic

Students transitioning to the consolidated alphabetic reading phase have built an integrated foundation to engage with texts for the purpose of better understanding the author's language and intended message. Teachers' earlier focus on decoding instruction must now give way to a focus on developing students' abilities to comprehend text—which begins with breaking down and processing the meanings of *all* the words students will read. That is, as much as we'd like to focus our instruction and attention on comprehension, we must first teach students to understand the *vocabulary* in the texts they'll be reading.

The consolidated alphabetic phase marks a turning point in students' reading development. They've built a strong foundation in phonemic awareness, phonics, and fluency to establish quick decoding skills and are turning the corner from "learning to read" to "reading to learn." When the basic reading skills of decoding and fluency have become smooth and accurate, this frees up working memory in the brain to focus on vocabulary and comprehension. Since decoding words requires less effort for consolidated alphabetic readers, they can use all their mental energy to read and understand longer, more complex text. This progression in reading development also marks a shift in a teacher's instructional focus from lower-level to higher-level skills on the hierarchy of reading skills (see figure 1.1, page 8).

When students transition from the full alphabetic to the consolidated alphabetic reading phase, they begin to read words in chunks and parts, but they don't completely master this word-solving strategy until the automatic reading phase. During the consolidated alphabetic phase, students automatically recognize words by their parts, as opposed to decoding words one letter and sound at a time. The word parts that students can quickly recognize consist of prefixes, base and root words, suffixes, morphemes, and syllables. Recognizing word parts allows students in the consolidated alphabetic phase to quickly and efficiently determine the meanings of new words. The process of chunking words to decode them and quickly determine their meanings prepares students to adequately comprehend the text.

Automatic

When students have developed sufficient automaticity with recognizing and correctly pronouncing most words they read without expending much mental energy on decoding, they've reached the automatic reading phase. In the automatic reading phase, students quickly and readily break words apart to read and pronounce them and are able to determine their meanings almost simultaneously, whereas in the earlier reading phases, this process is separate and involves students intentionally alternating their attention between decoding and comprehension. In this advanced phase of reading, no switching is necessary because students automatically deconstruct words and determine their meanings as they decode them (Ehri, 2005). Ehri (2020) refers to this reading ability as *unitization* because all of a word's identities (meaning, spelling, pronunciation) are immediately accessed and processed at once. Our brains recognize the spelling patterns within words, construct the pronunciation of the word, and determine its meaning. Because students' phonological and orthographic processing are so efficient, they're able to instantly know word parts and their pronunciations to automatically read words.

Ehri's phases of reading development are shown in figure 1.3.

Applying Reading Research to Small-Group Instruction

The development of early reading skills—phonemic awareness, phonics, and fluency—predicts early success in reading (Allington & McGill-Franzen, 2021; Caravolas et al., 2019; Foorman, Petscher, & Herrera, 2018; Foorman, Wu, Quinn, & Petscher, 2020; Kang & Shin, 2019; Kilpatrick, 2015; Poulsen, Protopapas, & Juul, 2023). We can ensure that all students receive high-quality reading instruction by designing instruction to equip students with the skills that will help them to become fully proficient readers.

Since students develop decoding skills at different rates—and because this impacts the reading skills at the top of the hierarchy—individualizing instruction based on decoding, fluency, and comprehension

Pre-Alphabetic	Partial Alphabetic	Full Alphabetic	Consolidated Alphabetic	Automatic
• Lacks knowledge of using letter names or sounds	• Knows most letters	• Has full letter-sound connections	• Recognizes letter patterns that occur in words (analogies to rimes, syllables, morphemes)	• Reads words quickly and effortlessly
• Does not use letter-sound connections to read words	• Begins to use blending skills	• Remembers how to read new words (blending becomes automatic)	• Retains words via morphemes (chunking) rather than by individual letter sounds	• Encounters most words as sight words
• "Reads" words by visual or context clues (logos, environmental print, their own name)	• Can use some letters and sounds to form connections between spelling and pronunciation	• Uses decoding as first strategy in reading unknown words	• Teaches themselves new connections and analogies to new words	• Decodes unfamiliar words with highly developed automaticity
• Uses visual features to remember words	• Uses letter-sound relationships to remember how to read and learn new words	• Integrates the highest levels of phonemic awareness with phonics	• Needs fewer connections to secure words in memory	• Expends little attention or effort in recognizing the pronunciations and meanings of new words
• May remember initial letters as cues	• Forms connections between some of the letters and sounds in words, often the first and final letter sounds	• Links spelling to pronunciation to enhance memory for words	• Facilitates automatic word reading with spelling patterns	• Processes larger units of words so internal patterns (prefixes, suffixes, roots) are retained in memory
• Exhibits poor phonemic awareness	• Lacks full knowledge of the alphabetic system, especially vowels	• Segments, blends, and substitutes phonemes	• Facilitates word reading speed with knowledge of letter patterns	• Connects phonological units to morphological units to activate semantic codes in memory (unitization)
• Attends to print-meaning correspondences, not print-sound	• Experiences much difficulty decoding unfamiliar words	• Secures words into memory with spelling, even irregularly spelled words	**Typical grade level:** Second grade	• Has a variety of word-solving strategies at their disposal
• Does not yet blend letter sounds	• Tends to leave out medial letters in writing using inventive spelling	• Retains complete spellings of words		**Typical grade level:** End of second grade and higher
• "Pretends" to read by using pictures	• Mixes up similarly spelled words due to weak letter-sound proficiency	• Learns new words rapidly		
• Memorizes familiar stories	**Typical grade level:** Kindergarten and early first grade	• Becomes proficient in word-level reading, increasing comprehension		
Typical grade level: Preschool and early kindergarten		**Typical grade level:** Late kindergarten through first grade and early second grade		

Source for phases: Ehri, 2020.

FIGURE 1.3: Ehri's phases of reading development.

can maximize potential for your students' overall reading success. Particularly for early reading instruction, research strongly supports implementing differentiated instruction "for promoting equity, optimization of quality[,] and effectiveness in teaching" (Valiandes, 2015, p. 17). Differentiating decoding, fluency, and comprehension instruction will provide all your students with opportunities to have their unique instructional needs met in a developmentally appropriate lesson format that follows an explicit and systematic progression.

To plan structured literacy lessons for students, it's crucial to translate the reading research into high-quality instruction. Well-designed research studies (IES, 2016) support the following practices for reading instruction.

- Directly teaching students the alphabetic principle (phonemic awareness and phonics)
- Developing students' efficient word-solving skills that lead to fluent reading (speed and prosody)
- Facilitating students' understanding of the language in text (vocabulary and comprehension)

As text difficulty increases, phonemic awareness, phonics, fluency, vocabulary, and comprehension skills develop together and reinforce one another in a cyclical manner. For many of us, teaching reading seems to be so difficult because these skills are moving targets—not only from year to year but from month to month, and even day to day. They're moving targets because, with each of these reading skills, there are distinct levels of difficulty.

This can make teaching reading seem very complex because each main reading skill—phonemic awareness, phonics, fluency, vocabulary, and comprehension—is taught at every grade level, and each has its own continuum of difficulty. Establishing the neural pathways in the brain to harness students' reading potential is influenced by how we teach students to read, so instructional approaches and teacher expertise play a pivotal role in helping all students become successful readers. Designing appropriate small-group instruction can be tricky—and can fail—if we don't focus on teaching the necessary skills that improve student reading outcomes in an evidence-based manner.

The correct amount and combination of activities that integrate each main reading skill are the essence of differentiating your reading instruction and designing high-quality small-group lessons. Research shows that instruction that's explicit, systematic, and consistent leads to the greatest student outcomes (Bulat et al., 2017; Burden & Byrd, 2019; Neitzel, Lake, Pellegrini, & Slavin, 2022; Stockard, Wood, Coughlin, & Rasplica Khoury, 2018; Treiman, 2018; Walpole & McKenna, 2017). This type of instruction is called *mastery learning* (Hunter, 1982). In this instructional approach, the teacher doesn't move on to teaching new skills until the students master the skills at hand. This ensures that teachers introduce foundational skills before they add in any complex concepts. It also prevents students from working on comprehension strategies with low-level text when they have weaknesses in decoding and fluency. When students need to improve decoding skills, teachers must address this need before fully turning their instructional focus to teaching vocabulary and comprehension.

Designing instruction based on the five skills while integrating reading and writing has been shown to produce the best outcomes for students (Conradi Smith, Amendum, & Williams, 2022; Diamond, n.d.; Hall & Burns, 2018; IES, 2016; Puzio, Colby, & Algeo-Nichols, 2020; Vaughn, Parsons, & Massey, 2020; Young, 2023). In this way, students are grouped primarily according to common reading skills. Skills-based grouping usually occurs according to decoding ability first, then fluency needs, and finally by vocabulary and comprehension capabilities. This grouping method requires assessing students in these specific areas and then determining which students need support with which reading skills, then grouping accordingly. When differentiated in this way, small-group instruction has consistently demonstrated positive effects (Conradi Smith et al., 2022).

The reading research also shows that, when compared to leveled, guided, or any other grouping arrangement of students, skills-based grouping is the most effective and equitable grouping format, increasing and advancing reading achievement for all students. Differentiation by other formats consigns students to simpler texts because the instruction doesn't focus on phonics or fluency—skill areas in which students need support to facilitate their growth (Conradi Smith et al., 2022). Teachers should group and teach students according to their phonics and fluency abilities before they turn their attention to teaching students vocabulary and comprehension. When Kristin Conradi Smith, Steven J. Amendum, and Tamara W. Williams (2022) examined twenty-six small-group research studies, they determined that instruction is more effective when teachers target lessons to a specific skill area. When grouping students using assessments that target specific skill areas—such as phonological knowledge, fluency, or vocabulary and comprehension—researchers find that the effectiveness of skills-based instruction nearly doubles in effect size. Again, this shows the importance of recognizing which skill areas of the hierarchy depicted in figure 1.1 (page 8) students need instruction in and grouping and designing instruction based on assessments targeted to those specific areas.

Fine-Tuning Your Reading Instruction

You may already use a format for small-group instruction, or maybe implementing a differentiated small-group format is a new instructional strategy for you. You may have pushed small-group instruction aside because you're not sure when and how to design lessons effectively so they align with a scientifically supported model. Small-group instruction could be the "crucial missing ingredient" in your literacy block, as educator Linda Diamond (n.d.) says is the case "in many core reading curricula" (p. 1). All too often, reading instruction occurs in a whole-group setting, which is markedly less effective and less equitable in developing reading skills (Diamond, n.d.).

How we form small groups, what assessments we use, and what skills we teach during small-group instruction can't be overlooked. According to Mark Seidenberg (2017), effective reading teachers must be adept at individualizing instruction based on careful and continuous formal and informal assessment of students. Successful reading teachers:

- Have an in-depth knowledge of the reading process and the research-based practices associated with the instruction and assessment process

- Possess in-depth understanding of their students' literacy needs

- Use valid, reliable, instructionally sound, and ongoing assessments to track how students are responding to instruction

If you haven't already made a shift to using small groups as part of your reading instruction, or if you're unsure how to group your students for small groups, the evidence from the reading research recommends that we differentiate instruction according to the reading skills that students need to master—namely, the five we've discussed here. Research consistently demonstrates that when we group students according to the targeted skills instruction they need, we see positive effects over all other formats for forming small groups (Gersten, Newman-Gonchar, Haymond, & Dimino, 2017; Neitzel, Pellegrini, & Slavin, 2022; Walpole & McKenna, 2017; Wanzek et al., 2017). When students are able to work in skills-based groups, where teachers attend to their individual needs and provide specific corrective feedback, their reading performance improves the most, so the instruction is effective and equitable.

When teachers emphasize all the processes that contribute to growth in reading, they'll have the best chance at making every student a successful reader (IES, 2016). Whether the goal is to provide high-quality intervention, prevent reading difficulties, or advance students' reading achievement, the reading instruction and learning process are the same. What differs is where you put the weight of your instruction—on the bottom half of the hierarchy (phonemic awareness, phonics, and fluency) or on the top half of the hierarchy (vocabulary and comprehension). In their meta-analysis of twenty-six studies on small-group instruction, Matthew S. Hall and Matthew K. Burns (2018) reveal that students who were grouped for early reading instruction according to skill need outperformed peers who were in traditional level-based reading groups. Students in skills-based groups also gained an average of two months of reading progress each following school year. The evidence is unequivocally clear that teachers should shift from instructing students in commonly leveled groups to forming skills-based groups where students receive scientifically-supported instruction. The following pages cover how to practically prepare for this shift: how to assess students for small-group instruction, group students and schedule small groups, choose appropriate texts for small groups, and determine activities for those students you aren't actively engaging with.

How to Assess Students for Small-Group Instruction

You can determine your students' strengths and areas of need with quick, readily available assessments that you may already have, or can obtain relatively easily. Use what you already have access to for curriculum-based assessments rather than over-testing students. It's important that you have assessment data for your students in the following areas.

- Decoding
- Fluency
- Vocabulary
- Comprehension

You can also use the assessments listed in table 1.1.

You don't need to administer each type of assessment listed in table 1.1 to every student. What assessments you use will depend on which areas of instruction your students need. Look to the skill area on the left of the chart to determine which assessments to administer. For students who need to work on phonemic awareness and phonics, administer the decoding assessment in appendices B, C, or D (pages 225, 241, or 259). For students in the full and consolidated alphabetic phases, you can administer a fluency assessment to determine if students need to continue to refine their decoding skills or if you can turn the focus of your instruction to teaching vocabulary and comprehension strategies. For students who need to advance their vocabulary and comprehension skills, administer the recommended assessments for those skills in table 1.1. If you're not sure which assessments to gather data from, refer back to figure 1.1 (page 8) to gauge where the focus of your instruction should be, taking into account fluency or decoding ability.

Fluency has long had the strongest correlation to reading achievement because it's a skill set that encompasses each reading skill represented in the hierarchy of reading skills. In terms of accuracy and speed, fluency is associated with phonemic awareness and phonics. In terms of prosody, fluency is associated with vocabulary and comprehension. As I conveyed earlier in the chapter, when students are fluent readers—or they're able to decode at an acceptable speed or rate—it frees up the working memory in the brain to focus on vocabulary and comprehension. When fluency is slow, it indicates that the decoding process is using most or all of the working memory in the brain. When this is the case, there will be little working memory left for learning vocabulary and sufficiently comprehending the text.

TABLE 1.1: Assessments for Forming Differentiated Reading Groups

Skill	Assessment Area	Possible Assessment
Decoding	Letter and sound knowledge	Letter-Sound Assessment (appendix A, page 197)
	Phonemic awareness and blending	Phonological Awareness Screening Test (https://thepasttest.com)
		Heggerty phonemic awareness assessments (https://tinyurl.com/2yh65nss)
	Decoding	Decoding assessments (appendices B, page 225, C, page 241, and D, page 259)
Fluency	Fluency speed	Grade-level screener (DIBELS) (https://tinyurl.com/mvz69az4)
		Fluency rating scale (table 5.13, page 145)
Vocabulary	Vocabulary knowledge	Vocabulary inventory (https://tinyurl.com/yj4yn8cx)
		Lexile measure
Comprehension	Background knowledge, inference, language comprehension skills	Retelling rubric (table 5.14, page 145)
		Lexile assessments
		Overall composite scores of comprehension

Working memory in the brain won't be freed up for learning vocabulary and comprehending text until the foundational skills of decoding have improved or are sufficient for individuals' grade-level expectancy. For this reason, fluency speed can indicate where you need to focus your small-group instruction. You can use fluency speed to gauge whether your students need more instruction in decoding and fluency or in vocabulary and comprehension. If a reader's decoding speed isn't at grade level, your instruction will focus on the lower areas of the triangle. If a reader's decoding speed is at the expected rate, your instructional focus will be at the top of the triangle.

To determine whether students' fluency is acceptable, have them read a grade-level-appropriate text and assess the number of words they read correctly in one minute (note that this assessment is appropriate only for students from the middle of first grade and higher, and only if they can decode words). If you already have access to these data, you can use those data to determine where the focus of your instruction should be. Otherwise, you can use a fluency norms chart.

Jan Hasbrouck and Gerald Tindal of the University of Oregon Behavioral Research and Teaching developed national grade-level fluency norms in 2006 and updated them in 2017 (Hasbrouck & Tindal, 2017). Table 1.2 shows sample rows of the norms chart for first grade, second grade, and third grade. The complete chart for first through sixth grades is available on the following websites.

- ERIC: https://eric.ed.gov/?id=ED605146

- Reading Rockets: www.readingrockets.org/article/fluency-norms-chart-2017-update

The benchmark for grade-level decoding speed is considered to be around the 50th percentile—the set of numbers located in the 50 row for each grade level in table 1.2. Pay particular attention to these figures for the 50th percentile. They're moving targets—they increase from the fall to the spring. This is because, as students continue to read more throughout the school year and from grade to grade, their decoding speed should also increase. If individuals are decoding far below the 50th percentile (below the 25th percentile), they're reading below the average number of words per minute read correctly for their grade level, and if they're decoding at or higher than the 50th percentile, they're reading more than the average number of words per minute read correctly for their grade level.

TABLE 1.2: Fluency Norms Chart Excerpt

Grade	Percentile	Fall WCPM*	Winter WCPM*	Spring WCPM*
1	90		97	116
	75		59	91
	50		29	60
	25		16	34
	10		9	18
2	90	111	131	148
	75	84	109	124
	50	50	84	100
	25	36	59	72
	10	23	35	43
3	90	134	161	166
	75	104	137	139
	50	83	97	112
	25	59	79	91
	10	40	62	63

*WCPM = Words Correct Per Minute

Source: Hasbrouck & Tindal, 2017.

If students aren't able to decode a grade-level text within the average range of words read correctly per minute, you should place the emphasis of your small-group instruction on the skills at the bottom of the hierarchy of reading skills (phonemic awareness, phonics, and fluency speed), while supporting students with vocabulary and comprehension instruction during those lessons.

If students are able to decode a grade-level text within the average range of number of words read correctly per minute, you can emphasize skills toward the top of the hierarchy—fluency prosody, vocabulary, and comprehension. Chapters 5 (page 117) and 6 (page 149) contain more detailed information about grouping students for vocabulary and comprehension instruction.

Note that it's not appropriate to administer a fluency assessment to students who read at a kindergarten to mid-first-grade level, since they're still establishing their decoding skills. For these beginning readers, your instruction should be based on the skills on the bottom portion of the hierarchy while supporting students in developing their vocabulary and comprehension skills. Table 1.3 is an easy reference for you when using fluency speed to determine where to focus your small-group instruction.

TABLE 1.3: Fluency Gauge

If. . .	Then. . .
Fluency speed is far below the 50th percentile (25th percentile or lower)	Focus instruction on decoding and fluency speed while supporting readers with vocabulary and comprehension.
Fluency speed is closer to the 50th percentile or higher	Focus instruction on fluency prosody, vocabulary, and comprehension using high-quality grade-level text.

How to Group Students and Schedule Small Groups

Your reading groups should be flexible enough that students move on or you regroup your students when they've mastered skills. Some students will progress more quickly than others, so you may need to move or regroup students sporadically. Hall and Burns (2018) recommend regrouping your students approximately every two weeks based on informal assessments, while other researchers recommend regrouping students every three to six weeks (Conradi Smith et al., 2022).

When forming small reading groups, also take into account your own anecdotal records, observational data, and notes based on students' social dynamics, classroom behaviors, and language and processing skills, as these factors all play a part in the impact of your small-group instruction. Take notes as your students read and use these informal and day-to-day formative assessment data to place or move students into the most appropriate groups.

You should plan to spend about twelve to fifteen minutes at a time with each of your small groups during your literacy block. You'll need to teach more lessons per week with groups of students who need more support to close larger learning gaps. Students who read at grade level or higher don't need as much direct instructional time in small groups, as they'll need time to analyze and synthesize text read independently or with one another. These students may be implementing a vocabulary or comprehension strategy, constructing a graphic organizer, or completing a writing piece, and will need less teacher support and more time working with complex text.

When and how often you meet with your small groups shouldn't disadvantage students by having them spend too much time unsupervised and working with simple text or not working with text at all. In addition, spending time teaching differentiated small groups shouldn't come at a detriment to other students working independently for the majority of the literacy block. The Reading Rockets website provides sample schedules that you can refer to when designing your reading block (Reading Rockets, n.d.).

The research evidence on formats for small-group instruction suggests allowing up to one hour per day for delivering differentiated reading instruction. You want to make sure that you afford your students in small groups enough time to read and receive corrective feedback. Then, for students working on vocabulary and comprehension strategies, you want to be sure to allot enough time for you to utilize the gradual release model (which we'll explore in chapter 6, page 149) so they can complete work with rich, complex text independently as you adjust and decrease your instructional support as needed.

How to Choose Texts for Small-Group Instruction

There are several types of texts that have been used to differentiate reading instruction in small groups, as shown in table 1.4.

TABLE 1.4: Types of Texts for Small-Group Instruction

Text Type	Purpose or Need
Decodable text	This is text that's used for students to practice phonics skills with controlled text. Between 90 percent and 95 percent of words in this text type are decodable, as they pertain to the phonics skill or pattern being taught (short vowels, digraphs, blends, and so on).
Vocabulary reader	This is text that contains controlled (specific) language and vocabulary constructs, along with decodable words that are appropriate for a particular grade level. Between 80 percent and 90 percent of words in this text type are decodable.
Leveled text / guided reading text	This is text that's determined to be a certain level by its word count, sentence length, and complexity. This type of text may or may not be controlled for specific vocabulary and phonics skills. Typically, between 60 percent and 70 percent of words in this text type are decodable.
Children's literature	This is text that's written to entertain, inform, or evoke a response from the reader. This type of text is typically used in read alouds and shared reading activities to build vocabulary and background knowledge, fluency and prosody, and higher-level comprehension skills, like making inferences.
Informational text	This is text that's usually based on a content-area topic or subject. This type of text usually contains vocabulary to develop background knowledge, and its decodability will vary.

Of course, you'll want to choose the type of text that best suits your students' needs and your instructional focus. But keep in mind that each type of text serves a different purpose, and it's advantageous to expose students of all reading phases to a variety text types (Gilakjani & Sabouri, 2016; Hedgcock & Ferris, 2018). In a report for The University of Newcastle, Australia, educators Rachel Birch, Heather Sharp, Drew Miller, Denyse Ritchie, and Susan Ledger (2022) explain that quality texts need to include multiple features and components to accommodate the complexity of the reading process, and the exclusive use of one type of text has a detrimental effect on reading development. Carefully select a variety of text types that will lead to a positive instructional outcome and attitude toward reading. For students working on fluency prosody, vocabulary, and comprehension, choose quality grade-level texts or higher. For students working on decoding and fluency speed, choose decodable text or vocabulary readers, with the goal of moving students into higher-quality grade-level text as soon as their decoding skills improve.

How to Determine Activities for Students Outside of Small-Group Instruction

There are few research findings on what types of activities yield the highest gains for young learners when they work independently. The general research consensus, though, according to literacy expert Timothy Shanahan (2020), is that activities should be authentic, engaging, and connected to other areas of learning. Students don't necessarily need to work in prearranged groups while you work with small groups of students. They may work independently at their seats or complete work in other configurations around the classroom—in pairs, alone, or in other small groups.

You don't need to group students in certain numbers and have their groups rotate through a concrete progression of work centers. You may have one group of two students and another group of six students. Ideally, what the other students are doing should align with skills, strategies, topics, and themes that you're teaching the whole group for reading, writing, vocabulary, comprehension, and word work, and can connect to the content areas. Even when students aren't with you, be sure that they're spending the maximum amount of time with their eyes on text—whether that be reading or writing about texts—as volume of reading predicts later reading achievement (Allington & McGill-Franzen, 2021). Advanced students can do the following tasks while not with the teacher.

- Read independently with accountability (see graphic organizers in chapter 6, page 149), read with a partner for fluency practice, or work in reciprocal teaching groups (see chapter 6)

- Write targeted responses to text read as a whole group

- Hunt for words (in the texts they're reading independently) that match a particular word study or vocabulary pattern

- Use words from the index, glossary, or table of contents to summarize facts about what they read and learned

- Practice and perform reader's theater

Meanwhile, beginning readers can:

- Practice "reading" text (for pre-alphabetic readers, pretending to read is a common best practice)

- Read independently or with a partner and then use Conversation Starter Comprehension Cards (appendices B and C, pages 221 and 247)

- Reread poems, songs, and nursery rhymes with a partner

- Work with a partner to sequence and retell stories

- Write or draw in response to text in a journal, a letter to another student, and so on (even if formal writing instruction hasn't taken place)

- Use stick puppets to retell well-known stories, poems, or nursery rhymes

- Practice phonemic awareness and phonics activities

- Trace and practice saying letters in an alphabet book

- Listen to stories being read aloud on technology

- Practice handwriting

- Practice various ABC activities—sorting letters, naming letters, putting letters in ABC order, stamping letters

- Sort and categorize picture cards

- Practice and perform developmentally appropriate reader's theater

Planning and Teaching Your Small-Group Lessons

As I noted in the introduction, each of the following chapters contains lesson plans to use with your small groups. Many of the activities in the lesson plans are similar to those in other chapters, but they increase in difficulty as students progress through the phases of reading development. What follows are instructions for how to plan and teach those repeating activities. You may want to keep these instructions nearby so you can easily refer to them.

Every reading phase contains several weeks or months of instruction, and your instruction will consist of a series of lessons. Every day that you meet with a particular group, you'll teach all the components of one lesson. Each lesson is designed to be completed in twelve to fifteen minutes, so you should be able to teach an entire lesson each time you meet with a group. How often you teach your lessons will depend on how often you see a particular group of students.

You'll cycle through each lesson on the plan (for example, teach lesson 1, then lesson 2, then lesson 3) and then start the cycle again (lesson 1, lesson 2, lesson 3). Teach one lesson each time you see a group, regardless of the day of the week. You might be on a lesson 1 on a Monday with one group and on a lesson 3 with another group. However, you don't necessarily have to teach a lesson with every group each day. Your students move to the next reading phase when they've mastered the skills within their current reading phase. In the sections that follow, you'll learn how to teach the lesson plan components that are common to multiple phases.

Letter Sounds

Throughout each of the lesson plans and reading phases, you'll need to pay particular attention to pronouncing sounds correctly when you teach them. It's imperative that when you teach students letter sounds, you enunciate (or pronounce them) correctly. Accurate pronunciation of letter sounds aids in students' development of phonemic awareness abilities—the blending and segmenting skills necessary for successful word reading. Before you begin instruction, practice the correct enunciation of each spoken phoneme (for example, /p/, not "puh") to ensure that you model correct pronunciation for students. Visit **go.SolutionTree.com/literacy** for a table of the forty-four English phonemes and the letters they represent.

Follow these three steps when teaching letter sounds.

1. Introduce the sound and the letter or letters it represents. Show students the letters on a small whiteboard or with magnetic letters or letter tiles.

2. Have students repeat the sound after you.

3. Be sure that students articulate the sound properly before you begin any of the activities on the lesson plans.

    a. Have students form their mouths, teeth, lips, and tongues in the correct manner to produce each sound.

    b. Use small mirrors, if necessary, so students can see how they are articulating the sound. You can also have them pay attention to your mouth movements and positions as you articulate each sound.

    c. Refer to sound wall cards with mouth positions that depict how the mouth, teeth, lips, and tongue form to produce each sound.

Phonics Rules

Phonics rules provide a foundational understanding of how letters represent sounds in words. This is essential for decoding words, helping early readers spell words, and figuring out the sounds and spellings for unknown words. Yet, spending too much time teaching rules rather than applying phonics skills in authentic reading opportunities can be detrimental to students. Many times, teachers substitute authentic reading practice for having students reiterate phonics rules, complete phonics activities that provide little to no decoding practice, require students to code words depending on their letters and sounds, or spend an exorbitant amount of time in direct phonics instruction each day, where the teacher is doing the majority of work. That instructional time for phonics, along with learning and applying common phonics rules, should include a wealth of reading practice for students.

Teaching phonics rules is beneficial for students because they learn about the predictable letter and sound properties of language. Yet, it isn't possible to teach all the rules of English necessary to become skilled readers. Proficient readers seem to implicitly acquire phonics knowledge through practice reading. Thus, research supports findings that some amount of decoding knowledge is learned implicitly (Arciuli, 2018), a process referred to as statistical learning. *Statistical learning* is the ability for students to learn about how words are decoded through a wealth of reading practice. Oral language skills, vocabulary knowledge, and decoding ability all contribute to statistical learning in reading (Arciuli, 2017; Kidd, 2012; Kidd & Arciuli, 2016; Spencer, Kaschak, Jones, & Lonigan, 2015). Therefore, it's critical that in addition to providing students with an understanding of basic and regular phonics rules, you afford students the opportunity to practice reading and discussing texts and building their background knowledge.

Word Building

During each word-building activity, students will learn how to read, spell, and write words that contain phonics patterns that follow a typically taught progression. For these activities, students will manipulate phonemes by making word chains, writing words in sound boxes, and substituting letters

in them to make new words that they'll read and write. Connecting reading and writing through phoneme manipulation when reading, building, and spelling words will promote the orthographic mapping
process and increase and strengthen students' orthographic memory.

Depending on the reading phase, students will need the word mats from appendices B, C, D, or E
(page 220, 232, 252, or 276), magnetic letters or tiles, and dry-erase markers to complete the word-building activities. There are several possible word lists for these word-building activities depending on what
phonics patterns students can read on the assessments you currently use or on the decoding assessments
for the full, consolidated, and automatic reading phases in the appendices.

Students will progress through the word-building activities gradually while mastering segmenting
and blending the phonemes of increasingly more difficult words. Phonics patterns in the word lists are
cumulative—as students master spelling patterns, the next set of spelling patterns will contain previous
spelling patterns so the words become more difficult as students progress through each word list. The
phonics patterns are also age and grade appropriate and correlate to common state literacy standards.
When students can quickly and easily write the words that you've dictated for a phonics pattern, you'll
move on to the next column of words or set of word lists.

The word-building component always consists of two tasks.

1. **Decoding:** For the first task, students will spell words and then read them. This will
   facilitate the decoding process of blending and segmenting letters and sounds.

2. **Encoding:** For the second task, students will substitute letters for sounds to spell new
   words. Manipulating phonemes in this way will promote the encoding—or spelling and
   writing—process of connecting sounds to letters.

Completing these two tasks reinforces the reciprocal relationship between letters and sounds and reading and spelling words.

For the first task, students will blend sounds to decode words. Table 1.5 contains the verbal directions
for completing this activity using the letters *i*, *t*, and *n* as an example.

TABLE 1.5: Verbal Directions for the Decoding Task

Step	Verbal Directions
1	*Take the letters* i, t, *and* n, *and line them up at the top of your word mat.*
2	*Pull down the* i *and the* n. *Or use sound boxes as a scaffold: Using the two sound boxes, place the* i *in the first sound box and the* n *in the second sound box.*
3	*Slide your finger under each letter and say the sounds.*
4	*Now slide your finger under each letter again and begin to blend the letter sounds together.* Students may need to repeat this step several times until they arrive at the pronunciation of the word *in*.
5	*What word did you make*? Students should respond with "in."
6	*Change the* n *to a* t. Repeat steps 3, 4, and 5.
7	Continue practicing with the next set of letters in the word list.

For the second task, students will associate sounds with letters to spell words. Table 1.6 contains the
verbal directions for completing this task using the same letters as in the preceding example. You can

work your way backward in the series of words that the students used during the first task or begin with the same first word you used for the first word-building task.

The goal of the word-building activities is for students to be able to decode (read) and encode (spell and write) each phonics pattern following the systematic progression I provided. Continue dictating the words for students to write independently on the dotted lines until they can correctly spell the words on the list for that phonics pattern. Once they can write the words correctly, they've mastered that pattern, and you can proceed to the next word list or phonics pattern. You can also use the lines on the word mats as an informal assessment before moving on to teaching the next word list.

TABLE 1.6: Verbal Directions for the Encoding Task

Step	Verbal Directions
1	*Line up your letters* i, t, *and* n *back at the top of your word mat.*
2	*Pull down the letters and make the word* in. Or use sound boxes as a scaffold: *Use two sound boxes and make the word* in.
3	*Slide your finger under each letter and say the sounds to make sure they match the letters you used to represent them.*
4	*Change a letter to make the word* it. Repeat step 3.
5	Continue practicing with the next set of letters in the word list.

As I suggested in the verbal directions, when progressing through the word lists, you may need to provide scaffolding for students to increase their ability to correctly write words with the patterns you dictate. The amount of support and scaffolding that you provide should decrease as students progress through the word-building activities in each reading phase. During the word-building activities, use the scaffolds from figure 1.4 (page 28) when necessary, keeping in mind that the goal for mastery of the word-building activities is for students to be able to correctly write the words independently or with little support and scaffolding (after the partial alphabetic phase).

On each planning template that contains word building, begin by listing the scaffold you'll use, if any. Start with magnetic letters or tiles in sound boxes and then adjust your instruction to provide more support (tap, snap, clap, or count phonemes on your hands) or less support (write phonemes or syllables in sound boxes). If students are missing letter sounds when completing the word-building activities, use a scaffold that provides more support higher up on figure 1.4. If students are proficient with applying their knowledge of letters and sounds using the scaffold you provide, decrease the amount of support by using a scaffold farther down on figure 1.4. More advanced students may not need any scaffolding, while other groups of students will need additional support using the scaffolds.

Once students are able to hear all the sounds in the words and build the words in sound boxes, have them build the words on the line under the sound boxes. When students are able to do this and include all the letter sounds, have them write the words in the sound boxes as you dictate each word. If they can write each letter of the words in the sound boxes, simply dictate the words and have students write them directly on the lines on the bottom of the word mat. These scaffolds provide a support system—from using manipulatives for building and reading words to writing words with little to no support.

Next, write the word list number and the phonics or spelling pattern you'll be teaching. These will be in bold on the headings for each column of words. Start on the left side of the word list and work your way down each list of words and across the chart. You'll progress through each pattern of words within a word list using the necessary scaffolds until students can write words when you dictate them with little to no scaffolding (after the partial alphabetic phase). At this point, they've mastered that phonics pattern, and you can proceed to the next column of words or word list.

Scaffold	Purpose
Picture cards	Develop background knowledge and context for words used in examples; sort letters and sounds; discriminate between letter and sound patterns
ABC chart	Refer to letter names and sounds and letter formation; use to teach letters and sounds through tracing
Your hands	Tap, snap, clap, count, blend, segment sounds
Chips (or other similar manipulatives)	Represent individual phonemes
Chips in sound boxes Example: 	Segment and blend sounds from left to right
Magnetic letters or tiles in sound boxes	Make words in sound boxes to show students how to segment and blend sounds
Magnetic letters or tiles	Make words to show students how to manipulate the phonemes in the words
Writing in sound boxes Example: 	Divide and write individual phonemes in boxes
Spelling boxes Example: 	Write and divide compound words, syllables, morphemes, onsets and rimes, and individual phonemes
Syllabication lines	Write and divide multisyllabic words
Word sorts	Sort cards with words to be categorized on a two- or three-column chart
Dictating word sort	Dictate words with phonics patterns for students to sort and write on a two- or three-column chart

FIGURE 1.4: Scaffolds for word-building activities.

It's also important to use as many visuals, pictures, and articulatory gestures as you can during your lessons. As you teach sounds, show students how to form them using tongue, teeth, lips, and mouth positions and movements. The reciprocal process of reading and writing can be difficult to grasp without physical and kinesthetic supports. Scaffolding instruction using these supports will give students a progressive understanding of how we connect letters and sounds in reading and writing, and it'll also help to increase their oral language skills. It's perfectly acceptable to use these scaffolds throughout the partial alphabetic and full alphabetic phases. For the consolidated alphabetic and automatic lesson plans and beyond, students should need little to no scaffolding. By using these scaffolds and supports, students will be able to discover a wealth of information about the relationship between letters and sounds in words.

Students will progress through the word-building activities at different rates. Some students will need extensive practice for each word list and pattern using every scaffold, while others will progress through the word lists and patterns quickly and effortlessly, requiring very little scaffolding. If students demonstrate mastery with the word-building activities quickly and easily, progress through the remaining word lists and patterns without scaffolds or only use writing the words in sound boxes as a scaffold (in the partial and full alphabetic phases). If students haven't mastered the words after completing a word list, provide additional support using the supplemental word lists for each reading phase in the appendices. Continue working in a word list or phonics skill until students have mastered that word list or skill.

High-Frequency and Sight Words

For students who need to practice reading and writing high-frequency (partial alphabetic phase) or sight words (full and consolidated alphabetic phases), focus on teaching one or two words per lesson. The lesson plans have spaces for you to write up to two words to teach. When choosing which words to teach your readers, don't select words that are so complex that they'll overburden students. Teach words that are in the text you're reading that your students won't be able to decode, are spelled irregularly, or contain phonics patterns that your students haven't yet learned. Follow these three steps to teach high-frequency and sight words.

1. **Teach and map:** Teach students the letter-sound correspondences for the word in a sensible manner. When words are phonetically irregular, use sound boxes. For example, with the word *said*, use sound boxes and teach students the letters that represent the three sounds in the word. The *s* would go in one box, the *ai* in the next box, and the *d* in the final box. When words are irregular because of their morphology, use spelling boxes to represent the parts of the word. For example, for the word *does*, write the word *do* in one box and put *es* in another box, then teach the pronunciation of the word.

    a. Build (with magnetic letters or tiles) or write the word on a dry-erase board.

    b. Identify which sounds correspond to which letters or explain the spelling of the word.

    c. Form boxes around the letters that correspond to the sounds or letters.

    d. Slide your finger under the boxes from left to right, one at a time, and have students stretch out and repeat the sounds after you.

2. **Build:** Build the word.

   a. Students then take their own magnetic letters or letter tiles and build the word on
       the word-building mat in the boxes.

   b. Students practice associating the letters and sounds and stretching them out to read
       the word (repeat step 1b).

3. **Write:** Write the word.

   a. Students push the letters up then write the corresponding letters in the boxes, or you
       dictate the word for them to write on the line below the boxes.

   b. Students erase the letter in the boxes or the word on the line.

   c. Students independently write the word again on the dotted lines after you dictate
       the word (without the letters as a scaffold).

Reading

For the reading component of each lesson plan, you'll choose a reading format. On a first reading, students should whisper-read independently so you can listen to them and provide corrective feedback and strategies and actions for decoding, fluency, and comprehension. On subsequent reads, when students' decoding and accuracy have improved, choose an echo, choral, or partner reading format. Consider the following regarding the four formats.

1. *Independent whisper reading* allows you time to individually teach and differentiate instruction based on every student's needs. Note what corrective feedback you provide for each student on the back of the lesson plan under Anecdotal Notes. Teach and provide feedback, actions, and strategies for decoding, then fluency and comprehension. The lesson plans list feedback prompts.

2. *Echo reading* provides the most fluency support for students because you model fluent reading, and they then "echo-read" the same part of the text. When the teacher models skilled reading first, readers hear how the text should sound with proper phrasing, speed, and expression. Echo reading also allows students to read manageable parts of sentences, usually in two- or three-word phrases. This offers them support and confidence during oral reading. Echo reading combines a fluency model with instant practice. This gradual release of responsibility provides the right support for partial and full alphabetic readers to develop accuracy, fluency, and comprehension.

3. *Choral reading* provides a moderate amount of support for students because you're reading the text at the same time. When students read aloud simultaneously as a group, partial alphabetic readers develop fluency by following the teacher's reading pace and expression. Readers may feel more secure with choral reading than they do reading independently. As the teacher, you can informally assess which students need more fluency support as you listen to them read along with you.

4. *Partner reading* provides the least amount of fluency support for students because you don't participate in the reading. During partner reading, students can echo- or choral-read with each other, or they can take turns reading one page or sentence each. Partners provide feedback, reinforcement, and modeling for each other. Providing readers with a supportive peer model can help build confidence through practice in a nonthreatening learning structure.

Teaching Vocabulary

Research suggests that explicit instruction in word analysis and vocabulary increases readers' awareness of language and the orthographic structures within words (Ehri, 2020). This understanding of words and their meanings underpins proficient reading comprehension abilities. Specifically, between 80 and 98 percent of comprehension is influenced by how well students understand the vocabulary they encounter in a text (Reutzel & Cooter, 2023; Schmitt, Jiang, & Grabe, 2011). Follow the steps in table 1.7 to teach vocabulary before, during, or after reading. An example is provided for each step.

TABLE 1.7: Steps and Procedures to Teaching Vocabulary

Step or Procedure	Example
Before Reading	
1. Pronounce the word and show it on your whiteboard, then have students repeat the word after you. Show students how to break the word apart by syllables or point out the base or root and any affixes.	*This is the word* cascading. *Say the word.* Students respond with "cascading." *The base word is* cascade, *the suffix is* -ing.
2. Introduce the word's meaning with a simple definition or synonym.	*When water cascades, it pours down rapidly and in large amounts.* Cascading *is the word used for when water is doing this.*
During Reading	
1. Ask the student if there were any words they didn't understand and need clarified.	*Were there any words on that page that you didn't understand?* Student responds, "I don't know what this word *fashioned* means here."
2. Provide the student with a simple definition or synonym.	*In this context,* fashioned *means "made" or "created."*
3. Ask the student to paraphrase what they read using the word.	*How did the author use the word* fashioned? Student responds, "It says that the dragons fashioned clouds of animals by breathing fire. The dragons made cloud animals."

continued ▶

After Reading						
1. Use a morpheme analysis chart to determine word meanings.	**Word**	**Root or Base**	**Prefixes and Suffixes**	**What Each Part Means**	**What Word Means**	**What It Means in the Sentence**
	disassemble	assemble	dis	not + put together	take apart	The boy took his bike chain apart.
2. Illustrate the words with examples and nonexamples. Have students put their thumbs up if the example is appropriate and their thumbs down when it's not.	• *Would you cascade down the steps?* • *Does water cascade down a waterfall?* • *Could water cascade down the sides of a fountain?* • *Do you ever cascade on your way to school?*					

	Situation	**Vocabulary Word**	**Example**
3. Provide students with situations that they have to associate the vocabulary word with.	Tell me if. . .	shuffling	Tell me if it would be safe to go shuffling across the sidewalk barefoot.
	How could you. . .	completely	How could you completely clean your room?
	Which would be. . .	supportive	Which would be supportive? • Talking to your friend if she's feeling sad • Yelling in your brother's ear

Sentence Dictation and Writing

In the partial and full alphabetic reading phases, students will write sentences that you dictate to them. Sentence dictation reinforces phonics and spelling patterns so students can actively think about and process letter-sound relationships and then apply them to correctly spell words. It also promotes further development of phonemic awareness skills. Phonemic awareness is a skill that requires students to process the connection from sounds to letters, while phonics requires students to process the connection from letters to sounds. These skills should develop simultaneously and continuously strengthen each other. The practice of writing dictated sentences helps students see the direct transfer between encoding (spelling or writing) and decoding (reading). You should continue to dictate sentences for students until they can write words with initial and final blends and can discriminate among all the short vowel sounds and spellings, which typically occurs midway through the full alphabetic phase.

To construct the dictated sentences, incorporate a few of the words from the book you'll be reading for lesson 2 or from the word-building lesson component with each of the high-frequency and sight words to create one or two sentences that are three to seven words long. Write the sentences you'll dictate in the spaces for sentence dictation on the lesson plan template. Students will use the lines at the word mat to write the dictated sentences, or they can write them in a writing journal.

It's important when you dictate sentences that you say them phrased, grouping two, three, or four words at a time. To practice fluency, have students reread the sentences they wrote, grouping two or three words at a time. Spend four to five minutes on sentence dictation and follow these five steps.

1. Say the sentence as a whole unit, pausing to phrase a few words at a time.
2. Have students repeat the sentence several times.
3. As students repeat the sentence, draw a line for each word on the students' word mats.
4. Have students stretch out each word, segment the sounds, and then write the letters on the lines that correspond to each sound.
5. Direct students to check each word by sliding a finger under the word and blend the letters and sounds to read the word.

Lesson Notes

At the end of each lesson plan component, there will be space for you to write notes to reflect on your instruction and how students responded to it. Use these daily informal notes to drive your next instructional decision regarding each literacy skill you've taught. These notes will help you adjust and plan for your next set of lessons. Note students' progress and mastery of concepts and adjust your instruction, student groups, activities, and pace if necessary.

Take these anecdotal notes into account when regrouping students so you place them in grouping arrangements that best facilitate their progress. Responsive planning and adjustment of instruction will enhance and maximize your small-group lessons and ensure optimal success for all your students. Don't move on to new skills and concepts until students have had sufficient time to practice and master the concepts you're currently teaching. Think about and reflect on the instructional concepts in table 1.8 (page 34) to direct the planning of your next lesson. Note that not every lesson plan component applies to each reading phase.

Your observations, anecdotal notes, and informal reading records will guide how you write your next plan. It's essential to reflect on your small-group instruction to assess the effectiveness of your lessons so you can make informed decisions about future lesson plans. This continuous improvement process helps you to enhance student learning outcomes over time.

TABLE 1.8: Instructional Concepts for Reflection

Lesson Plan Component	Questions to Consider After Teaching
Word Building	Are students ready to progress to the next scaffold, level, or word list? Note which word list you'll start your next lesson with.
High-Frequency or Sight Words	Do you need to repeat words to allow for more practice before introducing new or additional words? Note which word or words you'll teach next. Don't teach any new words until students can independently write and correctly spell the words you have taught.
	Were students able to read the high-frequency or sight words in the text, or did you need to use the responses for decoding as scaffolds? Note if you need to teach or reteach the words in your next lesson.
Prereading	Were students able to clarify any confusions they had and have all their questions answered before they began reading? Have you facilitated a discussion to build background knowledge and schema about the text they'll be reading? Have students made some connections to the text they'll be reading?
Text Reading	Was this text appropriate for the students' decoding abilities? Was it slightly challenging for students to read, or could they read the words quickly and effortlessly? Note the difficulty of the text and what you'll read for the next new text. Once the students can automatically read the words in the text, move on to a new text, preferably every lesson.
Teaching Decoding	Should you continue using the same phonics skill and pattern for the next lesson, or can you move on to a more challenging one? Note whether you need to increase the difficulty of the phonics skill or move to the next phonics pattern. Which scaffold will you use or progress to?
Teaching Vocabulary	Were students able to paraphrase and explain what these important words in the text mean? Could they explain how the author used the word in the text? Could they cite examples and nonexamples of the vocabulary and explain instances of when the words could be used appropriately?
Rereading	Were students able to read the text fluently with sufficient accuracy and pace? Which rereading format will you use for the next lesson? Note the students' proficiency with rereading the text.
Discussing the Text	Were students able to construct thoughtful responses for the comprehension sentence starters? Are they having more in-depth conversations about the texts they're reading?
Writing— Sentence Dictation	Were students able to transfer their letter-sound skills to writing and spelling? Were they able to write and correctly spell the high-frequency word you taught? What did you teach for editing? Note which of these skill areas students need additional support with and incorporate that into your writing instruction for lessons 1 and 3.
Comprehension	Were students able to paraphrase and remember what they rehearsed before they write? Did you pace your lesson so students rehearse and write only one sentence at a time?
Writing	Were students able to complete the writing with ease? Were you able to incorporate one to two of your language standards into the students' writing? Can you move to the next discussion strategy so students include more vocabulary and content in their writing?

Conclusion

The process of learning to read involves developing five main skills: (1) phonemic awareness, (2) phonics, (3) fluency, (4) vocabulary, and (5) comprehension. These skills aren't developed separately from one another—they strengthen and reinforce one another as they're developed. To achieve proficient comprehension, readers must be able to decode written words fluently and understand the vocabulary contained in what they're reading.

Readers apply phonemic awareness and phonics skills by blending the letters and sounds in words to decode them. To correctly pronounce decoded words, readers complete the process of orthographic mapping. These processes connect the visual and language processing areas of the brain. Orthographically mapping a large number of words aids in efficient and effortless decoding, which increases fluency. To increase vocabulary and comprehension skills, readers must develop sufficient reading fluency.

Transforming reading research into effective literacy instruction involves determining which skill areas your students need instruction in, how much and to what extent you need to provide these, and how you can implement a structured literacy format that aligns with the findings in the scientific research. This can be determined by assessing your students in decoding, fluency, vocabulary, and comprehension using common curriculum-based measures. Fluency speed is an appropriate assessment measure to determine whether the focus of small-group instruction should be on decoding (phonemic awareness and phonics) or vocabulary and comprehension.

Grouping formats for small-group reading instruction should be flexible so students can move on to subsequent skills when they've mastered the skills you've taught. Regrouping students should occur every two to six weeks, and you should form your small-group schedule based on which students need what type of instruction, for what length of time, and to what urgency.

Rather than limiting yourself to the type of texts used for small-group instruction, choose texts based on the students' skill areas of need. There are five types of text that are used in small-group instruction: (1) decodable text, (2) vocabulary readers, (3) leveled texts, (4) children's literature, and (5) informational text. Across various phases of reading development, students need exposure to a variety of texts.

When you're instructing students in small groups, the remaining students don't necessarily need to be in certain group formations rotating through work centers. Students should be completing assignments connected to the topics you teach in whole-group instruction. Their assignments should involve as much reading and writing as possible so they develop their decoding, fluency, vocabulary, and comprehension skills.

Using the lesson plan templates in the following chapters, you'll be able to design small-group differentiated reading lessons based on your students' specific reading needs. The lesson plan templates will provide you with the structure we crave as teachers while equipping you with the flexibility that you need as your daily instruction ebbs and flows. The lesson plans are designed to be simple and easy to complete while being scientifically grounded in the most effective practices for differentiating reading instruction.

Using targeted yet flexible differentiated small-group instruction, you can focus on teaching your students the literacy skills necessary for optimal reading success. This individualized instruction gives all your students equal access to the highest-quality literacy instruction; this minimizes inequities in education and maximizes the effectiveness of your literacy instruction for all students, taking a big step toward social justice and equity in education. Planning for, managing, and implementing small-group instruction while accounting for research-based factors can seem challenging, but these should be key components of the literacy block to ensure that you're meeting all students' needs.

CHAPTER 2

Preparing to Be a Reader: The Pre-Alphabetic Phase

[It's] not about helping children become better and more efficient hurdlers. It is about removing the hurdles from the track before the race even starts.

—David A. Kilpatrick

In this chapter, you'll learn how to build a foundation of phonological and phonemic awareness skills during the pre-alphabetic phase. First, I describe the characteristics of pre-alphabetic readers and the instructional focus of pre-alphabetic lessons. Next, I teach you how to assess and group your pre-alphabetic readers, then how to plan lessons for this phase. For most of the chapter, I sequentially explain lesson design by lesson plan component—phonological and phonemic awareness, letter and sound learning, reading and concepts of print, and writing. Next, I answer common questions about the pre-alphabetic phase. Finally, I conclude the chapter with instructions on how to determine whether students are ready to progress to the partial alphabetic phase. Appendix A (page 197) contains the resources to be used with the pre-alphabetic lessons.

Characterizing Pre-Alphabetic Readers

Pre-alphabetic readers are students who have had limited experiences with books. They may be students who have visually memorized some familiar environmental words, students with limited English language skills, or students whose written language isn't phonetic. Pre-alphabetic readers display the following characteristics.

- Guess words from context clues

- Memorize repetitive text or familiar stories

- Use environmental print

- Pretend "read" or "read" by talking about illustrations

- Have a limited knowledge of letters and sounds

- Don't use letters and sounds to read words
- Lack knowledge of sounds and connections to letters
- Exhibit poor phonological awareness skills
- Haven't developed the alphabetic principle
- "Pretend" write with no association between letters and sounds
- Don't know the difference between a letter and a sound
- Need to improve fine motor and handwriting skills
- May exhibit weak listening comprehension abilities
- May have weak oral language (speaking) skills

Teaching Your Pre-Alphabetic Readers

The instructional focus for pre-alphabetic readers will be on teaching book handling, print concepts, letter names, and handwriting; nurturing oral language development; developing students' phonological and phonemic awareness skills; and imparting the alphabetic principle—the understanding that written words are based on sets of letters that represent individual sounds in spoken language. Assessing your pre-alphabetic readers will involve determining which letters they can identify quickly and automatically and whether they can identify any sounds. Pre-alphabetic readers will fall into grouping categories based on how many letters they can identify. The grouping categories students fall into will determine the skills you teach to each group.

Where to Focus Instruction During Small-Group Lessons

It's important to teach skills for pre-alphabetic readers with reading and writing connected text rather than teach reading and writing in isolation. Your small-group lessons for pre-alphabetic readers will contain each of the following essential pieces.

- Constructing phonological and phonemic awareness
- Learning letter names with automaticity and speed
- Identifying sounds and associating them with the letters they represent
- Developing the alphabetic principle
- Establishing letter formation and handwriting routines
- Increasing print awareness and concepts of print
- Improving letter formation and handwriting
- Reinforcing listening comprehension skills
- Expanding oral language skills, such as speaking in complete sentences, asking and answering questions, and summarizing a text or illustration
- Increasing motivation to read—the desire to decode words and understand what's in a book

How to Assess Your Pre-Alphabetic Readers

The first time you assess your pre-alphabetic readers, you only need to utilize a simple letter-sound assessment. You can find a student copy and teacher score sheet in appendix A (page 197). Place a sheet of paper or a folder under each line. Point to each letter and ask the student to identify it and then mark the known letters on the teacher score sheet. It's important to pay particular attention to speed. Reaching a level of automaticity is key in reducing cognitive load and allowing for more space in students' working memory to decode new words when they get to the partial alphabetic phase (Poulsen, Protopapas, & Juul, 2023). Proceed to assess letter sounds for students who can identify at least forty-seven of the upper- and lowercase letters (about 90 percent). Students are considered to have mastered a letter name or sound when they can identify it in two or three seconds or less.

How to Group Your Pre-Alphabetic Readers

You can use the assessment record in appendix A (page 197) to keep track of the information on each of your pre-alphabetic readers. Once you've completed your assessments, you can use the grouping sheet in appendix A to determine which of the following three stages of pre-alphabetic reading your students are in.

- **Stage 1:** Students who can identify up to fifteen upper- and lowercase letters. These students have the least letter-naming knowledge and haven't yet developed the alphabetic principle. Students in this stage need specialized instruction in developing the alphabetic principle and will need small-group lessons more than other groups.

- **Stage 2:** Students who can identify between sixteen and thirty upper- and lowercase letters. These students can usually write and name the letters in their names and can identify some letters, so they're beginning to develop the alphabetic principle. They'll need to learn the rest of the letters and develop speed and fluency with naming them. They'll begin to implicitly learn sounds as they become more advanced with their letter knowledge.

- **Stage 3:** Students who can identify thirty-one or more upper- and lowercase letters. These learners have developed the alphabetic principle but need to build up speed and automaticity with naming letters. They usually can identify several sounds that they have learned implicitly through letter-naming activities. They can begin formal instruction on connecting sounds and letters. They will also need to increase the speed at which they connect letters and sounds.

Group students together according to their needs and in a manner that's manageable for you. The fewer students in a group, the more targeted and individualized your instruction can be. When you can manage the instruction and activities at hand, your students will grow and progress. As you begin to incorporate small-group instruction into your practice, start by meeting with students with the least letter knowledge and gradually work up to meeting with students who know more letters.

If we aren't responsive to our students, especially beginning readers, they're more likely to be left behind at the word-learning level, explain professors of literacy Nell K. Duke and Heidi Anne E. Mesmer (2018–2019). Some students will be in the pre-alphabetic phase for a week or two, but it's not uncommon for students to remain in the pre-alphabetic phase for two to three months as they establish a firm foundation for the next reading phase.

Planning Lessons for Pre-Alphabetic Readers

The pre-alphabetic lesson plan contains four components: (1) phonological or phonemic awareness, (2) letter and sound learning, (3) reading and concepts of print, and (4) writing. The tasks in each of the four lesson plan components are targeted at developing prereading literacy skills. The pre-alphabetic lesson plan template (appendix A, page 197) consists of a series of two lessons: Lesson 1 focuses on phonological awareness, and lesson 2 focuses on phonemic awareness.

The procedures for completing tasks associated with letter and sound learning, reading and concepts of print, and writing are the same in both lessons. There are also alliteration and oddity task activities, which are optional components that can be integrated if additional phonological practice is necessary. The structure of the pre-alphabetic lesson plan is shown in table 2.1.

TABLE 2.1: Pre-Alphabetic Lesson Plan Structure and Components

Lesson 1 Components	Lesson 2 Components
Phonological Awareness	Phonemic Awareness
Letter and Sound Learning	Letter and Sound Learning
Reading and Concepts of Print	Reading and Concepts of Print
Writing	Writing
	Alliteration or Oddity Tasks (optional)

When teaching phonological and phonemic awareness, complete the activities auditorily—focus students' attention on hearing sound units without teaching phonics. When you do need to write letters or use magnetic letters or tiles, be sure to focus on teaching the manipulation of sounds, not phonetic decoding. It's also important to use as many visuals, pictures, and articulatory gestures as you can. As you teach phonological units, show students how to form the sounds using tongue, teeth, lips, and mouth positions and movements. The concepts for pre-alphabetic readers are still abstract, which can be difficult for young learners to grasp without physical and kinesthetic supports. Scaffolding instruction using these supports will give students context, meaning, and a concrete understanding of how we produce sounds, and it will also help to increase their oral language skills.

Planning and Teaching Lesson 1

Explicitly teaching phonological awareness skills is key to establishing a strong foundation of literacy skills, so lesson 1 will emphasize building a foundation for phonology. Ehri (2020) suggests using gamelike listening and sound-manipulation activities to teach phonological awareness skills. These are skills that are inherently and commonly developed through singing and reciting silly phrases and nursery rhymes. Many students will need explicit instruction to further develop their phonological awareness and ability to process phonological sound units.

Phonological awareness skills are also integrated throughout all the pre-alphabetic lesson activities. Deficits in phonological awareness skills have long been correlated to later difficulties with decoding and orthographic mapping. These difficulties most often accumulate and impact students' ability to read fluently and acquire vocabulary and comprehension skills. In addition to phonological awareness skills, you'll also teach letter and sound knowledge, concepts of print, and writing.

The lesson 1 template is shown in figure 2.1.

Lesson 1
Phonological Awareness (2–3 minutes)

Word List:	☐ Isolating
	☐ Blending
	☐ Segmenting
☐ Rhyming Words	☐ Adding
☐ Compound words	☐ Deleting
☐ Syllables	☐ Substituting
☐ Rimes	

Notes:

Letter and Sound Learning (3–5 minutes)
Trace and Name Letters or Sounds:
Handwriting and Letter Formation:
Notes:

Reading and Concepts of Print (5 minutes)		
Text:		
Reading Format:	☐ Echo read	☐ Choral read
Teach a Concept of Print:		
Notes:		

Writing (3–5 minutes)			
Sentence From Text:			
Teaching Focus:			
☐ Letter names and formation	☐ Letter sounds	☐ Beginning sounds	☐ Final sounds
Notes for Next Lesson:			

FIGURE 2.1: Pre-alphabetic phase lesson 1.

*Visit **go.SolutionTree.com/literacy** to download a free reproducible version of this figure.*

Phonological Awareness

To increase students' phonological awareness skills, you'll have students work with four types of word and sound units: (1) words that rhyme, (2) compound words, (3) syllables, and (4) rime endings. Each phonological awareness task is meant to be completed auditorily by applying listening skills. Students may—but don't have to—see the letters for the words; they will not decode any of the words during these tasks. During this lesson component they are refining their ability to hear sounds in different positions within words. Use the scaffolds in figure 1.4 (page 28) whenever necessary; they don't prevent students from mastering phonological awareness tasks. For the first activity for lesson 1, you'll spend two to three minutes completing phonological awareness tasks.

On the planning template for lesson 1, you'll begin by teaching rhyming words. To do so, use a nursery rhyme for your text and focus on identifying words that rhyme during the reading and concepts of print component of the lesson plan. This way, you can use the word lists provided in the following subsections to teach compound words, syllables, and rimes. This sequence moves students from the largest and least complex units (compound words) to the smallest and most complex units (rimes). You'll spend two to three minutes of each lesson completing the phonological awareness tasks.

For each word unit you cover in lesson 1, write the word list you'll be using in the left-hand column of the lesson plan and check off the word unit contained in that list—compound words, syllables, or rimes. In the right-hand column, check off which phonological manipulation task the students will complete (isolating, blending, segmenting, adding, deleting, or substituting). These tasks are listed in the same order you will teach them from each of the word lists.

Students will vary in their development of phonological awareness skills, so it's important to adjust your next lesson for phonological instruction after you complete each lesson. Some students will master certain tasks more quickly than others. Move to the next column of tasks in the word list once students can complete a task with speed and accuracy. To master each phonological awareness task, students should be able to complete the task with speed and automaticity, even if scaffolding is needed. Phonological awareness tasks that are simple for some students may frustrate other students. If students haven't mastered a task, provide additional support using the supplemental lists in appendix A (page 197) until they have mastered it.

Compound Words

For your first lesson, write *1* next to Word List on the lesson plan, and in the left-hand column, check off *compound words*. In the right-hand column, check off *isolating*. For this first task, students will isolate each of the words in a compound word that you say aloud. Work vertically down the list of compound words in the Isolating column of table 2.2.

For each subsequent lesson 1 for word list 1, you'll again check off *compound words*, but if students have mastered isolating, you'll check off *blending* in the column to the right. For each subsequent lesson 1, you'll check off *compound words* and the next phonemic manipulation task (as long as students have mastered the previous one). Continue this progression until students master each phonological manipulation task—isolating, blending, segmenting, adding, deleting, and substituting—for compound words. The first row of table 2.2 contains an example of completing each task and the teacher language to use with the phonological manipulation tasks for compound words. Each column of word list 1 contains eight compound word units to complete for that phonological manipulation task.

Syllables

When students are proficient in each phonological manipulation task for compound word units, you'll proceed to the phonological manipulation tasks for syllable units. Breaking words apart into syllables helps establish the understanding that one word may contain two, three, or more parts. When we spell and write words, we can break them into syllables and write the letters for the sounds we hear in each syllable.

TABLE 2.2: Word List 1—Compound Words for Phonological Manipulation Tasks

Isolating (First Then Last Word)	Blending	Segmenting	Adding (Before Then After)	Deleting (First Then Second Word)	Substituting
sailboat	sun + set	birthday	add *board* after *card*; add *card* before *board*	racetrack – race racetrack – track	racetrack – track + way
What is the first word in sailboat? *What is the last word in sailboat?*	*What word do you get when you combine* sun *and* set?	*What are the two words in the word* birthday?	*What do you get when you add* board *after* card? *What do you get when you add* card *before* board?	*Say "racetrack." Now say "racetrack" without* race. *What word is left?* *Say "racetrack." Now say "racetrack" without* track. *What word is left?*	*Say "racetrack." Now say "racetrack," but instead of "track," say "way." What word do you have now?*
cobweb	gold + fish	homesick	air / plane	sun / set	birthday – day + mark
doorbell	out + side	airport	ear / drum	clock / wise	hillside – side + top
railroad	in + door	baseball	tooth / brush	life / guard	sideways – ways + step
playpen	life + guard	doorstep	saw / dust	fore / head	bookcase – case + shelf
bulldog	half + way	moonlight	some / day	ear / lobe	mailbox – box + man
seashell	some + thing	outlook	sea / shore	home / land	sailboat – sail + row
bookcase	love + bird	sideways	week / day	tight / rope	himself – him + her
football	air + craft	halfway	tooth / pick	hand / held	football – foot + base

Note: The example row in italics indicates what the teacher would say.

Pre-alphabetic readers should be able to recognize and manipulate the units in one-, two-, and three-syllable words when they hear them. Each phonological manipulation task for syllable units is meant to be completed auditorily. Continue to use the scaffolds in figure 1.4 (page 28) when necessary. Utilizing these scaffolds doesn't prevent students from mastering a phonological manipulation task.

For your first lesson with syllable units, begin by writing *2* next to Word List on the lesson plan, and in the left-hand column underneath, check off *syllables*. In the right-hand column, check off *isolating*. For the first task with syllables, students will isolate each of the syllables in a word that you tell them. Work vertically down the list of words for syllables in the Isolating column of table 2.3.

TABLE 2.3: Word List 2—Syllables for Phonological Manipulation Tasks

Isolating (First Then Last Syllable)	Blending	Segmenting	Adding (Before Then After)	Deleting (First Then Second Word)	Substituting
apple	ig + loo	pencil	add *one* after *every*; add *every* before *one*	over – o over – ver	begin – gin + fore
What is the first syllable in apple? *What is the last syllable in apple?*	*What word do you get when you combine ig and loo?*	*What are the syllables in the word pencil?*	*What do you get when you add one after every?* *What do you get when you add every before one?*	*Say "over." Now say "over" without o. What syllable is left?* *Now say "over" without ver. What syllable is left?*	*Say "begin." Now say "begin," but instead of "gin," say "fore." What word do you have now?*
baby	mon + key	water	thunder / storm	un / der	likely – y + ing
candy	pic + nic	circus	honey / bee	fa / ble	landline – line + lord
dimple	rab + bit	balloon	under / stood	lit / tle	monkey – key + day
wagon	wig + gle	person	silver / ware	nap / kin	market – et + er
giraffe	nois + y	empty	dragon / fly	dang / er	candy – y + le
under	tur + tle	rabbit	loud / speaker	fro / zen	homebody – body + sick
elephant	straw + ber + ry	colorful	sky / diving	mon / key	nimble – nim + fum
volcano	ham + burg + er	library	out / going	wind / ow	corner – corn + in

Note: The example row in italics indicates what the teacher would say.

For your next lesson 1, you'll again check off *syllables*, but if students have mastered isolating, you'll check off *blending* in the column to the right. For each subsequent lesson 1 for word list 2, you'll check off *syllables* and the next phonological manipulation task (as long as students have mastered the previous one). Continue with this progression until the students master each phonological manipulation task—isolating, blending, segmenting, adding, deleting, and substituting—for syllables. Each column of table 2.3 contains eight syllable sound units to complete for that phonological manipulation task.

Rimes

When students have mastered each phonological manipulation task with syllable units, you'll proceed to the phonological manipulation tasks for rime units. *Rime units* are words that contain two parts within one syllable—an onset and a rime. An *onset* is the first part of a syllable that can contain up to three consonant sounds. A *rime* is the final part of a syllable that begins at the vowel and contains up to four more letter sounds after the vowel. For example, in the word *cat*, the onset is *c* and the rime is *at*. In the word *scrap*, *scr* is the onset and *ap* is the rime. Onsets and rimes also occur in larger words with multiple syllables.

By completing these tasks, students will increase their understanding of the initial and final phonological units in words. They'll also come to understand the similarities in the endings of many simple words. This builds a solid conceptual framework for later decoding skills and processing phonemes for reading and writing. Although each phonological manipulation task for rime units will be completed auditorily, continue to use the scaffolds in figure 1.4 (page 28) when necessary.

To begin teaching rime units, write *3* next to Word List on the lesson plan, and in the left-hand column underneath, check off *rimes*. In the right-hand column, check off *isolating*. During these isolation tasks, students will listen to the words as you say each one, then complete the task for that column of words. Work vertically down the list of words for rimes in the Isolating column of table 2.4.

TABLE 2.4: Word List 3—Words With Rimes for Phonological Manipulation Tasks

Isolating (First Part [onset] Then Second Part [rime])	Blending	Segmenting	Adding (Before Then After)	Deleting (First Part [onset] Then Second Part [rime])	Substituting
bath	d + ad	fad	add *g-* before -*ap*; add -*ap* after *g-*	mad – m mad – ad	had – ad + op
What is the first part in the word bath? *What is the last part in the word* bath?	*What word do you get when you combine* d *and* ad?	*What are the two parts in the word* fad?	*What do you get when you add* g *before* ap? *What do you get when you add* ap *after* g?	*Say "mad." Now say "mad" without* m. *What is left? Say "mad." Now say "mad" without* ad *What is left?*	*Say "had." Now say "had," but instead of "ad," say "op." What word do you have now?*
gag	h + ag	jag	ch / at	j / am	nag – ag + ip
jam	P + am	ram	m / et	b / an	Sam – am + at
fan	m + an	pan	ch / ip	th / at	sat – at + it
nap	r + ap	sap	s / ip	t / in	tap – ap + op
pat	s + at	that	l / it	h / ot	mat – at + ud
wed	T + ed	bed	sh / ip	c / all	Ned – ed + ot
ten	wh + en	Ben	h / op	b / ill	men – en + ad
yet	s + et	pet	th / in	d / oor	bet – et + ot
big	d + ig	fig	th / is	m / ice	dip – ip + ot
chin	k + in	bin	w / ig	b / ear	bit – it + un

Note: The example row in italics indicates what the teacher would say.

For your next lesson 1, you'll again check off *rimes*, but if students have mastered isolating, you'll check off *blending* in the column to the right. For each subsequent lesson 1 for word list 3, you'll check off *rimes* and the next phonemic manipulation task (as long as students have mastered the previous one).

This continues until students have mastered each phonological manipulation task—isolating, blending, segmenting, adding, deleting, and substituting—for words with onsets and rimes. The first row of table 2.4 (page 45) contains an example for completing each task and the teacher language to use with the onset and rime phonological manipulation tasks. Each column of word list 3 contains ten words with rimes to manipulate for that phonological task.

Letter and Sound Learning

Pre-alphabetic readers who haven't developed the alphabetic principle typically identify very few or no letters, confuse letters that look similar, and aren't able to identify letter names or sounds quickly and automatically. In both lesson 1 and lesson 2, you'll spend time establishing and improving students' efficiency and mastery by tracing and identifying letter names and sounds. Then, you'll teach handwriting and correct letter formation. Figure 2.2 hones in on the activities for letter and sound learning in lesson 1.

Letter and Sound Learning (3–5 minutes)
Trace and Name Letters or Sounds:
Handwriting and Letter Formation:
Notes:

FIGURE 2.2: Pre-alphabetic phase lesson 1—Letter and sound learning.

*Visit **go.SolutionTree.com/literacy** to download a free reproducible version of this figure.*

Trace and Name Letters or Sounds

For the second activity of both lesson 1 and lesson 2, students will spend two to three minutes tracing and learning letter names. Then, have them spend two to three minutes practicing handwriting and letter formation with the letters or sounds that you're teaching for your small-group lessons that week. Each day that you teach a new letter, have students practice tracing it correctly following the proper writing strokes. Students will follow along with you and trace letters on the ABC chart (see appendix A, pages 208 and 209) and either name the letters or pronounce letter sounds (visit **go.SolutionTree.com /literacy** for a color version of the ABC chart). It's crucial to model correct letter formation throughout all the components for pre-alphabetic readers, as this will aid in their handwriting development. Visit **go.SolutionTree.com/literacy** for a chart of the sequence of strokes for letter formation. Provide corrective feedback during this lesson plan component and expect students to master letter naming and sound identification with speed and automaticity.

Use the phrases shown on the "Letter Formation Language" chart in appendix A (pages 210 and 211) along with the letter formation stroke sequences so students learn to say the letter formation language while they write each letter. When students say the phrases involved in the process of forming letters (*around and close, down, a*), connections along the neural pathways are formed in the brain for language, letter learning, and sounds. This process also helps connect an abstract concept with a concrete one. The verbalizing process gives students auditory cues to rely on as they first start learning how to write letters. The visual of demonstrating how to form letters while verbalizing how to form them reinforces a kinesthetic and sensorimotor experience and memory of letter formation. Providing explicit verbal directions for letter formation promotes students' ability to successfully replicate, which leads to handwriting mastery.

First, teach lowercase letter names, then sounds, and finally uppercase letter names. Teach students the letters in their names first, as their names are typically one of the first written words that pre-alphabetic readers identify with. Once students can identify the letters in their names, move on to teaching the remaining lowercase letters. Introduce and teach about four or five new letters per week, or one letter each lesson.

To teach each letter, simply trace it with your pointer finger on the ABC chart to model correct letter formation and then say the letter name. Students will repeat this process after you, naming the letters as they trace them with the pointer finger on their dominant hand. Monitor their letter tracing, formation, and letter naming and provide corrective feedback. Don't move on to introducing more letters until students have firmly mastered the letters you have previously taught. You may need to rearrange your pre-alphabetic groups at the end of each week depending on how quickly the students are mastering letter naming.

Decide on one order for teaching letter names and be consistent with it. You can teach letter names to your small groups in the order that you teach them to the whole group; in the order you prefer to teach sounds; according to which letters are easiest to form in handwriting; or in the order of utility—their usefulness in writing and speech. There's no scientific evidence that one sequence for teaching letters is superior to another (Shanahan, 2016). The key to successful letter learning is being thorough and systematic and practicing letter naming with fidelity and consistency to the level of mastery. Visit **go.SolutionTree.com/literacy** for several suggestions of sequences to teach letters and sounds.

Don't integrate teaching letter sounds during this part of the lesson until students have mastered naming most letter names with speed and automaticity (90 percent, or at least twenty-three of the most common letters). Focusing solely on letter names will help students learn them more quickly. Practicing correct letter formation will improve their fine motor skills for handwriting.

What follows are the verbal steps to take to form each letter correctly. Follow this progression when teaching letter formation.

1. Write the letter on a whiteboard, modeling correct letter formation.

2. Teach students to make the letter in the air and then on the table or desk with a finger, using phrases shown for that letter on the "Letter Formation Language" chart in appendix A (pages 210 and 211). Emphasize the motor patterns using short verbiage made up of simple prepositions for correct letter formation, like *up, down, in, over, out, around,* and so on. Be sure that students learn to say the verbiage (letter formation language) independently as they practice each letter. This will maximize handwriting legibility and will prevent students from reversing letters.

3. Ensure correct letter formation with finger movements before moving to the use of a marker or pencil.

4. Using a dry-erase marker, have students write the letter repeatedly across the bottom of the ABC chart as they repeat the language pathway.

Once students can identify letter names quickly and automatically, repeat letter tracing, but identify the letter sounds as you trace them. To teach each letter sound, simply trace it with your pointer finger to model correct letter formation, then pronounce the sound. Students will repeat this process after you, pronouncing only the sounds of the letters as they trace them with the pointer finger on their dominant hand. Monitor their letter tracing, formation, and pronunciation of sounds and provide corrective feedback. Introduce and teach about four or five new sounds per week, or one sound per lesson. Don't introduce more sounds until students have firmly mastered the sounds you've previously taught.

Note that there are several key reasons why it's beneficial for students to master letter names before learning letter sounds. Being able to automatically identify letter names provides meaning before students are expected to connect abstract sounds to the letters. Letter names provide a label for each letter. This helps students recognize and distinguish each letter from the others—a precursor to being able to decode words. Many letter names also contain their sound, which implicitly reinforces the natural connections between letter names and sounds. For these reasons, letter naming is to be taught along with handwriting and letter formation. When students have mastered letter names and how to correctly write each one, learning letter sounds smoothly piggybacks on previously mastered letter names. This prevents issues from occurring with letter reversals and confusion between letters and sounds. Research shows that learning letter names before learning sounds promotes faster acquisition of letter sounds (Ellefson, Treiman, & Kessler, 2009; Roberts, Vadasy, & Sanders, 2018; Shanahan, 2021a; Share, 2004; Treiman, Pennington, Shriberg, & Boada, 2008; Treiman, Sotak, & Bowman, 2001).

When students can name most of the lowercase letters and sounds, begin to teach uppercase letter names. If your students can't yet identify some of the less common lowercase letters (*j, k, w, x, y, z*), you can continue to teach them during the other lesson plan components. Introduce and teach about four or five new uppercase letters per week, or one letter each lesson. You'll follow the same procedures you did for learning lowercase letters and sounds.

To teach each uppercase letter name, simply trace it on the ABC chart with your pointer finger to model correct letter formation, then say the letter name. Students will repeat this process after you, naming the letters as they trace them with the pointer finger on their dominant hand. Monitor their letter tracing, formation, and letter naming and provide corrective feedback. Don't introduce more letters until students have firmly mastered the letters you've previously taught.

Students learn to name and write uppercase letters last during the pre-alphabetic phase because uppercase letters are used for only about 5 percent of writing activities. It has long been thought that uppercase letters should be taught before lowercase letters because they are made of horizontal and vertical lines—which are easier for young students to form. There's no research evidence to support this claim, and more than half of the uppercase letters include rounded and diagonal lines. Since barely 5 percent of writing activities contain uppercase letters, it's more useful to teach and practice lowercase letters first during your small-group lessons. Other than teaching the uppercase letters that are in students' names, focus on teaching lowercase letters first and then letter sounds. Last, teach the remaining uppercase letters. Letter and sound tracing and naming will be completed in both lesson 1 and lesson 2.

Handwriting and Letter Formation

For the next two or three minutes, students will practice writing the letter names or letters for the sounds you taught. If you're teaching and practicing letter names, have students practice writing those letters. If you're teaching letter sounds, dictate those sounds to students and have them write the letter that the sound represents. If you're teaching uppercase letters, students will write those letters as you dictate them.

Students should first learn to write the letters in their names. Make a simple name template and place it in a plastic sleeve. Students can use dry-erase markers to trace the letters. Visit **go.SolutionTree.com /literacy** for student handwriting paper. You can write students' names on the handwriting paper, and they can practice writing their names on the lines under your model. After students have learned the letters in their names and can write their names with proper letter formation, continue to practice handwriting for the letter names or letters for the sounds you've taught. You can use typical handwriting practice sheets easily available online. Handwriting and letter formation will be completed in lessons 1 and 2.

Reading and Concepts of Print

Students in the pre-alphabetic phase won't be reading independently, learning high-frequency or sight words, or learning how to decode during the reading portion of the lesson plan during this phase. Pre-alphabetic students haven't gained enough proficiency with phonological and phonemic awareness and letter knowledge to read books in which they'll need to decode words. Students in this reading phase are learning the alphabetic principle, so they'll echo- or choral-read the texts. Echo and choral reading are critical prereading behaviors for students who haven't developed the alphabetic principle and the ability to decode. Reading text along with students during this phase builds familiarity with text and reading behaviors.

The activities during this lesson plan component expose students to concepts of print and progressing through a story, song, or nursery rhyme. This early familiarity with learning concepts of print helps set the foundation for comprehension later. The activities contained in this component also support oral language and vocabulary development. Strong oral language and vocabulary abilities in prereaders are correlated with higher levels of reading proficiency. The activities in this lesson plan component will lay the groundwork to transition to conventional reading through decoding in the partial alphabetic reading phase. For these activities, you'll spend five minutes reading and teaching a concept of print. The activities for reading and learning concepts of print are shown in figure 2.3.

Reading and Concepts of Print (5 minutes)		
Text:		
Reading Format:	☐ Echo read	☐ Choral read
Teach a Concept of Print:		
Notes:		

FIGURE 2.3: Pre-alphabetic phase lesson 1—Reading and concepts of print.

*Visit **go.SolutionTree.com/literacy** to download a free reproducible version of this figure.*

You can choose from a variety of texts for the reading and concepts of print component of the lesson.

- Short books with one line of print on each page

- *Rebus books*—books with pictures to accompany some words

- Books with repetitive text

- Printed copies of nursery rhymes or songs your students are familiar with

- Printed copies of poems or songs for days of the week and months of the year, or any other concepts you're teaching
- Poetry appropriate for the students' grade level

If you use a nursery rhyme, song, or poem, you'll need to spend some time preteaching the language pattern and the rhythm of the text; making finger, hand, and arm motions; and helping students to pronounce the words in the text correctly. You may use one nursery rhyme or poem for instruction throughout an entire week of pre-alphabetic lessons. If you choose a nursery rhyme, this is the portion of the lesson where you'll integrate the phonological awareness skill of recognizing rhyming words.

Repeat the same steps for reading and teaching concepts of print for both lesson 1 and lesson 2. For these activities, you simply read a line of print and have students echo-read (repeat what you read) after you. If you use a text that you've practiced several times, students can choral-read (read at the same time) with you. Your focus will help students to:

- Establish *voice-to-print match*—saying a word each time they touch under the word
- Demonstrate *one-to-one matching*—moving their finger from word to word as they "read" the words
- Determine words that rhyme
- Learn about concepts of print

There are three parts to reading and teaching concepts of print. First, facilitate a conversation about the text you'll be reading. Listen to students as they take turns discussing the pictures in the text—or, you might need to read or sing the text to students so they can become familiar with it. You may need to explain the poem or nursery rhyme concepts that students aren't yet familiar with. Doing this will help build background knowledge and oral language skills.

Next, students will echo- or choral-read each line of print after or with you. Model one-to-one matching by placing your pointer finger under each word as you read it. Then, have students repeat the same actions. Be sure that students are using one-to-one matching as they repeat or follow along with your words. Once students are familiar with the text, you may prefer to choral-read. Students should also be practicing one-to-one matching during a choral read.

If you chose a nursery rhyme to read, practice teaching students to listen for words that rhyme. You can tell students two words from the nursery rhyme, and they can give you a thumbs-up or thumbs-down to show whether the words rhyme. You can also make or print pictures from the rhyme and have students group rhyming words together. Practice with rhyming takes the place of teaching a concept of print for this lesson.

Last, after the echo or choral reading, choose one or two concepts of print to begin teaching. Don't move on to teaching a new concept of print until students have grasped the current concepts. Following are the concepts of print, from least difficult to most difficult.

- **Book orientation:** Choose texts that have familiar pictures and clear lettering on the cover so holding the book or text upright and facing it frontward will be easier for students to understand. Demonstrate the difference between holding a text upside down and right side up. Have students practice doing the same.

- **Front and back covers and title:** Choose texts that have a clear difference between their front and back covers so students can easily identify the front or back of the book. Teaching this skill can be integrated with teaching students how to hold a book upright. Choose texts that have a large, clearly written and recognizable title. Demonstrate how to associate it with the front side and top of a book.

- **Author and illustrator:** Teach students to identify the author. A book's cover usually lists "Written by. . ." first so finding the author's name is a simple task. You can also teach them to look for the uppercase *W* for "Written by." Similarly, a book identifies the illustrator with "Illustrated by. . ." Teach students to look for the uppercase *I* to find the illustrator's name, which is usually written immediately beneath the author's name.

- **Concept of a sentence:** Have students count how many times they see an uppercase letter at the beginning of a sentence or a punctuation mark at the end of a sentence. You can also teach the students how to use both pointer fingers at the beginning and end of a sentence to make a "frame" around it.

- **Concept of a word:** Have students point to and count the number of words on a page or in a line of print. When we count a certain number of words, it's the same number of words that we then read on that page.

- **Left-to-right directionality:** Place a small sticker under the first word on a page so students learn where to start reading. As they learn left-to-right directionality, remove the sticker so they can do this independently.

- **Spaces or spacing:** Have students point to and count the number of spaces on a page. They can also practice moving their fingers from word to word, lifting their fingers in between the words where there is a space.

- **First word and last word in a sentence or line of print:** Relate the concept of first and last words to first and last lines, first and last pages in a book, and first and last sounds during phonological and phonemic awareness tasks.

- **First letter and last letter:** Point out the first and last letter in several sentences, then have students repeat this. Once students can identify the first and last letters of a sentence, show them the first and last letters in words. Have them identify the first and last letters in different words in the text.

- **Upper- and lowercase letters:** After teaching the concept of the first word, have students point out and count how many uppercase letters are on a page or in a line of print. Also, relate uppercase letters to the first letter in their names.

- **End punctuation:** Have students point out and count each end mark in every text you read. Teach the terminology for the end punctuation used—periods, exclamation marks, and question marks.

Writing

Writing is never a teaching practice to overlook or skip during small-group instruction. Practicing writing helps to reinforce phonological and phonemic awareness skills, knowledge of letters and sounds, the ability to connect sounds to the letters they represent, letter formation, and handwriting. Writing with pre-alphabetic readers also reinforces its reciprocal relationship to reading. Reading and writing skills should both flourish simultaneously. For this activity, you'll spend five minutes teaching writing. The writing portion of lessons 1 and 2 are shown in figure 2.4.

Writing (3–5 minutes)			
Sentence From Text:			
Teaching Focus:			
☐ Letter names and formation	☐ Letter sounds	☐ Beginning sounds	☐ Final sounds
Notes for Next Lesson:			

FIGURE 2.4: Pre-alphabetic phase lesson 1—Writing.

*Visit **go.SolutionTree.com/literacy** to download a free reproducible version of this figure.*

Handwriting and word and sentence dictation are key concepts and skills for pre-alphabetic readers. For this reason, you'll dictate a sentence from the text you just read and write it together with the students as a shared writing activity. Students will again practice letter formation, letter and sound naming, and handwriting throughout the writing activity.

To teach this lesson plan component, you'll use a dry-erase board or sentence strips to write a sentence from the text. Say the sentence aloud but leave out certain words or letters in words. Then, read the sentence back with the students and fill in missing words or letters. Follow these five steps to complete the writing portion of the lesson plan.

1. Choose one or two sentences or phrases from the text (approximately five to seven words each). Keeping the phrase or sentence short will ensure that students are able to remember it and repeat it on their own.

2. State the sentence or phrase to students and have them repeat it two or three times after you.

3. Write the sentence on a whiteboard or sentence strip, leaving out a few words or letters that contain initial and final sounds that are easy to hear.

4. Read the sentence or phrase to students as you point to and say each word.

5. When you come to the first blank space for a missing word, have students say the missing word. Ask them to enunciate the first, final, or medial sound. This is when you'll teach your focus skill.

   a. *Letter names and letter formation*—For students who may not be able to identify many letters yet, tell them which letter the word you are filling in the blank starts with. Have students point to the letter on their ABC chart, repeat the letter name, and trace it on their ABC chart. Then, using the language pathway phrases in the Letter Formation Language chart (see appendix A, pages 210 and 211), have students practice writing the letter at the bottom of their ABC chart. Students should repeat the language pathway phrase as they write the letter along with you on the bottom of their ABC chart. Internalizing these motor patterns will help make letter recognition and formation more automatic.

b. *Letter sounds*—Once students can identify and write all their lowercase letters with proper formation, teach letter sounds. First, teach initial letter sounds, then final sounds, and last, medial short vowel sounds.

  i. Initial sounds. Say the word and ask students what sound they hear at the beginning. Isolate the letter sound if you need to. Use your mouth to demonstrate how you make that sound. Point to your mouth as you say the sound to draw attention to listening to the sound. Use this process of associating the sound with the letter: "What sound do I hear? What letter is that?" Have students practice saying the sound and writing the letter on their ABC chart. Write the remaining letters to complete the word. Follow this process for each initial sound in the words you've left out.

  ii. Final sounds. Repeat the preceding process, focusing on the initial and final sounds in the words you've left out of the sentence or phrase.

  iii. Medial sounds. Repeat the preceding process, focusing on the initial, medial, and final sounds you've left out of the sentence or phrase.

Following is an example of a fill-in-the-blank writing activity.

Jack _____ nimble, Jack _____ quick

_____ jumped over the candle _____.

Completing a writing activity at the end of each lesson will give pre-alphabetic readers practice using letter and sound knowledge and will build their auditory memory. Building a strong auditory memory helps students remember words and phrases for when they'll write their own sentences or write sentences dictated to them.

Regularly practicing writing activities also establishes the process for spelling words and directs students' attention to letter-sound relations. Spending time on teaching the process of associating sounds with letters builds a system for inventive spelling so students don't rely on visually memorizing words. They learn how to break down words into syllables or individual sounds, then associate those sounds with the letters they represent. You'll repeat the steps for the writing activity for lessons 1 and 2.

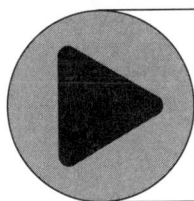

Use this QR code to watch a video of a teacher conducting a pre-alphabetic lesson 1.

Planning and Teaching Lesson 2

The focus for lesson 2 is on manipulating individual phonemes in words, or phonemic awareness. Manipulating individual phonemes through auditory activities helps pre-alphabetic readers develop skills for hearing and manipulating sounds in spoken language. This builds a foundation for connecting sounds with letters for reading and writing. As pre-alphabetic readers manipulate different sounds within different positions of words, they become aware that changing just one letter in a word creates an entirely new word. Students with stronger phonological and phonemic awareness skills often more easily learn how to decode words. They learn to decode and orthographically map new words quickly and efficiently. They also don't have to decode unknown words many times before they begin to recognize words automatically. This enables them to quickly learn an abundance of new words, which increases their fluency and ability to read words independently.

Proficiency with phonemic awareness at an early age is one of the strongest predictors of future reading success. I like to think of phonemic awareness as the glue that binds to later phonics skills. Maintaining a strong emphasis on phonemic awareness skills provides a strong foundation for not only later decoding but also spelling, writing, and vocabulary. In addition to phonemic awareness, you'll again teach letter and sound knowledge, handwriting, concepts of print, and writing.

Phonemic Awareness

Learning about individual sounds through phonemic awareness activities is essential to learn how to phonetically decode words and spell in the partial alphabetic phase. The Institute of Education Sciences (2016) recommends that beginning readers develop an awareness of the segments of speech sounds and how they link to the letters that represent them. Activities in which students practice phonemic awareness enable beginning readers to connect sounds with letters, which supports the orthographic mapping process.

It's also essential for pre-alphabetic readers to develop a conceptual framework for processing letters and sounds using left-to-right directionality. The phonemic awareness activities in lesson 2 promote the development of this concept. Having a strong conceptual framework for decoding every phoneme in words in order from left to right prevents readers from relying on whole-word visual memorization for reading. Visual memorization of words as wholes creates confusion with letter order in words and leads to poor reading accuracy.

For the phonemic awareness tasks, students will work with sounds that are in the initial, final, and medial positions of three-letter words. The words contain three sounds with a short vowel in the middle (or medial) position. Each phonemic awareness task is meant to be completed auditorily by applying listening skills. Students don't have to see the letters for the words. If you do use letters, don't emphasize the decoding process during these tasks. Use the scaffolds in figure 1.4 (page 28) whenever necessary; using these scaffolds doesn't prevent students from mastering the phonemic awareness tasks. You'll spend two to three minutes of each lesson completing the phonemic awareness tasks.

In the left-hand column of the planning template for lesson 2, begin by writing the word list you'll be using—4, 5, or 6—depending on which phoneme the students will be completing tasks for (initial, final, or medial). Then, check off the phoneme contained in the table you'll be using (initial, final, medial). The phonemes are in order from the easiest to learn (initial phonemes) to most difficult to learn (medial phonemes). In the right-hand column, check off which phonological manipulation task the students will be completing (isolating, blending, segmenting, adding, deleting, or substituting). The phonemic awareness activities for lesson 2 are shown in figure 2.5.

Some students may be able to complete the phonemic awareness tasks in one table within a few short lessons, while other students may need several series of lessons with a particular phonemic manipulation task. If students haven't mastered a task, provide additional support using the supplemental lists in appendix A (page 197) until they've mastered it.

Lesson 2
Phonemic Awareness (2–3 minutes)

Word List:	☐ Isolating
	☐ Blending
☐ Initial sounds	☐ Segmenting
☐ Final sounds	☐ Adding
☐ Medial sounds	☐ Deleting
	☐ Substituting
Notes:	

FIGURE 2.5: Pre-alphabetic phase lesson 2—Phonemic awareness tasks.

*Visit **go.SolutionTree.com/literacy** to download a free reproducible version of this figure.*

Initial Sounds

For your first lesson, write *4* next to Word List in the left-hand column of the lesson plan and check off *initial sounds*. In the right-hand column, check off *isolating*. For this first task, students will isolate the initial sound in a simple word with three sounds that you tell them. Work vertically down the list of words in the Isolating column of table 2.5.

TABLE 2.5: Word List 4—Words With Initial Sounds for Phonemic Manipulation Tasks

Isolating	Blending	Segmenting	Adding	Deleting	Substituting
cat	m + o + b	chub	add *k* before -*it*	Sam – S	mash – m + g =
What is the first sound you hear in the word cat?	*What word do you get when you combine the sounds /m/, /o/, and /b/?*	*What is the first sound in the word* chub?	*What do you get when you add /k/ before it?*	*Say "Sam." Now say "Sam" without /s/. What do you have left?*	*Say "mash." Now say "mash," but instead of /m/, say /g/. What word do you have now?*
cab	m + a + d	shag	add *b* before -*am*	ban – b	shut – sh + h =
bat	b + e + d	Ben	add *h* before -*ag*	shop – sh	bin – b + f =
dip	b + i + t	Bob	add *ch* before -*op*	dab – d	cot – c + b =
cup	b + u + g	bun	add *f* before -*in*	chop – ch	dad – d + b =
gash	h + a + m	can	add *th* before -*ug*	cat – c	fed – f + s =
den	g + e + t	dig	add *b* before -*ut*	hip – h	bit – b + l =
cob	d + o + g	cop	add *d* before -*ot*	big – b	dug – d + b =
shun	c + u + t	fab	add *f* before -*ad*	that – th	Jan – J + v =

Note: The example row indicates what the teacher would say.

For your next lesson 2, you'll again check off *initial sounds*, but if students have mastered isolating, you'll check off *blending* in the right column. For each subsequent lesson 2, you'll check off *initial sounds* and the next phonemic manipulation task (as long as students have mastered the previous one). Continue this progression until the students have mastered each phonemic manipulation task—isolating, blending, segmenting, adding, deleting, and substituting—for initial sounds. The first row of table 2.5 (page 55) contains an example for completing each task and the teacher language to use with the phonemic manipulation tasks for initial sounds. Each column of word list 4 contains eight words to use to complete that phonemic awareness task.

Final Sounds

When students are proficient in each phonemic manipulation task for initial sounds in words, proceed to the phonemic manipulation tasks for final sounds. Listening for the final sounds in words aids in building sound *correlation skills*—the ability to hear the sounds in words from left to right, or from beginning to end. This helps students to later map those final sounds to letters in reading and writing. Learning to listen for the final sounds in words also helps students hear the rimes in words, which enables them to learn more words through phonetic decoding in the partial alphabetic reading phase. Purposefully directing pre-alphabetic readers' attention to the final sounds in words strengthens their auditory discrimination skills and helps them break words down into sound units for later decoding. Continue to use the scaffolds in figure 1.4 (page 28) when necessary; utilizing these scaffolds doesn't prevent students from mastering a phonemic manipulation task.

For your first lesson with final sounds, begin by writing *5* next to Word List on the lesson plan and checking off *final sounds*. In the right-hand column, check off *isolating*. For the first task with final sounds, students will isolate the final sound in a word you tell them. Work vertically down the list of final sounds in the Isolating column of table 2.6.

TABLE 2.6: Word List 5—Words With Final Sounds for Phonemic Manipulation Tasks

Isolating	Blending	Segmenting	Adding	Deleting	Substituting
cap	d + u + g	dash	add *t* after *fi*	Sam – m	mash – sh + tch =
What is the last sound you hear in the word cap?	*What word do you get when you combine the sounds /d/, /u/, and /g/?*	*What is the last sound in the word* dash?	*What do you get when you add /t/ after* fi?	*Say "Sam." Now say "Sam" without /m/. What do you have left?*	*Say "mash." Now say "mash," but instead of /sh/, say /tch/. What word do you have now?*
bed	th + u + d	wax	add *g* after *pe*	shut – t	bun – n + d =
cub	y + a + k	hid	add *ch* after *mu*	tax – x	thin – n + ck =
fix	p + o + d	rim	add *d* after *so*	sap – p	cup – p + t =
gum	f + o + x	math	add *x* after *bo*	bid – d	mix – x + t =
rug	ch + u + g	yes	add *n* after *me*	hug – g	ham – m + d =
den	j + a + b	rip	add *m* after *su*	tam – m	bus – s + t =
job	m + o + m	back	add *sh* after *ma*	Max – x	cat – t + p =
kit	p + e + n	cob	add *d* after *co*	kid – d	hug – g + m =

Note: The example row in italics indicates what the teacher would say.

For your next lesson 2, you'll again check off *final sounds*, but if students have mastered isolating, you'll check off *blending* in the right column. For each subsequent lesson 2, you'll check off *final sounds* and the next phonemic manipulation task (as long as students have mastered the previous one). Continue with this progression until students have mastered each phonemic manipulation task—isolating, blending, segmenting, adding, deleting, and substituting—for final sounds. The first row of table 2.6 contains an example for completing each task and the teacher language to use with the phonemic manipulation tasks for final sounds. Each column of word list 5 contains eight words to complete for that phonemic awareness task.

Medial Sounds

When students have mastered each phonemic manipulation task for final sounds, proceed to the phonemic awareness tasks for medial sounds. Learning to hear the medial sounds in words helps pre-alphabetic readers notice the vowels that can be heard among a set of consonants. This lays the groundwork for decoding, expands vocabulary, and demonstrates to students how even simple words can differ by just one vowel sound. Learning to discriminate medial short vowel sounds prepares students to learn phonics rules. Recognizing medial vowel sounds builds familiarity with such patterns to facilitate decoding skills in the partial alphabetic reading phase. Although each phonemic awareness task for medial short vowels will be completed auditorily, continue to use the scaffolds in figure 1.4 (page 28) whenever necessary.

To begin teaching medial sounds, write *6* next to Word List on the lesson plan and check off *medial sounds*. In the right-hand column, check off *isolating*. For the first task, students will isolate the medial sound in a word you tell them. Work vertically down the list of words for medial sounds in the Isolating column of table 2.7.

TABLE 2.7: Word List 6—Words With Medial Sounds for Phonemic Manipulation Tasks

Isolating	Blending	Segmenting	Adding	Deleting	Substituting
big	m + u + t	math	m + a + d	top – o	mug – u + a =
What sound do you hear in the middle of the word big?	*What word do you get when you combine the sounds /m/, /u/, and /t/?*	*What sound do you hear in the middle of the word math?*	*What do you get when you add /a/ in the middle of /m/ and /d/?*	*Say "top." What two sounds do you have left if you remove the /o/ sound?*	*Say "mug." Now say "mug," but instead of /u/, say /a/. What word do you have now?*
has	l + e + d	had	j + a + m	sack – a	let – e + o =
tip	h + u + b	rob	y + e + t	dim – i	rub – u + o =
shot	b + i + t	lid	g + a + s	much – u	lash – a + u =
wet	h + u + t	mug	w + a + g	rod – o	hum – u + i =
rag	r + i + d	pod	b + a + ck	gap – a	sod – o + a =
jig	t + o + t	wed	n + o + d	six – i	shop – o + i =
cud	p + e + g	did	f + i + x	tub –u	jug – u + a =
lid	B + o + b	chop	p + i + ck	dip – i	fog – o + i =

Note: *The example row in italics indicates what the teacher would say.*

For your next lesson 2, you'll again check off *medial sounds*, but if students have mastered isolating, you'll check off *blending* in the right column. For each subsequent lesson 2, you'll check off *medial sounds* and the next phonemic manipulation task (as long as students have mastered the previous one). This continues until students have mastered each phonemic awareness manipulation task—isolating, blending, segmenting, adding, deleting, and substituting—for medial sounds. The first row of table 2.7 (page 57) contains an example for completing each task and the teacher language to use with the phonemic manipulation tasks for medial sounds. Each column of word list 6 contains eight words with medial sounds to manipulate for that phonemic awareness task.

Letter and Sound Learning

For letter and sound learning in lesson 2, repeat the same procedures for lesson 1 earlier in this chapter. Students will trace the letters on the ABC chart after you model them. Teach lowercase letter names before turning your attention to teaching sounds. Letter recognition builds visual familiarity so students are first able to distinguish between letters. This lays the groundwork for connecting visual letter representations to sounds. Letter names provide clues about sounds because many letter sounds are contained in their letter names.

Once students have mastered lowercase letter names, teach them most consonant sounds. Finally, teach students the names of the uppercase letters. Teach and practice handwriting and letter formation in this progression as well. The letter names or sounds you teach in this component should be the letter names and sounds you practice writing. Use the letter formation charts in the online resources along with the letter formation language for teaching students how to form each letter.

At the end of each week, or after you've completed a series of lessons, assess students for letter or sound knowledge before introducing new letters or sounds the following week. You may need to regroup students weekly or biweekly, as they'll learn and master letters and sounds at different paces. Use the "Letter-Sound Assessment" in appendix A (page 204) as often as needed. Follow the same steps in completing the Letter-Sound Assessment as you did for your initial assessment. Point to each letter and ask the students to identify the corresponding letter or sound. Mark the known sounds on the teacher score sheet. Students have mastered a sound when they can identify it in two or three seconds or less. Regroup your students when necessary, and plan your next set of lessons based on student progress and proficiency with letter and sound knowledge.

Reading and Concepts of Print

You'll repeat the procedures from lesson 1 earlier in this chapter for text reading and teaching a concept of print. You'll choose a short book, song, nursery rhyme, or poem and either echo- or choral-read it with the students. Then, you'll teach a concept of print. Pre-alphabetic students who don't yet have knowledge of letter-sound relationships still benefit greatly from reading experiences in which they learn about concepts of print. During this lesson plan component, pre-alphabetic students learn that print carries meaning, and they develop the alphabetic principle.

If you used a short book with repeated text, choose a different book for both lessons 1 and 2. Or, if you chose a song, poem, or nursery rhyme, continue reading that same text from lesson 1. This will allow you time to teach the rhyming words and rhythm of the text and help students become familiar with the meanings of the words. You'll either repeat the reading procedures and teach a new concept of print or continue to teach the same concept of print if students haven't yet mastered that concept.

Through the process of reading and engaging with texts, students learn that there's a connection between the words we read and the words we speak. Echo and choral reading expand oral language and build vocabulary and language skills essential to reading comprehension. While pre-alphabetic readers don't yet decode or necessarily recognize letters and sounds, instruction focused on reading texts plays a pivotal role in establishing the essential concepts reading success is built on.

Writing

You'll repeat the same procedures for lesson 1 earlier in this chapter for writing. You'll choose one or two sentences or phrases from the text that you read during your lesson. Using a whiteboard or sentence strips, you'll write short sentences or phrases and leave words or letters out. You'll then read the phrases with students, determine which words are missing, and write the missing words or letters in the blank spaces. The focus for the writing activity is for students to learn to listen to the initial, final, and medial sounds in familiar words. You'll also target correct letter formation and handwriting during the writing component.

This type of shared writing activity is extremely important for pre-alphabetic readers. When you complete this writing activity with students, it reinforces the concepts of print you're teaching during the reading portion of the lesson. You'll also build familiarity with sounds and the letters they correspond with. The action of filling in the blanks with the missing words helps establish the understanding that print represents the words we say and reinforces the concept of matching the words we say to printed words. This shared writing process creates a foundation for students' transition from oral language to decoding printed words.

After you've completed the activities for lessons 1 and 2, plan what text you would like students to read next. Using a variety of books, poems, songs, and nursery rhymes will familiarize students with various texts and genre types and will facilitate ongoing engagement for pre-alphabetic readers. Exposing pre-alphabetic readers to a variety of text types builds their comfort with the functions and features of many types of text. They begin to recognize key elements of narrative structures, poetry, and informational text. Teaching varied topics that students encounter and read about increases their academic knowledge and nurtures their spoken vocabulary and oral language skills. A sample completed lesson plan for the pre-alphabetic phase is shown in figure 2.6 (page 60).

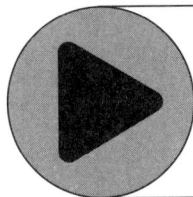

Use the QR code to watch a video of a teacher conducting a pre-alphabetic lesson 2.

Pre-Alphabetic Phase	
Lesson 1	**Lesson 2**
Phonological Awareness (2–3 minutes)	**Phonemic Awareness (2–3 minutes)**

Word List: 2		Word List: 4	
☐ Rhyming words	☐ Isolating	☐ Initial sounds	☐ Isolating
☐ Compound words	☑ Blending	☑ Final sounds	☐ Blending
☑ Syllables	☐ Segmenting	☐ Medial sounds	☐ Segmenting
☐ Rimes	☐ Adding		☑ Adding
	☐ Deleting		☐ Deleting
	☐ Substituting		☐ Substituting

Notes: Segmenting next	Notes: Review adding, move to deleting
Letter and Sound Learning (3–5 minutes)	**Letter and Sound Learning (3–5 minutes)**
Trace and Name Letters or Sounds: a, c, i, n, p, t	Trace and Name Letters or Sounds: a, c, i, n, p, t, u, f
Handwriting and Letter Formation: a, n, p, t	Handwriting and Letter Formation: a, n, p, t, u, f
Notes: Add *u* and *f*	Notes: Continue to practice using letter formation language
Reading and Concepts of Print (5 minutes)	**Reading and Concepts of Print (5 minutes)**
Text: "Little Boy Blue"	Text: "Little Boy Blue"

Reading Format:	☑ Echo read	☐ Choral read	Reading Format:	☐ Echo read	☑ Choral read

Teach a Concept of Print: First word / last word	Teach a Concept of Print: First word / last word
Notes: Listening for last word / rhyming words	Notes: Listening for last letter of words and rhyming words
Writing (3–5 minutes)	**Writing (3–5 minutes)**
Sentence From Text: The <u>cow's</u> <u>in</u> the <u>corn</u>.	Sentence From Text: He's <u>under</u> the haystack, <u>fast</u> <u>asleep</u>.
Teaching Focus:	Teaching Focus:

☐ Letter names and formation	☑ Letter sounds	☐ Beginning sounds	☐ Final sounds	☐ Letter names and formation	☑ Letter sounds	☐ Beginning sounds	☐ Final sounds

Notes for Next Lesson: Practice letter formation—n	Notes for Next Lesson: Practice letter formation—s, p

Source for text: Poetry Foundation, n.d.

FIGURE 2.6: Sample completed pre-alphabetic lesson plan.

Visit **go.SolutionTree.com/literacy** *to download a free reproducible version of this figure.*

Planning and Teaching Alliteration and Oddity Tasks (Optional)

If students need more practice with phonemic awareness activities, you can integrate alliteration and oddity tasks into your lessons, either at the end of each lesson or on an additional day of instruction. *Alliteration* is when the same letter sound occurs at the beginning of all—or most of—the words in a phrase. *Oddity tasks* are activities in which students decide which word in a set of words doesn't belong, since their initial, final, or medial sounds differ. These additional activities help students build their sound discrimination abilities. These exercises will also aid with decoding in the partial alphabetic phase. Visit **go.SolutionTree.com/literacy** for alliteration activities and directions for completing oddity tasks.

Answering Common Questions About the Pre-Alphabetic Phase

Having a strong grasp of the pre-alphabetic phase allows you to understand the foundational skills required for successful literacy instruction. Differentiating instruction based on students' needs and delivering targeted instruction will help students establish a firm understanding of how letters and sounds work in reading and writing. What follows are the most common questions about the pre-alphabetic reading phase that may not have been addressed in this chapter.

Why Should I Teach Letter Names Before Letter Sounds?

When learning to read and write in English, we typically teach letter names before letter sounds because English is one of the most opaque languages—letters can represent more than one sound. English is an extremely complicated language to learn, as it's not completely phonetic—it is considered *morphophonemic*. That is, words in English are composed of phonemic units, but they're also composed of *morphological units*—the smallest units of words that carry meaning. Therefore, letter and sound learning needs to be approached differently in English than in other languages that have a more regular correspondence between sounds and letters. Since letters in English are used to represent different sounds, we have to be able to confirm a word's spelling by naming which letters represent which sounds. For this reason, when learning to read in English, we must know letter names. Letter names are typically learned before sounds because identifying a letter name is an easier skill than recalling a sound.

Once students have mastered letter names with speed and automaticity, we can quickly turn the focus of instruction to letter sounds. Many letter names in English also contain the sound at the beginning or the end of the letter name (for example, the letter name *b* starts with /b/, and the letter name *m* ends with /m/). When students have become proficient in naming letters, they tend to implicitly learn letter sounds through a wealth of interaction with naming the letters.

Letter knowledge at the beginning of kindergarten strongly predicts later reading ability. By the end of kindergarten, students' knowledge of sounds most accurately predicts their reading ability, which indicates that knowledge of letters precedes knowledge of sounds in beginning readers. Knowing letter names provides students with a consistent visual anchor for then learning sounds. In English, knowing letter names implicitly helps with learning sounds.

When students enter school in the pre-alphabetic phase, the focus should be on learning letter names with speed and automaticity, then attaching sounds to the letter names. This will help reduce letter naming and sound confusion, letter reversals in handwriting and spelling, and confusing the difference between letters and sounds.

Why Do Students Need to Be Able to Identify Letters and Sounds So Quickly?

Letter-naming speed has long been considered one of the most important indicators to predict early reading development. This is referred to as *rapid automatized naming*, or RAN. In prereaders, RAN measures how quickly students can identify objects (letters, numbers, shapes, objects, and so forth). It indicates how quickly students can recall information. The speed at which students can retrieve and identify their letters and sounds depends on their visual processing skills, working memory, attention, processing speed, and motor skills.

Students' ability to name their letters and sounds strongly predicts decoding and fluency measures consistently through the second grade (Georgiou, Papadopoulos, Fella, & Parrila, 2012; Martinez, Georgiou, Inoue, Falcón, & Parrila, 2021; Wolff, 2014). The speed at which students can identify their letter names and sounds influences how quickly they can process the two when learning to decode words.

Not only does RAN reflect how quickly students can retrieve letter and sound names, but it also measures how efficiently they can process them in order from left to right for decoding words. RAN also involves the oral production of decoding words, and research suggests that this skill indicates later reading fluency and may be the most dominant skill underlying the relationship between RAN and reading (Georgiou & Parrila, 2020; Georgiou, Parrila, Cui, & Papadopoulos, 2013; Protopapas, Altani, & Georgiou, 2013).

It's possible to improve RAN speed with additional and adequate practice. Pre-alphabetic students should continue to trace and name their letters or sounds on the ABC chart and practice a variety of alphabet activities during and outside of small-group instruction. Pre-alphabetic students should remain in this phase until they can identify their letters and sounds quickly and automatically. Once they've attained success with this skill, and have developed phonological and phonemic awareness skills and concepts of print, it's appropriate to progress to the partial alphabetic phase and begin decoding words.

Overlooking the importance of letter and sound identification skills will only delay development of the orthographic mapping process. This expectation may demand more instructional and practice time for students who are acquiring letter and sound knowledge more slowly. If your more advanced pre-reading students are able to identify their letters and sounds quickly and automatically, why would you lower that expectation for any other students? Allowing students ample time to develop letter and sound naming ensures that all prereaders are equipped with the skills necessary for future reading success.

Transitioning Students to the Partial Alphabetic Phase

When students have successfully completed the phonemic awareness manipulation tasks with initial, final, and medial sounds and with the activities in lessons 1 and 2, you can assess whether they're prepared to transition to the partial alphabetic reading phase. Use the reproducible "Assessment to Transition to the Partial Alphabetic Phase" (appendix A, page 212) to determine whether students have mastered the pre-alphabetic reading phase. This assessment will aid you in pinpointing any gaps or inconsistencies in the foundational literacy skills, from the pre-alphabetic phase and onward. If students need continued instruction in the pre-alphabetic phase, use the supplemental word lists in appendix A (page 197) to complete additional phonological and phonemic manipulation tasks. Continue to teach letter names and sounds, concepts of print, and writing until students can reach a sufficient level of proficiency to progress to the partial alphabetic phase.

Students ready to transition to the partial alphabetic phase should be proficient in the following skills. Pre-alphabetic students may require the scaffolds in figure 1.4 (page 28) to complete the tasks; this is completely acceptable for this reading phase.

- Identify upper- and lowercase letter names with speed and automaticity

- Connect twenty-three or more letter sounds to letter names

- Blend compound words, syllables, onsets and rimes, and two to three individual phonemes of familiar words

- Isolate initial and final letter sounds in two- to three-phoneme words

- Segment sounds in two- to three-phoneme words

- Write their names and letters legibly with correct formation

- Identify concepts of print

- Discriminate between a letter name and a sound

- Follow directions within the small-group lesson

- Ask and answer questions about a text used in small-group instruction

- Retell or describe what they've read in small-group instruction

Conclusion

Before individuals can learn to read well, they need to master prereading skills to lay a proper foundation to be able to orthographically map letters and sounds successfully. The pre-alphabetic phase is arguably the most critical phase of reading and literacy development. Prereading skills are crucial to literacy development because they set students up to decode words independently and read with understanding. The skills contained in the pre-alphabetic lesson plan need to be established and developed before formal decoding instruction can begin. The stronger these prereading skills are, the more proficient students are in reading moving forward. Building a strong prereading foundation of phonological and phonemic awareness skills strengthens not only later decoding abilities but also encoding skills.

CHAPTER 3

Beginning to Read: The Partial Alphabetic Phase

Oh, magic hour when a child first knows it can read printed words!

—Betty Smith

In this chapter, you'll learn how to teach students to use phonetic decoding as their first strategy for reading words. I describe the characteristics of partial alphabetic readers and present the components of the partial alphabetic lesson plan. You'll learn how to assess and group your partial alphabetic readers, then, you'll learn how to teach students to decode similar words with four, five, six, and seven different changing phonemes. Students will learn to read and write the most common high-frequency words used in reading and writing. You'll learn how to incorporate phonetic and high-frequency words into sentences that you dictate for students to write. Next, I answer common questions about the partial alphabetic phase. Finally, the chapter concludes with instructions on how to determine whether students are ready to progress to the full alphabetic phase. Appendix B (page 217) contains the resources to be used with the partial alphabetic lessons.

Characterizing Partial Alphabetic Readers

Students entering the partial alphabetic reading phase may have some experience with books, but they aren't adept with the discrete skills involved in early reading development—segmenting and blending letters and sounds in printed text. They typically can identify their letters and sounds but aren't skilled in blending them to decode words. Partial alphabetic readers:

- Can identify most upper- and lowercase letters with speed and automaticity
- Can identify most letter sounds
- Can link most sounds to their letter names
- Can connect some of the letters and sounds in words—often first and last letters
- Can discriminate between a sound and a letter
- Use initial sounds to attempt to decode words

- Use some letters accurately when writing and begin to associate sounds to letters in writing
- Have limited ability to decode new words
- Display a short, labored decoding process
- Easily confuse short vowel sounds
- Mix up similarly spelled words in reading and writing

One characteristic that partial alphabetic readers won't display is quick and effortless reading skills, as their decoding abilities haven't fully emerged. Sometimes, partial alphabetic and beginning readers begin to develop a coping mechanism to offset their inability to phonetically decode words. They may attempt to read words solely by sight, memorization, or using context clues, such as guessing words based on pictures. These behaviors are characteristic of pre-alphabetic readers, but in the partial alphabetic phase, readers must shift their attention and working memory to phonetically decoding words. Memorizing words as whole units should never be a substitute for mastering letter names and sounds, and blending and segmenting to decode words. A formal assessment is included in appendix A (page 197) to determine whether students are prepared for the partial alphabetic reading phase. Students should be able to identify 90 percent of their letters and sounds and complete each of the tasks on the Assessment to Transition to the Partial Alphabetic Phase (see appendix A, page 212) with at least 80 percent accuracy, using any of the scaffolds in figure 1.4 (page 28).

Teaching Your Partial Alphabetic Readers

Partial alphabetic readers still have a limited ability to blend sounds together to read and segment words into sounds to spell and write. They need practice establishing their decoding skills to read words that confirm the letter-sound relationships they know. This is a fundamental switch from relying on pictures and environmental print for the reading they did prior to the pre-alphabetic phase. Continuing to teach the relationship between letter sounds is critically important during this reading phase. Systematic and explicit instruction focused on relating sounds to print, blending letter sounds, and manipulating phonemes lays the foundation for advancing to the full alphabetic reading phase. Meeting partial alphabetic readers based on their proficiency in letter-sound skills is key to maximizing decoding instruction.

Where to Focus Instruction During Small-Group Lessons

Although the focus of instruction for your partial alphabetic readers will be on decoding, isolated skills instruction in decoding doesn't produce effective learning outcomes, according to researcher Susan Brady (2020). Learning to read isn't a process that occurs in and of itself. The process of learning to read is dependent on transferring reading skills among four areas of literacy—(1) reading, (2) writing, (3) speaking, and (4) listening—within a variety of types of literacy activities. Each lesson on the partial alphabetic lesson plan contains a variety of literacy activities designed to develop reading, writing, speaking, and listening skills concurrently, rather than treat them as isolated skill sets. It's vital that your small-group instruction occurs within reading and writing connected text rather than learning to read words in isolation. Your small-group lessons for partial alphabetic readers will contain each of the following essential pieces.

- Mastering letter names and sounds with speed and automaticity

- Constructing orthographic mapping abilities through systematic phonics activities (isolating, blending, segmenting, deleting, and substituting individual letter sounds)

- Connecting letter sounds with letter names through writing and word-building activities

- Blending letters and sounds to read words with two and three sounds

- Developing left-to-right visual and auditory processes during reading and writing

- Learning to read and write at least ten high-frequency words necessary to construct basic sentences

- Linking the spelling and pronunciation of written words with meaning

- Strengthening letter formation and handwriting skills

How to Assess Your Partial Alphabetic Readers

Utilize the letter-sound assessment for pre-alphabetic readers in appendix A (page 204) to determine whether there are any remaining letters and sounds students may still need to master. Students should be able to name most upper- and lowercase letters in two to three seconds and identify most consonant and short vowel sounds. Use the results from the Assessment to Transition to the Partial Alphabetic Phase (appendix A, page 212) to be certain that students are prepared for the instruction in the partial alphabetic phase. The importance of students developing a basic level of phonemic awareness before they begin to phonetically decode words cannot be overlooked. If students aren't able to complete most tasks on this assessment, continue instruction using the pre-alphabetic lesson plan.

In addition to a letter-sound and phonemic awareness assessment, you can evaluate students' fine motor skills by administering a letter formation assessment. Use your own handwriting paper or make two copies of the Letter Formation Assessment (visit **go.SolutionTree.com/literacy** to download a free reproducible copy) to assess upper- and lowercase handwriting. Use this assessment piece to determine the amount of time to spend on handwriting during your lessons.

How to Group Your Partial Alphabetic Readers

There are several factors to consider when grouping students in the partial alphabetic phase that impact how quickly or slowly they'll progress through this phase.

- Identification of letters and sounds with speed and automaticity

- Speed in associating letter names and sounds

- Proficiency in manipulating phonemes

- Oral language skills

- Handwriting and letter-formation skills

- Amount of redirection or repetition needed during small-group-lesson tasks

Group students together in a needs- and skills-based arrangement that's manageable for you. During this phase, groups of up to six students at a time is manageable. Students with strong phonemic awareness abilities will progress more quickly through this phase. Therefore, phonemic awareness ability should be the major factor that dictates how you group students for small-group instruction. Grouping students according to how well they perform on the Assessment to Progress to the Partial Alphabetic Phase (page 212) will provide you with sufficient data to form your partial alphabetic groups. There are 141 items total on the assessment. You can group students by the following scores.

- 113–121 items correct (lower third of passing scores)

- 122–131 items correct (middle third of passing scores)

- 132 or more items correct (top third of passing scores)

The partial alphabetic phase is the opportune time to remediate difficulties for students who are struggling with phonemic awareness and phonics. For students of differing proficiency in phonemic awareness, small-group decoding instruction has been shown to be most effective in these early phases of reading development (IES, 2016). This phase is also the perfect time to provide advanced instruction for students who excel in these foundational reading skills. Small-group lessons provide greater opportunity for giving feedback and corrections, promptly modifying instruction, and adjusting the pace of learning for all your partial alphabetic readers.

Planning Lessons for Partial Alphabetic Readers

The partial alphabetic lesson plan contains three lessons. Lesson 1 focuses on word building, teaching high-frequency words, and writing; lesson 2 focuses on reading, teaching decoding skills, and discussing the text; and lesson 3 focuses on word building and reviewing high-frequency words, rereading, and writing. The lesson components within these series of lessons contain a variety of activities that connect the reading and writing processes and maximize the transfer of literacy skills to other activities throughout the school day. Each lesson is constructed to be completed in approximately twelve to fifteen minutes. The structure and components for the partial alphabetic lessons are shown in table 3.1.

TABLE 3.1: Partial Alphabetic Lesson Plan Structure and Components

Lesson 1	Lesson 2	Lesson 3
Word Building	Reading	Word Building and Review High-Frequency Words
High-Frequency Words	Teaching Decoding	Rereading
Writing—Sentence Dictation	Discussing Text	Writing—Sentence Dictation

Planning and Teaching Lesson 1

The activities in the partial alphabetic lessons are designed to piggyback on the phonemic tasks that students completed in the pre-alphabetic lessons. In this reading phase, students will use magnetic letters or tiles and sound boxes to manipulate phonemes so they learn to read and write simple words with short vowels. During each series of lessons, students will manipulate phonemes in words using three to seven sounds and the scaffolds in figure 1.4 (page 28). In addition, throughout each set of lessons, students will learn to read and write about ten high-frequency words (*the*, *and*, *is*, *I*, *a*, and so on). Students will also begin to write short sentences that you dictate to them that contain high-frequency and phonetic words.

The lesson 1 template is shown in figure 3.1.

Lesson 1			
Word Building (4–5 minutes)	Word List:	Level:	Scaffold:
High-Frequency Words (4–5 minutes)			
Complete Each Step:	Teach and map	Build	Write
Writing—Sentence Dictation (4–5 minutes)			
Teaching Focus:			

☐ Handwriting and letter formation	☐ Phonetic spelling	☐ High-frequency words	☐ Spacing	☐ Capitalization	☐ End punctuation

Notes for Next Lesson:

FIGURE 3.1: Partial alphabetic phase lesson 1.

*Visit **go.SolutionTree.com/literacy** to download a free reproducible version of this figure.*

Word Building

The purpose of the word-building activities is for students to learn how to read, spell, and write consonant-vowel-consonant (CVC) words. Activities that require students to build words, segment and blend words using manipulatives, and write words promote the orthographic mapping process by connecting reading and writing through phonemic manipulation. For the word-building activities, students will manipulate phonemes by making word chains and substituting letters in them to make new words. Students will each need a copy of the word mat in appendix B (page 220) and magnetic letters or tiles. Students may also need to refer to the ABC chart in appendix A (page 208 and 209) to review and practice letter names and sounds. Partial alphabetic readers may require much support and scaffolding while completing the word-building activities. Use the scaffolds from figure 1.4 (page 28) whenever necessary. The goal for mastery of word building by the end of the partial alphabetic phase is for students to be able to independently write the words used in the word-building activities.

There are four word lists for the word-building activities, numbered 1, 2, 3, and 4. Similar to the process of phonemic awareness development for pre-alphabetic readers, when students are learning to decode, they first master the connection between letters and sounds in the initial position of words, then in the final position, and finally in the medial position. The word lists are arranged in this format. Students will progress through the decoding process gradually while mastering the blending and segmenting of phonemes in each phoneme position. When they reach word list 4, they should be able to manipulate any phoneme in the initial, final, or medial position of any CVC word. The word lists and the phonemes to be manipulated for that list are shown in table 3.2 (page 70).

TABLE 3.2: Word Lists and Phonemes to Manipulate

List	Phonemes to Be Manipulated
1	Initial
2	Final
3	Medial
4	Initial, final, and medial

For each word list, there are up to four difficulty levels (labeled A, B, C, and D) depending on how many phonemes students will use for the words to build for that activity. The word building lists follow a progression in order of difficulty based on the number of phonemes for manipulation. Words where there's a choice of only four possible phonemes (level A) will be easier for students to work with than words where there's a choice of six (level C) or seven (level D) possible phonemes to manipulate. The number of phonemes for each level is shown in table 3.3.

TABLE 3.3: Level and Number of Phonemes

Level	Number of Phonemes Used
A	4
B	5
C	6
D	7 or more

Not every word list contains words at every level, but students must be able to complete the words given for every level before moving on to the next word list. Each word level contains up to five sets of words to build. Complete both the reading and phonemic manipulation tasks following the directions in tables 1.5 (page 26) and 1.6 (page 27). Use the scaffolds from figure 1.4 (page 28) as necessary. Work down the word lists until students can write the words independently with little scaffolding. If students are skilled with manipulating multiple phonemes in words, you don't need to begin at level A for word list 3—you can begin at level B or C. When students can quickly and easily write the words from a level, move on to the next level in that word list.

The words on the word lists were designed so that each letter sound in the initial position is a conso-nant sound that can be stretched. A *stretch sound* is a sound that can be elongated when pronounced, such as the sounds that represent the letters *f, h, j, l, m, n, r, s, v, w, y,* and *z*. Each sound in the final position of the words is a *stop sound*—a letter sound that has a definite ending to it (without adding "uh" to the end). The stop sounds in the word lists are *b, d, g, p, t,* and *x*. Words that contain these sounds in the initial and final positions lend themselves to being blended with ease. The use of these words will facilitate the orthographic mapping process as smoothly as possible.

Follow the directions for completing the word-building lesson plan component provided in chapter 1 (page 7) for both decoding and encoding. In lesson plan 1, you'll write the scaffold and word list you'll start teaching with. Next, circle *level A*. For each word list (tables 3.4–3.7), spend three to four minutes completing the word-building activities (both the reading and phonemic manipulation tasks) with each set of words, using the scaffolds from figure 1.4 (page 28) as needed.

Table 3.4 contains word list 1. Word list 1 consists of words in all four levels—A, B, C, and D. In this word list, all words have the same final sounds to blend. Students will only substitute the initial consonant before the rime unit.

TABLE 3.4: Word List 1

Word List 1			
Rime Unit	**Initial Letters to Be Substituted**	**Letters Needed**	**Words to Make**
Level A			
-eb	j, w	b, e, j, w	jeb → web
-eg	l, M	e, g, l, m	leg → Meg
-ib	f, l	b, f, i, l	fib → lib
-od	r, s	d, o, r, s	rod → sod
-ud	m, s	d, m, s, u	mud → sud
Level B			
-ub	h, r, s	b, h, r, s, u	hub → rub → sub
Level C			
-ab	f, j, l, n	a, b, f, j, l, n	fab → jab → lab → nab
-ig	f, j, r, w	f, g, i, j, r, w	fig → jig → rig → wig
-ip	h, l, s, z	h, i, l, p, s, z	hip → lip → sip → zip
-op	h, l, m, s	h, l, m, o, p, s	hop → lop → mop → sop
-ut	h, j, n, r	h, j, n, r, t, u	hut → jut → nut → rut
Level D			
-ot	h, j, l, n, r	h, j, l, n, o, r, t	hot → jot → lot → not → rot
-id	h, l, m, r, S	d, h, i, l, m, r, s	hid → lid → mid → rid → Sid
-ug	h, j, l, m, r	g, h, j, l, m, r, u	hug → jug → lug → mug → rug
-et	j, l, m, n, s, v, w, y	e, j, l, m, n, s, t, v, w, y	jet → let → met → net → set → vet → wet → yet
-ag	h, j, l, m, n, r, s, w, z	a, g, h, j, l, m, n, r, s, w, z	hag → jag → lag → mag → nag → rag → sag → wag → zag

Table 3.5 (page 72) contains word list 2. Word list 2 consists of words in all four levels—A, B, C, and D. For these words, students will substitute the final consonant in words that have the same two sounds at the beginning of the word.

TABLE 3.5: Word List 2

Word List 2			
Unit	Final Letters to Be Substituted	Letters Needed	Words to Make
Level A			
ja-	b, g	a, b, g, j	jab → jag
mo-	b, p	b, m, o, p	mob → mop
su-	b, d	b, d, s, u	sub → sud
ve-	t, x	e, t, v, x	vet → vex
wi-	g, t	g, i, t, w	wig → wit
Level B			
fo-	b, g, x	b, f, g, o, x	fob → fog → fox
ha-	d, g, t	a, d, g, h, t	had → hag → hat
ru-	b, g, t	b, g, r, t, u	rub → rug → rut
zi-	g, p, t	g, i, p, t, z	zig → zip → zit
Level C			
li-	b, d, p, t	b, d, i, l, p, t	lib → lid → lip → lit
fi-	b, g, t, x	b, f, g, i, t, x	fib → fig → fit → fix
ra-	d, g, p, t	a, d, g, p, r, t	rad → rag → rap → rat
ri-	b, d, g, p	b, d, g, i, p, r	rib → rid → rig → rip
sa-	d, g, p, t	a, d, g, p, s, t	sad → sag → sap → sat
Level D			
lo-	b, g, p, t, x	b, g, l, o, p, t, x	lob → log → lop → lot → lox
ma-	d, g, p, t, x	a, d, g, m, p, t, x	mad → mag → map → mat → max
la-	b, d, g, p, t, x	a, b, d, g, l, p, t, x	lab → lad → lag → lap → lat → lax

Table 3.6 contains word list 3. Word list 3 consists of words in only three levels—A, B, and C. For these words, students will substitute the medial short vowel in words that have the same initial and final consonants. This is one of the more difficult phonological tasks, as students tend to master the medial sound in CVC words last. Short vowel sounds are also similar depending on dialect, and learning to discriminate between these discrete sounds can take some students additional instructional time to master.

Table 3.7 contains word list 4. Word list 4 consists of words in only two levels—C and D. For each of these words, students will substitute the initial, final, or medial sound. These are the most advanced phonemic awareness tasks and shouldn't be used until students are proficient in word building using lists 1, 2, and 3 with very little scaffolding. Students should be able to independently write the words from level C or D after you dictate them. Students must know which sound they need to substitute and in what position of the word—initial, final, or medial—to complete each task in word list 4.

TABLE 3.6: Word List 3

Word List 3			
Initial Letter	Medial Letters to Be Substituted	Letters Needed	Words to Make
Level A			
f	a, i	a, f, i, t	fat → fit
h	i, o	h, i, o, p	hip → hop
j	a, u	a, g, j, u	jag → jug
m	a, e	a, e, m, t	mat → met
n	e, o	d, e, o, n	Ned → nod
Level B			
f	a, i, o	a, b, f, i, o	fab → fib → fob
l	a, e, i	a, d, e, i, l	lad → led → lid
r	i, o, u	b, i, o, r, u	rib → rob → rub
s	a, i, o	a, i, o, p, s	sap → sip → sop
m	a, e, u	a, e, g, m, u	mag → Meg → mug
Level C			
h	a, i, o, u	a, h, i, o, t, u	hat → hit → hot → hut
l	a, e, o, u	a, e, g, l, o, u	lag → leg → log → lug
l	a, e, i, o	a, e, i, l, o, t	lat → let → lit → lot
r	a, e, i, o	a, d, e, i, o, r	rad → red → rid → rod
s	a, i, o, u	a, d, i, o, s, u	sad → Sid → sod → sud

TABLE 3.7: Word List 4

Word List 4		
Letters Needed	Starting Word	Substitute Initial, Medial, or Final Letter to Make the Next Word
Level C		
a, b, d, o, r, s, t	rot	→ rat → rad → sad → sod → sob
Level D		
a, b, g, h, j, o, t	hat	→ hot → hog → jog → jag → jab
a, e, g, j, r, t, u	rut	→ rat → rug → jug → jut → jet
a, g, i, n, p, r, u	nip	→ rip → rap → rag → rug → rig
a, b, h, i, r, t, u	hub	→ rub → rut → rat → hat → hit
e, d, h, i, l, o, p, t	led	→ lid → lip → hip → hop → hot

If time permits, after you've taught the word-building component, spend time reviewing letter names and sounds, teaching any remaining letter names or sounds, or having students build the simple CVC words that they'll read in the book you choose for lesson 2. Use the scaffolds from figure 1.4 (page 28) and have students practice blending the letter sounds to decode the words. Students physically building words that they'll decode helps reinforce the phonetic decoding process and build their confidence when they read during lesson 2. Constructing words that they'll then read orally gives partial alphabetic readers practice connecting letters and sounds and builds their confidence with decoding—a novel process for partial alphabetic readers.

High-Frequency Words

Since partial alphabetic readers haven't developed the orthographic proficiency to have a large bank of words that they recognize quickly and automatically, using the term *sight word* isn't appropriate for this lesson plan component. The term *high-frequency word* will be used instead. *High-frequency words* are the words that appear most often in texts, and they can differ based on which list is used (Dolch or Fry).

Focus on teaching one or two high-frequency words per lesson. In lesson plan 1, there are spaces for you to write up to two high-frequency words to teach. When choosing which words to teach your partial alphabetic readers, don't choose words that are so complex that they'll overburden students. Teach only the high-frequency words that are in the text you're reading that your partial alphabetic readers won't be able to decode because they may contain irregular phonics patterns or phonics patterns you haven't taught yet. Spend four to five minutes of lesson 1 teaching sight words using the steps outlined in the section High-Frequency and Sight Words in chapter 1 (page 7).

Linda Farrell, Michael Hunter, and Tina Osenga (n.d.) recommend first teaching the simple high-frequency words in table 3.8 to partial alphabetic readers. These words are the most common words in texts for partial alphabetic readers. With these words, students can use the first letter sound and the letter names to easily recognize them. They also contain letters that are easier to identify and form in writing.

TABLE 3.8: High-Frequency Words for Beginning Readers

Word	Dolch Frequency Rank	Fry Frequency Rank
a	5	4
I	6	20
the	1	1
to	2	5
and	3	3
was	11	12
for	16	13
you	7	8
is	22	7
of	9	2

Source: Adapted from Farrell et al., n.d.

Once students have mastered these first few high-frequency words, choose which high-frequency words to teach based on what matches your readers' needs. Also, consider your text because you'll want students to be able to write these words in a dictated sentence. If you have a high-frequency word list that you already use, proceed to teach those words after students can read and write the ten words in table 3.8.

Writing—Sentence Dictation

Having students practice writing simple sentences that you've dictated is a critical component of the partial alphabetic phase. Phonemic awareness activities through writing tasks that systematically progress through the phases of the orthographic patterns targeted during phonics instruction enhance letter and sound awareness and spelling knowledge (Brady, 2020). This component of the lesson plan also gives you the opportunity to reinforce the spelling of high-frequency words that contain irregular phonics patterns. Sentence dictation will be repeated during lesson 3. Follow these four steps for sentence dictation.

1. Say the sentence phrased and have students repeat it several times.
2. Have students count the number of words in the sentence or in each phrase.
3. As each student does this, write a blank line for each word on the student's writing page or word mat for each word.
4. Have students go back to the beginning of the phrase or sentence, say it orally, then begin to write it one word at a time.

As students progress through the partial alphabetic phase, you may begin to have them write each word without your writing the lines first. You'll need to teach proper spacing between words. You may need to construct sound boxes for the words in the sentences on the lines to support students' segmenting and blending to write and read the words. Direct students to always say words out loud as they write the corresponding words; also, make sure they slide from one sound into the next without pausing between and that they simultaneously write the letter or letters that match the sounds coming out of their mouths to tightly integrate phoneme-grapheme connections.

Differentiate the support you provide for students during writing based on their individual needs. Some students may need scaffolding to connect sounds to the letters they represent, while others will need to practice improving handwriting or using end punctuation. Use the skills across the bottom of the lesson plan template as a progression for differentiating your instruction for each student. After students finish writing the sentence, choose a teaching point as your focus for students to edit their sentences. The teaching points are in developmental order from left to right on the lesson plan. Students should edit their sentences for handwriting and letter formation first; then phonetic spelling and high-frequency words; and finally, spacing, capitalization, and end punctuation. Focus on one skill per lesson after writing the dictated sentences. Don't move on to editing for the next skill until students have mastered the writing skill you're currently teaching.

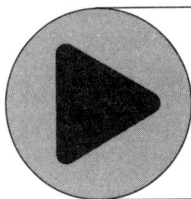

Use the QR code to watch a video of a teacher conducting a partial alphabetic lesson 1.

Planning and Teaching Lesson 2

In lesson 2, students will read a text, and you'll explicitly teach the process of decoding words. You'll then facilitate a discussion about the text. When deciding which text types are best for partial alphabetic readers, begin by using decodable texts. Beginning readers by nature are prone to trying to read words by guessing based on context, their knowledge of environmental print, and pictures (Ehri, 2020). If they continue reading texts that contain repetitive phrases and don't promote phonetic decoding, it'll reinforce their innate habit of guessing words through context. This will delay their ability to learn to decode words phonetically and develop the orthographic mapping process. After you teach decoding skills, you'll facilitate a discussion about the text.

Lesson 2 is shown in figure 3.2.

Lesson 2	
Text Title:	Phonics Skill:
Reading (8–9 minutes)	
Give Overview and Introduce Phonics Skill or High-Frequency Words:	
Strategies and Actions for Decoding (Check box when used during the lesson):	
☐ Stretch / blend the letter sounds.	☐ Chunk the word at the onset and rime.
☐ Try this sound. . .	☐ Dictate or make word via sounds → letters.
☐ Have student blend sounds aurally, then read.	☐ Does that make sense?
Strategies and Actions for Fluency and Comprehension (Check box when used during the lesson):	
☐ Frame two to three words for student to practice fluency.	☐ What did you read? Tell me about it.
☐ Read along and then repeat after me.	☐ What was the most important part?
Teaching Decoding (2–3 minutes)	
Examples:	
Discussing Text (2–3 minutes; use cards in appendix B, page 221)	
Notes for Next Lesson:	

FIGURE 3.2: Partial alphabetic phase lesson 2.

Visit **go.SolutionTree.com/literacy** *to download a free reproducible version of this figure.*

Reading

During lesson 2, students will read and reread decodable text to promote the orthographic mapping process. The book you choose for students to read will contain your phonics skills or focus for this lesson. Follow the scope and sequence that you use to teach your whole-group phonics. Like teaching individual letter sounds, the most important aspect is that your lessons are consistent and that you teach phonics with fidelity, differentiating where and when necessary. Regroup students when you notice their progress with decoding changes and place them in groups of students with similar needs.

The book you choose may also contain the high-frequency words you teach throughout the three lessons. Choose high-quality decodable texts that promote the use of letter-sound relationships as the first action to take when reading unknown words and reinforce phonics skills being taught. The controlled vocabulary of decodable texts also helps build fluency because readers are less likely to guess words or read them incorrectly. This motivates readers, builds their confidence, and increases their accuracy and fluency. Students get the repetitive practice they need to orthographically map letter-sound patterns, which aids in automatizing sound-spelling patterns.

Give students a quick overview of the book—character names and a one-sentence summary are sufficient for a literary text. For an informational text, in a single-sentence summary, tell students what they'll read to learn about. Allow students to look through the text and examine the illustrations or text features to activate their *schema* (or understanding) and background knowledge and connect to the text. Use this time to introduce any new vocabulary or high-frequency words contained in the text. Simply point them out, tell students the sounds in the words, and have them blend the sounds to pronounce each word you're introducing. Explain to students that they'll read the text independently by blending the letter sounds and pronouncing each word.

Spend the next eight to nine minutes listening to each student read. Take anecdotal notes or an informal reading record on the back of the lesson plan. Students should whisper-read independently to practice blending letter sounds on their own. During this reading phase, blending letter sounds may take several seconds, and students will need to blend letter sounds aloud—this is expected and completely normal. After much practice, students in the partial alphabetic phase will be able to decode a CVC word within a few seconds. Provide strategies and actions first if students need support in decoding, then for fluency, and finally, only for comprehension if the student doesn't make any decoding errors. If students finish reading the text early, they can reread it or read other decodable texts with the same phonics skill or pattern.

If students read words incorrectly, use the following six decoding strategies and actions to provide feedback. They are in the lesson plan in two columns in order from the most amount of support in left-hand column (top to bottom) to the least support in the right-hand column.

1. Stretch and blend the letter sounds.
2. Tell the student the correct sound to try.
3. Segment the letter sounds on your fingers for the student to blend auditorily first. Then, bring their attention back to letters in the word in the text and have them blend the letters and sounds themselves.
4. Divide, or chunk, the word at the onset and rime.
5. Use the word mat and dictate the sounds in the word for the student to write in the sound boxes. Have the student slide their finger under the word and blend the letter sounds. Direct the student to do the same with the word in the text.
6. Once the student has reread and corrected the word and finished reading the sentence, ask whether that makes sense. This will promote the student's ability to self-monitor and self-correct any decoding errors.

If students decode each word correctly, then provide responses for them that promote fluency. The fluency strategies are in the lesson plan in the left-hand column. The following two responses require students to practice fluency.

1. Place your fingers around two to three words at a time for students to practice phrased reading. You can also drag your finger and scoop underneath two to three words at a time.
2. Read a page and have students reread and repeat after you.

Be sure that students can read the text fluently, using appropriate phrasing, before asking them comprehension questions. Choose one of these two comprehension questions to ask from the column on the right-hand side of the lesson plan.

1. "What did you read? Tell me about it." This response to students' reading is open-ended and gives them an opportunity to expand their thinking.

2. "What was the most important part?" This response allows students to justify and summarize what they've read.

Each time you complete lesson 2, mark your anecdotal notes on the back of the lesson plan. This will help you to tailor your future feedback for decoding strategies and actions so they specifically meet each student's needs and abilities.

Teaching Decoding

For the second component of lesson 2, you'll model phonetic decoding for students using words to demonstrate the process of segmenting and blending phonemes. Teacher modeling is an invaluable instructional strategy for supporting early decoding skills. When teachers explicitly show how to decode words, it helps students understand the step-by-step process for reading unknown words. This demonstration helps demystify what can be an abstract process for many partial alphabetic readers. Spend two to three minutes modeling how to phonetically decode some words from the text students read. Choose two or three words from the text as examples for teaching phonetic decoding and jot them down on the lesson plan. Follow these four steps to model decoding like a think-aloud.

1. Write a word on a small whiteboard.

2. Slide your finger under it and begin pronouncing the letter sounds and blending them.

3. Repeat this process and have students stretch and blend the letter sounds along with you until you together arrive at the correct pronunciation of the word.

4. Repeat this process for one or two more words from the text.

You can also write letters in sound boxes to demonstrate blending letter sounds or write one letter at a time on the whiteboard while students blend the sounds to pronounce the word. You could also use magnetic letters or tiles and push them up one at a time to model how to blend letter sounds. Refer to the scaffolds in figure 1.4 (page 28) and use additional supports if you need to.

Verbalizing letter-sound relationships also helps cement basic phonics rules for decoding. Modeling the decoding process allows teachers to illustrate the self-monitoring process, like rereading when errors occur and self-correcting pronunciation inaccuracies. For example, in the word *has*, the *s* makes a /z/ sound. When reading *has* in the context of a sentence, the reader needs to self-correct and adjust their pronunciation of the word to sound like "haz." Demonstrating the processes of self-monitoring and self-correcting aids students in practicing these strategies regularly in their own decoding. Making the decoding process concrete and visible for students promotes mastery through imitation and repetition and helps students internalize good reading habits.

Discussing Text

The third component of lesson 2 consists of facilitating a comprehension discussion about the text. Many times, texts for partial alphabetic readers are so simplified, they don't lend themselves to rich, thought-provoking discussions. For this reason, use the Conversation Starter Comprehension Cards in appendix B (page 221) to guide your discussion about the text. These open-ended discussion starters provide more insight into students' thinking than "teacher asks and students answer" types of questions.

Asking open-ended questions where students must support their thinking and make connections promotes higher-order literacy skills. These questions encourage a meaningful discussion and serve as a springboard for a more in-depth conversation about the text. This comprehension discussion is an ideal time for students to refine their oral language skills while discussing the text. Spend two to three minutes leading a discussion about the text students read.

Use the QR code to watch a video of a teacher conducting a partial alphabetic lesson 2.

Planning and Teaching Lesson 3

Lesson 3 is composed of a combination of the same activities completed in lessons 1 and 2, so it has four components. You'll continue in the progression of word-building activities from lesson 1 and again complete the steps for teaching high-frequency words with the same words you taught in lesson 1. Students will reread the text to practice fluency. You'll again dictate one or two sentences for students to write and will choose a teaching point to integrate as an editing practice after they've completed the dictated sentence. Figure 3.3 shows the components for lesson 3.

Lesson 3			
Word Building (3–4 minutes)	Word List:	Level:	Scaffold:
Review High-Frequency Words (3–4 minutes)			
Complete Each Step:	Teach and map	Build	Write
Rereading (3–4 minutes)			
Reading Format:	☐ Independent read	☐ Echo read	☐ Choral read	☐ Partner read
Strategies and Actions for Fluency and Comprehension (Check box when used during the lesson):			
☐ Frame two to three words for student to practice fluency. ☐ Read along and then repeat after me.		☐ What did you read? Tell me about it. ☐ What was the most important part?	
Writing—Sentence Dictation (3–4 minutes)			
Teaching Focus:			
☐ Handwriting and letter formation	☐ Phonetic spelling	☐ High-frequency words	☐ Spacing	☐ Capitalization	☐ End punctuation
Notes for Next Lesson:			

FIGURE 3.3: Partial alphabetic phase lesson 3.

*Visit **go.SolutionTree.com/literacy** to download a free reproducible version of this figure.*

Word Building

For the word-building component, you'll spend three to four minutes teaching students to build word chains like you did for lesson 1. First, based on how students did with building words in lesson 1, decide on the appropriate scaffold and record it on the lesson plan. If the scaffold you used was appropriate, you can continue to use it for your next set of words or provide less support by choosing the next scaffold from figure 1.4 (page 28). If students need more support, use the same word list you used in lesson 1 with a scaffold that offers more support for students. Then, write the word list number and phonics pattern. If students are proficient in writing the words you dictated on a list, move to the next level or word list. You can use a set of words and move down the list of scaffolds until students can write the words independently as you dictate them. Then, try dictating another set of words for students to write from that list and level. If they can write the words independently, move on to the next level or word list. If students haven't mastered a word list, provide additional support using the supplemental lists in appendix B (page 222) until they have mastered each word list pattern.

Review High-Frequency Words

After students have completed the word-building task, choose another high-frequency word from table 3.8 (page 74), choose a high-frequency word from the text the students read, or continue to practice the high-frequency word or words from lesson 1 if students can't yet write them independently. Spend three to four minutes and follow the same three steps for teaching high-frequency words as you did for lesson 1.

Rereading

Rereading familiar text is incredibly valuable for reinforcing decoding skills for partial alphabetic readers. Revisiting previously read texts gives students more decoding practice so you can ensure mastery before moving on to more complex phonics and spelling patterns.

For the rereading lesson component, first decide which format you'd like to use. If students were successful with their decoding during lesson 2, choose an echo, choral, or partner read for the rereading, as explained in chapter 1 (page 7). If students need additional practice with decoding words, provide strategies and actions for them as you listen to them read independently.

Writing—Sentence Dictation

For the writing lesson plan component, plan for students to write one sentence that you dictate that includes the phonics skills and high-frequency words you've taught. The process of encoding (or spelling) requires that students pay attention to the relationship of sounds to the letters they represent, which is a more difficult process in the brain than decoding words. Writing phonetic and high-frequency words within the context of sentences helps increase working memory, which enables the brain to concentrate on the next set of skills. Research studies that showed the best results used a combination of phonemic awareness within the context of reading and writing. Students in these studies who had previously displayed difficulty in their reading and writing reached a level of expected reading proficiency (Suggate, 2016).

When students practice correct letter formation when writing words and phrases, it adds fine motor planning and memory to the writing process, which helps them orthographically map words faster and more efficiently. Follow the same process from lesson 1 to dictate one sentence for students to write. Incorporate a few words from the word-building lesson component with one or two high-frequency words you've taught to create one sentence containing three to seven words. Students can use the dotted lines at the bottom of the word mat to write the sentence, or they can write it in a writing journal. When you dictate the sentence for students to write, say them phrased, grouping two or three words at a time. To practice fluency, have students reread their sentence, grouping two or three words at a time when they read it.

After students finish writing the sentence, choose a teaching point from those listed under Teaching Focus in lesson plan 3 for students to edit their sentence. Focus on the next skill if students are proficient in the skill you taught during lesson 1. If students aren't proficient in applying the skill you taught during lesson 1, repeat editing sentences with that skill as your focus. Don't move on to editing for the next skill until students have mastered the writing skill you're currently teaching. A sample completed lesson plan for the partial alphabetic phase is shown in figure 3.4.

Use the QR code to watch a video of a teacher conducting a partial alphabetic lesson 3.

Partial Alphabetic Phase			
Lesson 1			
Word Building (4–5 minutes)	Word List: 4	Level: C	Scaffold: Magnetic letters
High-Frequency Words (4–5 minutes)	was		you
Complete Each Step:	Teach and map	Build	Write
Writing—Sentence Dictation (4–5 minutes)			
The cub was wet from snow.		Do you like when the cubs play?	
Teaching Focus:			
☐ Handwriting and letter formation / ☑ Phonetic spelling / ☑ High-frequency words	☐ Spacing	☐ Capitalization	☐ End punctuation
Notes for Next Lesson: Word list 4, level C, and assess students to progress to full alphabetic phase			
Lesson 2			
Text Title: *Cub Fun*		Phonics Skill: CVC words and plurals	
Reading (8–9 minutes)			
Give Overview and Introduce Phonics Skill or High-Frequency Words: play			
Strategies and Actions for Decoding (Check box when used during the lesson):			
☐ Stretch / blend the letter sounds.		☐ Chunk the word at the onset and rime.	
☐ Try this sound . . .		☐ Dictate or make word via sounds → letters.	
☐ Have student blend sounds aurally, then read.		☐ Does that make sense?	

FIGURE 3.4: Sample completed partial alphabetic lesson plan.

continued ▶

Strategies and Actions for Fluency and Comprehension (Check box when used during the lesson):	
☐ Frame 2–3 words for student to practice fluency. ☐ Read along and then repeat after me.	☐ What did you read? Tell me about it. ☐ What was the most important part?

Teaching Decoding (2–3 minutes)
Examples: cubs, pals, get, hot, mud (short *e, o, u*)

Discussing Text (2–3 minutes; use cards in appendix B, page 221)
Notes for Next Lesson: Choose text with CVC words and all five short vowels.

Lesson 3			
Word Building (3–4 minutes)	Word List: 4	Level: C	Scaffold: None
Review High-Frequency Word (2–3 minutes)	was		you	
Complete Each Step:	Teach and map	Build	Write

Rereading (3–4 minutes)				
Reading Format:	☐ Independent read	☐ Echo read	☐ Choral read	☐ Partner read

Strategies and Actions for Fluency and Comprehension (Check box when used during the lesson):	
☐ Frame 2–3 words for student to practice fluency. ☐ Read along and then repeat after me.	☐ What did you read? Tell me about it. ☐ What was the most important part?

Writing—Sentence Dictation (3–4 minutes)	
The cub was hot in the sun.	Did you see the cubs swim?

Teaching Focus:					
☐ Handwriting and letter formation	☐ Phonetic spelling	☐ High-frequency words	☐ Spacing	☑ Capitalization	☑ End punctuation

Notes for Next Lesson:

Source for text: Cub Fun

*Visit **go.SolutionTree.com/literacy** to download a free reproducible version of this figure.*

Answering Common Questions About the Partial Alphabetic Phase

Most of your focus for instruction during the partial alphabetic phase will be on helping students develop efficient blending and segmenting skills to decode words. Having a deep understanding of the process by which partial alphabetic readers begin to read and write simple words allows you to understand the process of building the neurological system for orthographic mapping. Differentiating instruction based on students' needs and delivering targeted instruction will help students establish a firm understanding of how letters and sounds work in reading and writing. It also supports students learning at their own pace, eliminating gaps in literacy skills. What follows are the most common questions about the partial alphabetic reading phase that may not have been addressed in this chapter.

Should I Use a Word Wall in My Classroom?

There is very little research that supports using a word wall to assist in spelling and writing words. A word wall encourages students to look for and copy how to spell and write words rather than to process the letters and sounds to promote orthographic mapping. For students to write and approximate the correct spelling of words, we want them to be able to segment the sounds in a word and think, "What sound do I hear? What letter is that?" This process of connecting sounds to the letters they represent reinforces decoding and spelling skills and provides students with a process for writing words on their own using phonological skills. Displaying a word wall doesn't promote that process as a first choice; instead, it promotes the visual memorization of words as whole units—an ineffective practice. A word wall encourages students to look for shortcuts in writing and spelling words correctly rather than using their own phonological abilities to connect sounds to the letters they represent.

A sound wall is considered a more effective tool for spelling and writing than a word wall. A sound wall displays the mouth positions we make to produce each sound and the letters that can be used to represent those sounds in spelling. Using a sound wall when spelling and writing reinforces the process used in writing—segmenting words into their own individual sounds and then associating the sounds with the letters they represent. This encoding helps increase phonological processing abilities for students. The mouth formation cards on a sound wall help students process and write each sound in the words they want to write. For these reasons, a sound wall is a better option than a word wall.

Because a sound wall can take up a lot of the wall space in your classroom, you could create a personal file folder "sound wall" for each student. You can shrink down the mouth position cards and letter representations so the vowels and consonants are each on one side of the folder. You can purchase high-quality sound wall materials from companies such as hand2mind (www.hand2mind.com), the Institute for Multi-Sensory Education (https://imse.com), Oxford Speech Plus (www.oxfordspeechplus.ca), 95 Percent Group (https://store.95percentgroup.com), or Learning By Design (https://shop.learning bydesign.com).

What Can I Do if My Students Can Blend Letter Sounds but Then Can't Read the Word Correctly?

There are a few possible reasons why students may be able to say the individual sounds in a word but not the full word itself. Putting individual sounds together into a full word requires blending abilities that may still be emerging for some partial alphabetic students. Typically, students have to sound out a word one to four times before they can read the word automatically (Kilpatrick, 2015). Students with weak phonemic awareness skills will require additional exposure to words and more opportunities to blend letters and sounds during reading and word building.

Even when students know letters and sounds, retrieving and sequencing the sounds from memory can pose a challenge for some. With targeted, persistent, individualized practice focused on blending, word analysis through word building, and word retrieval, students often improve in their ability to read unfamiliar words over time. This reinforcement of letter and sound skills typically improves word reading over time. If partial alphabetic readers aren't saying a word correctly after blending its isolated sounds, try the other blending techniques in table 3.9 (page 84).

TABLE 3.9: Blending Techniques

Technique	Procedures
Sequential blending	Begin by having the student blend the first two letter sounds together. Once the student can smoothly blend the first two sounds together, add on the third sound without segmenting the first two sounds that you blended. Practice blending the first two sounds (as a cluster) with the third sound until the student can smoothly pronounce the blended cluster of three phonemes. Continue adding on one phoneme at a time in this progression until students can smoothly pronounce the entire word.
Auditory blending	Have the student blend the letter sounds auditorily first, then have them pronounce the word. Next, uncover the letters in the word one at a time and have the student blend and pronounce the word again.
Isolated blending	Say the first sound the loudest and then speak softer as you get to the end of the word. Students tend to start blending with the loudest sound they heard.
Snap blending	Have the student blend the first two sounds together, then snap your finger and have them produce the last sound, then the word.
Stretch blending	Stretch the medial short vowel in the word. This will help students to store the initial letter sounds in short-term memory before pronouncing the last sound.

In addition to these blending techniques, be sure to use the words from the word-building components of the lesson plan. They contain words that are easiest to blend: They begin with a stretch sound and end with a stop sound. All medial short vowels are stretch sounds. When pronounced correctly, none of the words in the lessons should contain a schwa sound ("uh") at the end; for example, the sound for the letter *t* is /t/, not "tuh." Using these words ensures that students are blending letter sounds without adding an extra "uh" to words.

Transitioning Students to the Full Alphabetic Phase

For students to transition to the full alphabetic phase, they should be proficient in several skills. Students transitioning to the full alphabetic phase shouldn't need the word-building scaffolds in the lesson plans when reading CVC words. Students have acquired the reading and spelling skills necessary to transition to the full alphabetic phase when they've established an orthographic memory for independently reading CVC and common high-frequency words. An orthographic memory has been constructed when students are able to remember and retain the letter and sound (or orthographic) patterns in words. The orthographic mapping process typically leads to an orthographic memory for words after students have decoded phonetically regular words one to four times. Students with weak phonemic awareness skills will require additional exposure and blending and segmenting activities to establish their orthographic memory for each word.

Partial alphabetic readers may need some of the scaffolds in figure 1.4 (page 28) during writing, which is acceptable for this phase. To transition to the full alphabetic phase, students should be able to do the following.

- Identify each letter name and its individual sounds with speed and automaticity
- Decode a CVC word with any short vowel sound

- Segment the phonemes in a CVC word to write it with and without sound boxes

- Manipulate the initial, medial, and final sounds in a CVC word (isolate, blend, segment, add, delete, and substitute)

- Discriminate between similar letters and sounds

- Write legibly with correct letter formation, free of any letter reversals

- Use decoding as the first strategy to read new words

- Spell and write ten to twelve high-frequency words

In addition to being proficient in the activities in the lesson plan components for the partial alphabetic phase, you can use the decoding assessment to be sure that students are proficient in reading CVC words before they progress to the full alphabetic phase. The decoding assessment contains a combination of real and nonsense words. The purpose of assessing students using nonsense words is to create multiple consonant patterns with each short vowel. Sometimes this produces a nonsense word, with the intent to assess the student's ability to segment and blend letters and sounds regardless of whether they're familiar with the word.

Follow the directions for administering the decoding assessment in appendix B (page 225). You'll begin by having students read the list of words similar to those they read and wrote in the partial alphabetic phase. The word list contains twenty words, and some of the words are nonsense words. Students will read each word as you point to it. Students have read the word correctly when they can read it within two to three seconds.

The decoding assessment contains a teacher score sheet that you can use to record which words the student reads correctly. If the student correctly reads at least sixteen (80 percent) of the words (within two to three seconds), proceed to lessons in the full alphabetic phase. When the student isn't able to read at least fifteen words correctly, you will stop your assessment at that list.

Students who can read fourteen or fifteen words correctly will need a few additional lessons in the partial alphabetic phase. Students who read fewer than fourteen words correctly will need several more lessons in the partial alphabetic phase. Assess students again when they successfully complete the activities in the partial alphabetic lessons with very little scaffolding.

Taking time to instruct students in small groups will allow you to accelerate reading instruction for those who have already developed the skills for this phase and are ready to progress to the full alphabetic phase. In the full alphabetic phase, more advanced readers will have the opportunity to increase their volume of reading, improve fluency, develop more advanced vocabulary, and begin to transition into reading instruction that focuses more heavily on comprehension.

Conclusion

Students in the partial alphabetic phase know most letters and many letter sounds, but you'll need to address and fill in the gaps in their learning so they master all letter names and individual sounds during this reading phase. Your students may be able to sound out some words but may struggle segmenting and blending the letter sounds for others. It's critical to complete each component of the three lessons on the lesson plans. They balance decoding, spelling, phonics, and writing instruction so students can transfer their literacy knowledge across speaking, listening, reading, and writing activities. Development through the partial alphabetic phase occurs more rapidly for some students than others, and you may need to regroup students every two to three weeks to tailor your instruction more effectively. Instruction during this phase should be individualized and specialized because the rate at which students develop decoding skills can differ greatly. Addressing needs and individualizing instruction during the partial alphabetic phase are essential for student success.

CHAPTER 4

Well on Their Way: The Full Alphabetic Phase

*To learn to read is to light a fire; every syllable that is spelled
out is a spark.*

—Victor Hugo

In this chapter, you'll learn how to teach students to decode words with more complex phonics patterns, monitor their word pronunciation, build their self-correcting and self-monitoring skills, and increase their fluency. I describe the characteristics of full alphabetic readers and present the components of the full alphabetic lesson plans. You'll learn how to assess and group your full alphabetic readers; then you'll learn how to teach students to decode words with various letter patterns. Students will learn to read and write the most common sight words used during this phase, and you'll learn how to incorporate phonetic and sight words into sentences for them to write that you dictate. Next, I answer common questions about the full alphabetic phase. Finally, the chapter concludes with instructions on how to determine when students are ready to progress to the consolidated alphabetic phase. Appendix C (page 229) contains the resources to be used with the full alphabetic lessons.

Characterizing Full Alphabetic Readers

Full alphabetic readers can name all letter names and their individual sounds with speed and automaticity and use their decoding skills to read CVC words and some high-frequency words. They rely on phonics skills as their first strategy for reading new words. This is a key shift in strategic decoding that full alphabetic readers developed during the partial alphabetic reading phase. Their knowledge of letter and sound connections and patterns allows for fluent reading and writing of words. Full alphabetic readers:

- Associate all letters with their individual sounds quickly and automatically
- Employ letter-sound skills to decode new words
- Recognize some phonetically irregular high-frequency words

- Can fully manipulate (isolate, blend, segment, delete, add, and substitute) individual phonemes in CVC words
- Learn and remember new words using the orthographic mapping process to secure words in memory through spelling and pronunciation
- Retain complete spelling and decoding of CVC words with phonemes in all positions—initial, medial, and final
- Read simple text with sufficient fluency

Like partial alphabetic readers, students just transitioning to the full alphabetic reading phase won't be fast, effortless readers. Although they should be able to decode most CVC words with some ease, they haven't yet completely developed a vast word reading, or decoding, knowledge. The neural pathways in the brain for letters, sounds, word pronunciation, and meaning haven't yet completely formed. Students should have established basic orthographic memory of common CVC words and some high-frequency words but still need to increase their amount of reading and learn more complex phonetic patterns to solidify the orthographic mapping process.

Teaching Your Full Alphabetic Readers

As students progress through the full alphabetic phase, their orthographic memory, reading fluency, and ability to self-correct should increase and strengthen. When students are able to monitor their own decoding and correct decoding errors and mispronunciations, they're building their set for variability. *Set for variability*, according to researchers Laura M. Steacy and colleagues (2019), is one of the most powerful predictors of early reading development. It denotes a person's ability to self-correct or fix any mismatch between a word's pronunciation when reading using a combination of common decoding rules and how the word is actually pronounced. Sometimes when readers decode a word, they have to think about if a word sounds right and make a minor adjustment in its pronunciation. This adjustment builds and expands a reader's set for variability. For example, when a beginning reader decodes the word *dogs*, in the context of a sentence, they tend to self-correct and pronounce the *s* as /z/ instead of /s/ because the word *dogs* is in the reader's listening and speaking vocabulary. A set for variability helps full alphabetic readers develop flexibility in their decoding ability. When students self-correct pronunciation and decoding mismatches, those words become orthographically mapped in the reader's brain alongside phonetically regular words.

When students have this flexibility with their decoding ability and begin to unconsciously construct a set for variability, they increase the amount of text that they read which in turn promotes self-teaching. According to David L. Share's (2011) self-teaching hypothesis, once students have established their basic knowledge of letter and sound relationships and the essential processes of segmenting and blending phonemes, they apply this knowledge to new words and greatly increase the number of words they're able to read by implicitly applying phonics skills and essentially teaching themselves how to decode new words.

Where to Focus Instruction During Small-Group Lessons

Throughout the full alphabetic reading phase, students begin to inherently use their knowledge of letters and sounds to decode and pronounce new words and, in doing so, teach themselves new spelling patterns. During small-group instruction, you'll need to facilitate these processes and reinforce them during your lessons. Your small-group lessons for full alphabetic readers will contain each of the following essential pieces.

- Creating a self-monitoring and self-correcting system

- Facilitating the development of a set for variability

- Increasing statistical learning

- Developing a self-teaching process to learn new words

- Promoting proficiency in orthographic mapping abilities through phonemic manipulation activities

- Fully mapping letter combinations through writing and word-building activities

- Blending complex letter and sound combinations to read words with digraphs, blends, silent *e*, inflected endings, contractions, and common long vowel patterns

- Increasing sight vocabulary and fluency

- Mastering letter formation and handwriting skills

It's important during the full alphabetic phase to vary the type of texts that students read. Students who can blend and segment quickly and easily should transition to reading more vocabulary readers, informational texts, grade-level texts, articles, poetry, and texts with a lower percentage of decodable words. The goal of decoding instruction is for students to apply phonics knowledge to authentic texts, allowing them the opportunity to read multiple words with various phonics patterns. For students with quick and proficient segmenting and blending skills, reading practice can shift away from decoding specific phonics patterns in decodable texts to decoding via blending and segmenting across a variety of text types and a wider array of phonics patterns.

For students who continue to need practice with a small number of phonics patterns and skills at a slow pace, continue to read decodable texts until their abilities with blending and segmenting improve and they develop an increased fluency. Refer to the fluency norms in table 1.2 of chapter 1 (page 7) to gauge whether students have reached the average fluency rate expected for reading their grade level of text. Once they have, begin to vary the type of texts you use during small-group instruction.

How to Assess Your Full Alphabetic Readers

Utilizing the decoding assessment is especially helpful during the full alphabetic reading phase because you'll be able to determine which letter-sound patterns students know and which ones they need to learn. For students who are just exiting the partial alphabetic phase, you can simply begin instruction with word list 1 (page 93).

The decoding assessment in appendix C (page 241) will help inform your small-group instruction and enable you to identify gaps in phonics knowledge, as well as how to strategically group students for instruction. Knowing exactly where individuals are in their decoding ability allows you to target a specific focus for your small-group instruction and provide your students with systematic, explicit progression for building their phonetic decoding skills.

Follow the directions in appendix C (page 241) for administering the decoding assessment. Students will read words containing the following.

- Digraphs and final double consonants
- Initial and final blends
- Consonant clusters
- Long vowel sounds that end in silent *e*
- Inflected endings
- Contractions
- Common long vowel digraphs

The words students will read on the assessment contain cumulative phonics patterns. For example, a word that ends in silent *e* may contain a consonant digraph, or an initial blend. A word that contains the vowel pattern *oa* may also contain an initial or final digraph or blend. This accumulation of phonics skills follows the expectations set forth in common state literacy standards. Carefully follow the directions on the decoding assessment to ensure that you group your students and plan your lessons accordingly.

How to Group Your Full Alphabetic Readers

Although the decoding assessment for full alphabetic readers contains a variety of phonics spelling patterns, you can group students together with similar needs. For example, you can group students who need instruction in similar phonics patterns, such as digraphs and blends, words with silent *e* and inflected endings, or words with long vowel patterns. Each phonics skill stretches four to eight weeks in a typical instructional sequence. Therefore, it's feasible to group students together with similar needs, and they'll be within about two months of each other's progressive decoding and orthographic mapping development. This grouping format will make your instruction efficient and effective. As long as you informally assess students' needs and periodically reassess and regroup students as needed, skills-based phonics groups allow you to provide efficient, targeted, ability-appropriate instruction. This approach to small-group instruction has been shown to help all students improve their reading proficiency.

Full alphabetic readers need to increase the amount of reading and writing they do to continue to build an orthographic memory for reading and remembering words. Increasing the complexity of phonics patterns is critically important during this reading phase. A systematic and explicit focus on further developing more advanced orthographic mapping skills will provide a secure foundation for transitioning students to the consolidated alphabetic phase. Differentiating your instruction based on students' phonemic awareness, phonics, and fluency needs is key to enabling each of them to reach their full potential by proficiently decoding new words with ease.

Planning Lessons for Full Alphabetic Readers

The full alphabetic lesson plan contains three separate lessons. The focus for lesson 1 is on word building, teaching sight words, and writing; lesson 2 focuses on reading, teaching decoding skills, and discussing the text; and lesson 3 focuses on word building and reviewing sight words, rereading, and writing. The components within these series of lessons contain a variety of activities that will continue to promote the connection between the reading and writing process to increase the transfer of literacy skills and other activities throughout the school day. The structure and components for the full alphabetic lessons are shown in table 4.1.

TABLE 4.1: Full Alphabetic Lesson Plan Structure and Components

Lesson 1	Lesson 2	Lesson 3
Word Building	Reading	Word Building and Review Sight Words
Sight Words	Teaching Decoding	Rereading
Writing—Sentence Dictation	Discussing Text	Writing—Sentence Dictation

Planning and Teaching Lesson 1

The activities in the full alphabetic lesson plan are designed to teach students some predictable and regular phonics patterns, as this aids in facilitating self-teaching so full alphabetic readers can learn hundreds of very similar words. Because these activities cover a wide span of decoding abilities, your students may differ greatly in their ability to manipulate these letters and sounds. The goal of the activities in the full alphabetic lessons is for students to simultaneously develop their reading and writing abilities with these phonics patterns. Words that were referred to as *high-frequency words* in the partial alphabetic lesson plan develop into *sight words* in this reading phase—words we would like students to be able to read quickly and easily. Students will also begin to write short sentences that you dictate to them that contain phonetic and sight words. Lesson 1 is shown in figure 4.1.

Lesson 1				
Word Building (4–5 minutes)	Scaffold:			
Word List:		Phonics Skill:		Patterns:
Sight Words (4–5 minutes)				
Complete Each Step:	Teach and map		Build	Write
Writing—Sentence Dictation or Sentence Starter (4–5 minutes)				
Teaching Focus:	☐ Handwriting	☐ Spacing	☐ Phonetic spelling	☐ High-frequency words
☐ Noun-verb agreement	☐ Sentence structure	☐ Possessives	☐ Irregular plural nouns	☐ Irregular verbs ・ ☐ Past-, future-, present-tense verbs
Notes for Next Lesson:				

FIGURE 4.1: Full alphabetic phase lesson 1.

Visit go.SolutionTree.com/literacy to download a free reproducible version of this figure.

Word Building

During the full alphabetic phase, students will continue to develop their blending and segmenting skills with phonemes within words that have digraphs, blends, consonant clusters, long vowel sounds in words with silent *e*, common long vowel teams (vowel digraphs), inflected endings, silent consonants, and contractions. By completing the word-building activities, students will learn to read, spell, and write words that contain these phonics patterns. Connecting reading and writing through phoneme manipulation when reading, and constructing and spelling words and writing sentences, will continue to promote the orthographic mapping process and increase and strengthen students' orthographic memory.

In lesson plan 1, you'll write the scaffold and word list you'll begin teaching from. Then, note which of the following phonics skills and spelling patterns you'll begin your teaching with based on how students performed on the decoding assessment.

- Digraphs

- Floss words

- Initial blends

- Final blends

- Initial and final blends

- Consonant clusters

- Long vowels with silent *e*

- Silent letters

- Inflected endings

- Contractions

- Common long vowels (digraphs)

Follow the directions for completing the word-building lesson plan component provided in chapter 1 (page 7). For each word list (tables 4.2–4.13), spend four to five minutes completing the word-building activities (both the reading and phonemic manipulation tasks) with each set of words, using the scaffolds from figure 1.4 (page 28) as needed.

Table 4.2 contains lists of words with the most common consonant diagraphs. For the words you'll be working with, be sure to first teach the sounds for digraphs following the steps described in chapter 1 (page 7).

Here are some helpful hints and rules for digraphs.

- In a one-syllable word with a short vowel that ends with the /k/ sound, the sound is represented by the letters *ck*.

- For words spelled with *wh*, I recommend making a chart with *wh* words. Until students gain more experience and fluency with spelling and writing the *wh* words correctly, it helps to be able to reference the most common words spelled with *wh*.

- The letters *th* make a voiced sound (like in the word *that*) and an unvoiced sound (like in the word *thin*). There are five rules for when the *th* is voiced versus unvoiced. Through statistical learning when reading, writing, speaking, and listening, students will implicitly learn for which words the voiced or the unvoiced sound is expected.

TABLE 4.2: Word List 1—Skill: Digraphs

Word List 1					
Spelling Patterns					
ch	**sh**	**ck**	**th (unvoiced)**	**th (voiced)**	**wh**
chad	lash	lack	bath	than	whack
chop	mesh	shack	thin	that	wham
chum	shin	check	thick	them	when
much	shock	thick	thug	then	whip
inch	shop	mock	moth	this	which

Table 4.3 contains lists of words with the most common *floss* phonics pattern—single-syllable words that end in a double *f, l, s,* or *z.* Here is a helpful hint and rule for floss words.

- When we add an inflectional ending (*-ed* or *-ing*) on to a floss word—such as *huffed* or *messing*—the final *l, f, s,* or *z* remains doubled.

TABLE 4.3: Word List 2—Skill: Floss Rule

Word List 2			
Spelling Patterns			
ll	**ff**	**ss**	**zz**
wall	tiff	pass	jazz
shell	whiff	chess	razz
gill	cuff	less	fizz
shill	huff	diss	whizz
hull	puff	miss	buzz

Table 4.4 (page 94) contains lists of words with the most common initial consonant blends phonics pattern. A consonant blend can occur at the beginning or end of a word.

Here are some helpful hints and rules for initial blends.

- Students typically master initial blends first (for example, the word *flag*); then final blends (for example, the word *bank*); and last, words with initial and final blends (for example, the word *bring*).

- Consonant blends can be especially tricky for young readers and writers to learn because the second sound of an initial blend and the second-to-the-last sound of a final blend (the nondominant sounds) aren't stressed, so they're more difficult to hear. It may take some students more time than others to learn to hear and identify these discrete sounds.

- Teach only two initial blends at a time for students who have difficulty hearing each of the two distinct sounds in blends.

Table 4.5 contains word lists with the most common final consonant blends.

Here is a helpful hint and rule for final blends.

- Teach only two final blends at a time for students who have difficulty hearing each of the two distinct sounds in blends.

Table 4.6 contains the word list for phonics patterns with both initial and final blends. For these lists, the final blend in each word is the same and the initial blend changes from word to word.

Table 4.7 contains word lists for phonics patterns with both initial and final blends in which the initial blend is the same and the final blend changes from word to word.

TABLE 4.4: Word List 3—Skill: Initial Consonant Blends

Word List 3									
Spelling Patterns									
bl	**br**	**cl**	**cr**	**dr**	**fl**	**fr**	**gl**	**gr**	**pl**
blab	brag	clad	crab	drab	flap	frap	glam	grad	plan
bless	brass	clash	crash	dress	flex	fresh	glib	gram	pled
bliss	bred	cliff	crib	drill	flit	fret	glob	grin	plop
blog	brim	clog	cross	drop	floss	frizz	gloss	grit	plug
blush	brush	club	crush	drum	flush	frog	glum	grub	plush

pr	**sc**	**sk**	**sl**	**sm**	**sn**	**sp**	**st**	**sw**	**tr**
pram	scam	skid	slab	smash	snag	span	stab	swag	tram
prep	scan	skiff	sled	smell	snap	spell	stash	swell	trash
press	scat	skill	slip	smog	snip	spill	stiff	swig	trek
prom	scuff	skip	slop	smug	snob	spot	still	swim	trip
prop	scum	skull	slush		snug	spun	stuff	swish	trop

TABLE 4.5: Word List 4—Skill: Final Consonant Blends

Word List 4					
Spelling Patterns					
ft	**lf**	**lk**	**lp**	**lt**	**mp**
daft	golf	bulk	help	belt	champ
shaft	gulf	hulk	gulp	kilt	chimp
left	self	milk	kelp	pelt	wimp
theft	shelf	sulk	pulp	welt	chomp
tuft	wolf	silk	yelp	wilt	thump

nd	ng	nk	nt	sk	st
bond	fang	yank	chant	bask	cost
fund	sang	honk	font	mask	past
land	thing	think	tint	task	rest
tend	long	gunk	went	whisk	list
wind	rung	chunk	lent	dusk	must

TABLE 4.6: Word List 5—Initial and Final Blend (Initial Blend Changes)

Word List 5								
Spelling Patterns								
ft	**lp**	**mp**	**nd**	**ng**	**nk**	**nt**	**sk**	**st**
craft	scalp	scamp	bland	clang	crank	grant	flask	blast
draft		blimp	brand	bring	prank	spent	whisk	crest
graft		skimp	gland	cling	blink	glint		grist
drift		stomp	blend	sting	clink	blunt		frost
swift		clump	trend	swung	stunk	stunt		trust

TABLE 4.7: Word List 6—Initial and Final Blend (Final Blend Changes)

Word List 6								
Spelling Patterns								
bl	**br**	**cl**	**cr**	**dr**	**fl**	**fr**	**gl**	**gr**
bland	brand	clamp	craft	draft	flank	frost	gland	graft
blast	bring	cling	crank	drank	flask		glint	grant
blend	brink	clomp	crest	drift	fling			grump
blimp		clump	crimp	drink	flint			grunt
blunt		clung	crust		flung			grist

pl	**pr**	**sc**	**sk**	**sl**	**sp**	**st**	**sw**	**tr**
plank	prank	scalp	skimp	slang	spank	stand	swift	trend
plant	primp	scamp		slant	spend	stank	swing	trunk
plonk	print	scant		sling	spent	sting	swung	trust
plump				slump	spunk	stink		
plunk				slung		stomp		

After you've completed the word-building activities for initial and final blends, I recommend administering a spelling assessment containing about twenty various words with both initial and final blends.

Don't move on to teaching any more complex phonics skills until students can achieve at least 80 percent mastery with writing words with different initial and final blends and each of the short vowels.

Being proficient in reading and writing words with beginning and final blends is a crucial point in students' literacy skills that impacts later skills because advanced phonetic patterns will be cumulative. Words containing initial and final blends consist of about five to six letters that students need to hold in their short-term (working) memory for reading and spelling. When students can easily remember these sounds and read and spell accurately, they're prepared to attack more complex words with additional consonants, syllables, and inflected endings. If students haven't mastered the words on the lists up to this point, provide additional support using the supplemental lists in appendix C (page 234) until they master each word list pattern through word list 6.

Table 4.8 contains lists of the most common words that have *trigraphs*, or clusters of three consonants. Trigraphs contain blends and digraphs, so they combine to create either two or three sounds.

Here is a helpful hint and rule for consonant clusters.

- The letters *-tch* are used at the end of a one-syllable word or a syllable when the sound before it is represented by a short vowel (for example, *match* or *matching*).

TABLE 4.8: Word List 7—Skill: Consonant Cluster (Initial and Final)

Word List 7								
Spelling Patterns								
scr	**spl**	**spr**	**str**	**shr**	**thr**	**-tch**	**-lch**	**-nch**
scram	splash	spring	strand	shred	thresh	scratch	belch	branch
scrap	splish	sprung	stress	shrink	thrift	stretch	gulch	drench
script		split	strict	shrill	throb	stitch	mulch	trench
scrub		splint	strong	shrimp	thrush	blotch		hunch
scruff		sprint	struck	shrub	thrust	crutch		scrunch

Table 4.9 contains lists of the most common words that have long vowel sounds and end with silent *e* (*a, e, i, o, u*). Words containing long vowel sounds that end in silent *e* that have a *c* or *g* change the sound of those consonants to make what we call *soft sounds*. A soft *c* sound is /s/, and a soft *g* sound is /j/. These lists also contain words with the *dge* spelling pattern that represents the /j/ sound.

Here are some helpful hints and rules for silent *e* words.

- When *c* or *g* is followed by silent *e*, it makes its soft sound—/s/ or /j/.

- Silent *e* provides a "cushion" so that words in English don't end in *v, i, u,* or *z*.

- Silent *e* after *th* represents the voiced sound of /th/.

- Silent *e* adds a vowel to a syllable (every syllable must have at least one vowel)—for example, *table*.

TABLE 4.9: Word List 8—Skill: Silent *e* Long Vowels, Soft *c*, and Soft *g*, *-dge*

Word List 8										
Spelling Patterns										
a	**e**	**i**	**o**	**u**	**c**		**Soft *g***			
					Long Vowel, Soft *c*	**Short Vowel, Soft *c***	**-dge**	**Long Vowel, Soft *g***	**Short Vowel, Soft *g***	**Soft *g***
chase	eve	chime	choke	cube	grace	since	badge	huge	hinge	gel
frame	these	spine	globe	dune	space	dance	lodge	range	lunge	gem
haste	theme	while	those	mule	price	glance	smidge	grange	cringe	germ
scrape		stride	whole	crude	twice	chance	dredge	stage	binge	gist
trade		thrive	throne	flute	spruce	prance	smudge	strange	plunge	gym

Table 4.10 contains the most common words with silent letters and the spelling pattern *qu*. The spelling pattern *qu* isn't considered a blend or a digraph—it simply produces the /k/ and /w/ sounds. Most spelling patterns contained in the *qu* words have already been taught, so they're grouped with the words with silent letters.

Here are some helpful hints and rules for *qu* words and words with silent letters.

- In 100 percent of words in English, the letter *u* follows the letter *q*.
- The *g* is silent when it's followed by the letter *n* at the beginning or end of a word.
- The *k* is silent when it's at the beginning of a word with the letter *n*.
- When a word ends with *mb*, the *b* is always silent.
- The letter *w* is silent when it's followed by an *r*.

TABLE 4.10: Word List 9—Skill: Silent Consonants and *qu*

Word List 9				
Spelling Patterns				
gn	**kn**	**mb**	**wr**	**qu**
gnat	knelt	lamb	wrath	quit
gnash	knot	limb	wreck	quack
gnome	knoll	numb	wring	quest
	knock	crumb	wrong	quilt
	knack	thumb	wrote	squint

Table 4.11 contains the word list for the most common phonics patterns with inflected endings. Here are some helpful hints and rules for words with inflected endings.

- The letters *ed* make the /id/ sound when they follow a base or root word ending with the sounds /d/ and /t/.
- The letters *ed* make the /t/ sound when they follow a base or root word ending with the sound or spelling *k, p, sh, ch, gh, th, s, c, x*.
- The letters *ed* make the /d/ sound when they follow a base or root word ending with the sound or spelling *l, n, r, g, v, s, w, y, z*.
- When a single-syllable word ends with a short vowel and a consonant, the consonant is doubled before adding the inflectional ending.
- When a word ends with a silent *e*, drop the *e* before adding a morpheme that begins with a vowel, such as *-ed* or *-ing*.

TABLE 4.11: Word List 10—Skill: Inflected Endings, Doubling, and *E*-Drop

Word List 10						
Spelling Patterns						
ed = /id/	ed = /d/	ed = /t/	**Doubling With -ed**	**Doubling With -ing**	**E-Drop With -ed**	**E-Drop With -ing**
planted	yelled	bumped	grabbed	dotting	blamed	chasing
drifted	pledged	fussed	hugged	grinning	scraped	trading
glided	chimed	glanced	dropped	planning	shined	piling
shifted	closed	cracked	skipped	skipping	thrived	chiming
trusted	trudged	picked	trapped	trapping	choked	whining

Table 4.12 contains the word list for the most common words used to form contractions. Here are some helpful hints and rules for words that can form contractions.

- When the verb is *are*, an apostrophe takes the place of the *a*.
- When the verb is *had* or *would*, an apostrophe takes the places of all letters except the *d*.
- When the verb is *have*, an apostrophe takes the place of the letters *ha*.
- When the verb is *is* or *has*, an apostrophe takes the places of all letters except the *s*.
- When the verb is *not*, an apostrophe takes the place of the letter *o*.
- When the verb is *will*, an apostrophe takes the places of the letters *wi*.

TABLE 4.12: Word List 11—Skill: Contractions

Word List 11							
Spelling Patterns							
am	**are**	**had and would**	**have**	**is and has**	**not**	**will**	**us**
I'm	they're	I'd	I've	it's	can't	I'll	let's
	we're	he'd	we've	he's	isn't	it'll	
	you're	she'd	you've	she's	don't	he'll	
		we'd	they've	who's	didn't	she'll	
		who'd	could've	how's	aren't	we'll	
		you'd	should've	here's	wasn't	you'll	
		they'd	would've	that's	hasn't	they'll	
		there'd		what's	hadn't		
				there's	haven't		
				where's	doesn't		
					weren't		
					couldn't		
					shouldn't		
					wouldn't		

Table 4.13 (page 100) contains the word list for the most common phonics patterns with long vowels. These are single long vowels (in the word *find*) and vowel digraphs (two vowels representing one sound, like in the word *beach*).

Here are some helpful hints and rules for words with long vowels.

- The letters *ay* are used at the end of a word or syllable to represent the long *a* sound.

- The letters *ai* are used at the beginning or middle of a word or syllable to represent the long *a* sound.

- There are no reliable rules for when to use *ea* or *ee* in spelling the long *e* sound.

- Long *i* is typically spelled with a *y* when it comes at the end of a one-syllable word.

- Many times, long *i* and *o* are spelled as single letters when they're followed by two consonants.

- There are no reliable rules for when to pronounce *oo* as in *boot* (long *oo*) or as in *book* (short *oo*).

- The long *oo* sound is typically spelled with *ue* in a one-syllable word, or at the end of a syllable.

TABLE 4.13: Word List 12—Skill: Common Long Vowels

Word List 12									
Spelling Patterns									
ay	**ai**	**ee**	**ea**	**y**	**iCC***	**oa**	**oCC***	**oo**	**ue**
slay	claim	cheek	leash	pry	mind	coax	jolt	boost	hue
sway	snail	greed	knead	shy	sign	coach	volt	groom	sue
spray	quaint	queen	weave	sly	child	boast	ghost	scoop	clue
stray	sprain	sleeve	scream	wry	climb	groan	scold	swoop	glue
tray	strain	screech	squeak	spry	grind	throat	stroll	smooth	true

CC = Consonant Consonant

Sight Words

A high-frequency word is a word that appears most often in certain texts—usually divided or organized by grade-level word lists—the most common being the Dolch and Fry lists. On the other hand, a sight word can be any word that a reader recognizes automatically when they read it, without having to decode it letter by letter. These are words that are phonetically regular and irregular. Words become sight words when we sound them out over and over (orthographically mapping them) when we read until we can read them automatically. Words for beginning readers don't become sight words until students have formed the pathways in the brain necessary for orthographic mapping. Proficient adult readers encounter most words as sight words. The goal in reading instruction is to make as many words as possible sight words for students. This leads to effortless decoding, increases fluency, and allows for further development of vocabulary and comprehension skills.

Whether the spelling of a word is phonetically regular or irregular, proficient readers pay attention to the phonological structure of words and orthographically map letters and sounds to fully connect a word's sounds, spelling, pronunciation, and meaning. Words that are phonetically irregular will require additional practice with sound-to-letter mapping, but they shouldn't be taught as whole units to be read or memorized. When we teach high-frequency words, we need to fully analyze the letter-sound relationships within them, whether the word is composed of expected—or regular—letter-sound relationships or not (Duke & Mesmer, 2018–2019).

The belief that students learn to read words by sight is a common misconception. When proficient readers store a large number of words through orthographic mapping, they read so quickly and efficiently that they appear to be able to read words "by sight." This may lead us to think that this must be how those words were learned—by visually memorizing whole units. Sight words aren't the memorization of a group of letters (Ehri, 2014). We know through brain imaging scans that this isn't how students learn to read words. Students who decode regular and irregular words quickly and easily can do so because they have a highly efficient orthographic memory for reading; mapping letter sounds, pronunciations, and remembering words.

As mentioned in chapter 2, English isn't entirely a phonetic language—it's a morphophonemic language. Many English words can be read phonetically, but many others can be tied to their *morphology*—or the meaning of the parts in the word. Rooted in the morphology of words is their *etymology*—their origin. The English language consists of mostly Latin, French, and Germanic language origins, with some traces from Greek. There's a very small percentage of words with unknown origin. For these reasons, I like to take what are considered to be "sight words" and categorize them in three different ways.

The first category of sight words is words that are phonetically regular, such as *can*, *am*, and *it*. Along with all other phonetically decodable words, those words should become sight words quickly and easily when students learn their letters and sounds and develop phonetic decoding skills.

The second category of sight words is words that are phonetically decodable, but students in that phase of reading haven't learned the phonics skill that corresponds to decoding the words. These are words such as *see*, *play*, *like*, and *look*. Those words can be easily decoded phonetically, but the phonics skills that correspond to them aren't taught until the full alphabetic reading phase—so for students in the partial alphabetic reading phase, those could be considered sight words.

The third category of sight words is words that have irregular phonics patterns. The sounds and spellings of these types of words are rooted in morphology and etymology, and not so much in phonics. Examples of these words include the following.

- When we form the past tense of a verb that ends in the letter *y*, we change the *y* to *i* and then add *ed*. For example, the past tense of the word *carry* is *carried*. In the case of the word *said*, the letter preceding the *y* in the base word *say* is an *a*. When following this rule, we end up with the word *saied*—a word with three vowels. The *e* was dropped and—over time, and due to regional dialects—the pronunciation of the *ay* in *said* became a short *e* sound, which is how we now pronounce the word *said*.

- In the word *come*, the *o* is pronounced as a schwa. A *schwa sound* is an alternate, weak, or unaccented vowel sound. A schwa sound is actually the most common vowel sound in English, and it can occur among all vowel sounds. Words like *done*, *love*, *some*, *was*, *around*, *away*, and many others are all pronounced with the schwa sound.

- The word *does* is formed by adding the second person Latin morpheme *es* on to the verb *do*. When pronounced, the *oe* spelling takes on a schwa sound. The word *goes* follows the same spelling patterns as *does*, but the *oe* in *goes* retains the long *o* sound.

Irregular sight words are usually only irregular by one or two sounds. Most of the word is still usually phonetically or morphologically regular. We can easily and seamlessly teach these common sight words by either explaining their morphology or pointing out the part of the word that's different or unexpected, then relating it to other similar words. For example, I don't explain the morphology or etymology of the word *said* to students; I simply explain to them that the medial sound in *said* is the short *e* sound spelled with an *ai*. This spelling is similar to the letter sounds in the middle of the words *again* and *against*. This explanation demystifies the spelling and phonetic patterns of these irregular sight words and helps students understand and learn how words are similar to many others. There are very few words that are true sight words, so learning about morphology becomes extremely important in vocabulary development.

According to Duke and Mesmer (2018–2019), when we teach words that we'd like to become sight words, we need to fully analyze the letter and sound relationships within them, whether the words are composed of expected letter and sound relationships or not. I recommend teaching phonetically irregular words by relating their letters and sounds to their morphological patterns, then relating the word to similar words when possible (for example, *go*, *no*, and *so*; *does* and *goes*; *like* and *bike*; *look* and *book*; and so forth). Teach irregularly spelled high-frequency words alongside more commonly known words and incorporate a wealth of authentic, meaningful reading and writing practice.

Table 4.14 consists of the most common sight words for students in the full alphabetic phase that contain phonics patterns they haven't yet learned or are irregular due to their morphology. For words that contain phonetically regular letter-sound correspondences, teach students which letters and sounds in the words are regular. Then, teach them what is irregular about the letter-sound correspondences in the word. Whether spellings are regular or irregular, literacy and language specialist Jan Wasowicz (2021) explains that students must learn to pay attention to the phonological and morphological structure of words to connect them to their meanings. Words with similar spelling patterns and sounds are grouped together. You can easily find the morphological explanation and etymology online for each word.

TABLE 4.14: Common Irregular Sight Words

about, round	even	only, open, over
after	very, every	our, out
said, again	far	one
also	first	own
are	or, for, four	put
any, many	found, round	of, off
away	from	they
been	full, pull	too, two
by, my, try, why	good, look	use
come, done, some	grow, know, show	saw, draw
could, would, should	her	want
do, to	here, where, there	was
does, goes	little	what, who
how, down	new	you, your

For full alphabetic readers, focus on teaching one or two sight words per lesson. In lesson plan 1, there are spaces to write up to two sight words to teach. When choosing which words to teach your full alphabetic readers, teach sight words that are in the text you're reading that your full alphabetic readers won't be able to decode.

Spend four to five minutes of lesson 1 teaching sight words using the steps described in in chapter 1 (page 7).

Writing—Sentence Dictation

Writing is an essential component of literacy and is the modality through which phonics and spelling, pronunciation, and sound connect for the most effective and efficient orthographic mapping. Writing permeates phonics patterns and sight words in orthographic memory. The most effective way to teach the correct spellings of regular and irregular words is to read and write them many times within connected text (Ehri, 2020). Writing instruction reinforces the reciprocal relationship between reading and spelling, or decoding and encoding. Writing practice allows students to apply phonemic awareness, phonics, handwriting, and text comprehension skills, which strengthen and increase overall reading achievement gains.

Research supports the idea that we can improve reading proficiency through writing instruction (Celik, 2019). Infrequent writing practice and a lack of explicit writing instruction impact reading achievement. The benefits of systematic and explicit writing instruction are especially significant for students who are less proficient in reading. When the basic writing skills contained in the full alphabetic reading lessons become effortless for students, they can focus on developing and transforming their writing with rich vocabulary and clearly communicating the content and context of their ideas.

Having students practice writing simple sentences that you've dictated continues to be a critical spelling and writing component during the full alphabetic phase. Continue to dictate sentences to students until they can correctly spell words with consonant clusters and any short vowel (through blends). When students can blend and segment several letter sounds and discriminate among the five short vowels, they've built a strong orthographic memory for reading, writing, and remembering each separate sound in words, or the largest number of letter sounds that would be in a syllable. At this point, use the Comprehension Discussion Starter Cards in appendix C (page 247) as sentence starters, and students can complete the one, two, or three sentences.

Sentence dictation is a useful way to reinforce the phonics skills from the word-building and sight-word components of the lesson plans. Having students write sentences that you've dictated strengthens phonetic connections between sounds and letters, builds automaticity with applying phonics and spelling rules, and helps develop self-monitoring skills in reading and writing. Sentence-level dictation allows full alphabetic readers to integrate the layers of letter-sound rules, spelling conventions, and self-monitoring and self-correction strategies involved in the skilled reading and writing of connected text.

To construct the dictated sentences, incorporate some words from the book you'll be reading for lesson 2 or from the word-building lesson component with each sight word to create one or two sentences that are five to seven words long. Write the sentences you'll dictate in the spaces on the lesson plan template for lesson 1. Students will use the handwriting lines at the bottom of the word mat to write the dictated sentences, or they can write them in a writing journal. Spend four to five minutes of lesson 1 dictating sentences and teaching editing by using the steps described in chapter 1 (page 7).

You may need to construct sound or spelling boxes on the lines for the words in the sentences to support students' segmenting and blending to write and read the words. Direct students to always say words out loud as they write the corresponding letters, making sure they slide from one sound to the next without pausing between and they simultaneously write the letters that match the sounds coming out of their mouths to tightly integrate phoneme-grapheme connections. Differentiate the support you provide for students during writing based on their individual needs. Some students need more support with handwriting, while others need to focus on writing the correct letters for the sounds they represent.

Use the skills across the bottom of the lesson plan template (under Teaching Focus) as a progression for differentiating your instruction for each student. After students finish writing the sentence, choose a teaching point as your focus for them to edit their sentences. The teaching points are in developmental order from left to right on the lesson plan. Students should edit their sentences in the following order:

(1) handwriting and letter formation, (2) proper spacing of words, (3) phonetic spelling, (4) writing sight words, (5) capitalization, and (6), end punctuation. Focus on one skill per lesson after writing the dictated sentences. Don't move on to editing for the next skill until students master the writing skill you're currently teaching.

Use the QR code to watch a video of a teacher conducting a full alphabetic lesson 1.

Planning and Teaching Lesson 2

In lesson 2, students will read a text, and you'll explicitly teach the process of decoding words. You'll then facilitate a discussion about the text. Begin your instruction using decodable texts until students can quickly and easily decode words containing about four to five sounds. When students are able to read at a sufficient fluency rate, they should begin to read other types of texts. Varying the type of text students read during small-group instruction will help them flexibly apply their decoding skills across many different words with various phonics patterns. During lesson 2, students will read while you listen to them, and you'll teach the decoding skills of segmenting and blending and facilitate a discussion about the text. Lesson 2 is shown in figure 4.2.

Lesson 2	
Text Title:	Phonics Skill:
Reading (8–9 minutes)	
Give Overview and Introduce Phonics Skill or Sight Words:	
Vocabulary:	
Strategies and Actions for Decoding (Check box when used during the lesson):	
☐ Stretch / blend the letter sounds. ☐ Try this sound. . . ☐ Have student blend sounds aurally, then read. ☐ Chunk the word or break it into syllables.	☐ Dictate or make word via sounds → letters. ☐ You know this word. . . (write an analogy). ☐ Does that make sense? ☐ Reread the sentence and tell me what it means.
Strategies and Actions for Fluency and Comprehension (Check box when used during the lesson):	
☐ Swoop three to four words for student to practice fluency. ☐ Read along and then repeat after me.	☐ What did you read? Tell me about it. ☐ *What* happened to *who, where, when,* and *why*?

Teaching Decoding (2–3 minutes)	Skills:
Examples:	
Discussing Text (2–3 minutes; use cards in appendix C, page 247)	
Notes for Next Lesson:	

FIGURE 4.2: Full alphabetic phase lesson 2.

*Visit **go.SolutionTree.com/literacy** to download a free reproducible version of this figure.*

Reading

The book you choose to read may contain your phonics skills or focus for this lesson, depending on whether or not the students are reading on grade level. Students typically learn to decode words using the same or a similar scope and sequence to the progression in the word-building component of lesson 1. You can follow the scope and sequence that you use to teach your whole group phonics if you prefer, but you'll need to adjust your word-building activities so the scope and sequence you use aligns. The most important conditions are that your lessons are consistent and that you teach phonics with fidelity, differentiating where and when necessary. In addition, regroup students when you notice their progress with decoding changes and place them in groups of students of similar needs. The book you choose should also contain the sight words you'll teach throughout the three lessons.

For students who decode at a slower, more laborious rate and need to practice increasing their fluency, continue to use high-quality decodable texts that promote the use of letter-sound relationships as the first action to take when reading unknown words and reinforce the phonics skills being taught. The familiar phonetic patterns in decodable text are controlled so as to not overwhelm students with too many new spelling patterns to decode. This controlled approach allows students to focus on building fluency, strengthens orthographic mapping, and increases orthographic memory. For students with quick and efficient decoding abilities, begin to incorporate a variety of text types into your small-group lessons so they can practice segmenting and blending with many different phonics patterns.

Spend a brief minute or two to give students an overview of the text. For a literary text, pointing out character names and proper nouns and providing a one-sentence summary is sufficient. For an informational text, tell students what they will read about in a one-sentence summary. Allow students to look through the text and examine the illustrations or text features. Use this time to introduce any new vocabulary or sight words contained in the text. Direct students to the page the word is on, tell them the sounds in the word, and have them blend the sounds to pronounce each word you introduce. If the sight word is irregular, explain the spelling pattern to students and have them locate and read the word along with you. If you need to formally introduce new and unknown vocabulary words, follow the steps in table 1.7 of chapter 1 (page 31).

Spend the next seven to eight minutes listening to each student read. Take anecdotal notes or an informal reading record on the back of the lesson plan. Students should whisper-read independently so they have the opportunity to practice segmenting and blending letter sounds on their own. Independent whisper reading provides each student with practice connecting letters and sounds to reinforce the orthographic mapping process, helps to promote building a set for variability, and promotes statistical learning and the self-teaching process. Whisper reading is an invaluable reading strategy that supports self-monitoring and self-correcting, which promote fluency and automaticity with sound and spelling patterns. Provide strategies and actions for students first for decoding, then for fluency, and finally for comprehension (if the student doesn't make any decoding errors).

When students read words, allow them time to blend the letters and sounds and arrive at the correct pronunciation of the word instead of interrupting and correcting them. You may even need to wait until the student finishes reading the sentence and has the opportunity to go back to their misread or mispronunciation and correct it. Interrupting students while they're reading during the full, consolidated, or automatic phases disrupts fluency and comprehension and teaches them to read one word at a time and then look to the teacher to confirm that they read the word correctly. This hampers their ability to develop self-monitoring and self-correcting skills, which are both necessary for maximum reading success.

After the student has read a sentence, if they read words incorrectly, bring their attention to their mistake and use the following decoding strategies and actions to provide feedback. They're in the Strategies and Actions for Decoding section on the lesson plan (see figure 4.2, page 104) in two columns in order from the most support (left-hand column, top to bottom) to the least support (right-hand column, top to bottom).

1. Stretch and blend the letter sounds.

2. Tell the student the correct sound to try.

3. Segment the letter sounds on your fingers for the student to blend auditorily first. Then, bring their attention back to letters in the word in the text and have them blend the letters and sounds themselves.

4. Divide, or chunk, the word at the onset and rime or into syllables.

5. Use the word mat and dictate the sounds in the word for the student to write in the sound boxes. Have the student slide their finger under the word and blend the letter sounds. Direct the student to do the same with the word in the text.

6. Show the student an analogy to a similar word they would know. For example, if the word is *hive*, use *five* as an analogy. Break the word apart at the onset and the rime and show them that the rime is the same in both words, so they only need to substitute the *h* for the *f*.

7. Once the student has reread and corrected the word and finished reading the sentence, ask whether that makes sense. This will help develop the student's set for variability and build their ability to self-monitor for comprehension.

8. Have the student reread the sentence or page to completely map the spelling, pronunciation, and meaning of the word.

If students decode each word correctly but lack fluency, then provide strategies and actions to increase fluency. The fluency responses in the left-hand column of the Strategies and Actions for Fluency and Comprehension section of the lesson plan (see figure 4.2, page 104). The following responses will require students to practice fluency.

1. Place your fingers around three to four words at a time for students to practice phrased reading. You can also drag your finger and swoop underneath three to four words at a time.

2. Read a page and have students reread and repeat after you.

Be sure that students can read the text fluently, using appropriate phrasing, before asking them comprehension questions. Choose one comprehension question to ask in the right-hand column of the Responses for Fluency and Comprehension section of the lesson plan.

1. "What did you read? Tell me about it." This response to students' reading is open-ended and gives the students an opportunity to expand their thinking.

2. "*What* happened to *who, where, when,* and *why*?" This gives students the opportunity to briefly summarize the text.

Each time you complete lesson 2, mark your anecdotal notes on the back of the lesson plan. This will help you tailor your future responses and feedback so they specifically meet each student's needs and abilities.

Teaching Decoding

The second component for lesson 2 is teaching and demonstrating the decoding process. Spend two to three minutes modeling how to phonetically decode some words from the text students read and how to segment and blend the phonemes. When teachers explicitly demonstrate how to decode words, it helps students understand the step-by-step process for reading new words. This helps demystify what can be an abstract process for full alphabetic readers. Choose a few words from the text to use as examples for teaching phonetic decoding and jot them down on the lesson plan. Choose one or two strategies from the Strategies and Actions for Decoding section of the lesson plan and write them in the space next to Skills. You'll model the decoding process using these strategies with the words you've chosen. Write your example words on a small whiteboard and model one or two of the eight decoding strategies (page 106).

You can also write letters in sound boxes to demonstrate blending letter sounds or write one letter at a time on the whiteboard while students blend the sounds to pronounce the word. Another option is to use magnetic letters or tiles and push them up one at a time to model how to blend letter sounds. As students move through the full alphabetic phase, you can begin to demonstrate how to chunk or break apart words as the onset and rime or by morphemes or syllables. Refer to the scaffolds in figure 1.4 (page 28) and use additional supports if you need to.

Modeling the decoding process aloud for students helps them recognize how this process mirrors what they do when they read. This also allows teachers to demonstrate the self-monitoring and self-correcting process. Modeling the self-correction process to build a set for variability is critically important for students to develop flexibility when decoding new words. They learn to focus on pronunciation and word meaning in addition to phonetic decoding, promoting the complete process of orthographically mapping new words.

Discussing Text

The third component of lesson 2 consists of facilitating a discussion about text comprehension. Spend a few minutes discussing the text with students. Use the Conversation Starter Comprehension Cards in appendix C (page 247) to guide these discussions. Open-ended discussion starters where students must make an analysis, support their thinking, and make connections and inferences promote higher-order literacy skills. These starters encourage a more meaningful discussion and serve as springboards for an in-depth conversation about the text. Consider using only one or two discussion starters at a time and introducing a new one with each lesson.

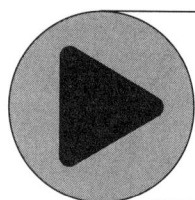

Use the QR code to watch a video of a teacher conducting a full-alphabetic lesson 2.

Planning and Teaching Lesson 3

Lesson 3 is composed of a combination of the same activities completed in lessons 1 and 2, so it will have four components. Figure 4.3 shows the components for lesson 3.

Word Building

For the word-building component, you'll spend three to four minutes teaching students to build word chains like you did for lesson 1. First, based on how students did with building words in lesson 1, decide on the appropriate scaffold and record it on the lesson plan. If the scaffold you used was appropriate, you can continue to use it for your next set of words or use a lesser degree of support by choosing the next scaffold from figure 1.4 (page 28). If students need more support, continue to teach the same word list you used in lesson 1 with a scaffold that provides more support for them. If students were proficient in writing the words you dictated with a phonics pattern, move to the next phonics pattern or skill. You can use a list of words and move down the list of scaffolds until students can write the words independently as you dictate them. If students haven't mastered a word list, provide additional support using the supplemental lists in appendix C (page 234) until they master each word list pattern.

Lesson 3			
Word Building (3–4 minutes)		Scaffold:	
Word List:	Phonics Skill:		Patterns:
Review Sight Words (3–4 minutes)			
Complete Each Step:	Teach and map	Build	Write
Rereading (3–4 minutes)			
Reading Format:	☐ Independent read	☐ Echo read	☐ Choral read	☐ Partner read

Strategies and Actions for Fluency and Comprehension (Check box when used during the lesson):

☐ Swoop three to four words for student to practice fluency.	☐ Read along then repeat after me.
☐ Try to sound like you are talking.	☐ Were there any words or parts you didn't understand?
☐ Read to the punctuation before stopping.	☐ What did you read? Tell me about it.
☐ Make your voice go up for a question.	☐ What new information did you learn?
☐ Read it the way the character feels (exclamation).	☐ Why do you think. . .?

Writing—Sentence Dictation or Sentence Starter (3–4 minutes)				
Teaching or Editing Focus:	☐ Handwriting	☐ Spacing	☐ Phonetic spelling	☐ High-frequency words
☐ Noun-verb agreement	☐ Sentence structure	☐ Possessives	☐ Irregular plural nouns	☐ Irregular verbs	☐ Past-, future-, present-tense verbs
Notes for Next Lesson:				

FIGURE 4.3: Full alphabetic phase lesson 3.

*Visit **go.SolutionTree.com/literacy** to download a free reproducible version of this figure.*

Review Sight Words

After students have completed the word-building task, choose another sight word from table 4.14 (page 102) or from the text the students read, or continue to practice the sight word or words from lesson 1 if they can't write them independently yet. Spend three to four minutes and follow the same three steps for teaching sight words as you did for lesson 1.

Rereading

Students will reread the text from lesson 1 to practice fluency. Full alphabetic readers need to increase their automaticity and reading rate, so rereading familiar text is vitally important during this reading phase. Students can also reread texts that you've previously used for instruction before moving on to more complex phonics and spelling patterns. For the rereading lesson component, first decide which format you'd like to use. If students need additional practice with decoding words, have them reread the text independently. If they were successful with their decoding during lesson 2, choose an echo, choral, or partner read for the rereading.

Students' decoding skills with the text should be stronger, especially if they've practiced reading the text several times. If they make decoding errors, refer to the responses and feedback on lesson 1. Provide your decoding strategies and actions after the student has finished reading the sentence. If they don't recognize their decoding errors, bring their attention to the mistake and use the decoding strategies and actions to help them fix it.

If students decode each word correctly, then provide strategies to increase fluency. The fluency strategies and actions are in the lesson plan in the left-hand column and to the top of the right-hand column. The following five strategies require students to practice fluency.

1. Place your fingers around three or four words at a time for the student to practice phrased reading or drag your finger and swoop underneath three to four words at a time.
2. Direct the student to practice reading the phrases in the sentence as if they're talking.
3. Have the student read up to the comma or end of the sentence without stopping.
4. Demonstrate to students how your voice raises at the end of a question and goes down for a sentence that ends with a period or read with energy for an exclamation.
5. Read a page and have the student reread and repeat after you.

Be sure that students can read the text fluently, using appropriate phrasing, before asking them comprehension questions. Choose one of the comprehension questions to ask on the bottom right column of the lesson plan.

1. "What new information did you learn?" This gives students time to explain the facts and information they learned from the text.
2. "What was the most important part?" This allows students to justify what they thought was most important in what they read.

Each time you complete lesson 3, mark your anecdotal notes on the back of the lesson plan. This will help you to tailor your future responses and feedback to meet each students' needs and abilities.

Writing—Sentence Dictation

Writing is a crucial component of developing sufficient literacy skills. For the writing lesson plan component, plan for students to write one or two sentences that you dictate that include the phonics skills and sight words you've taught. Or, provide sentence starters for students using the Conversation Starter Comprehension Cards (page 247). Compared to phonetic decoding practice, when students practice writing and spelling words, there is a greater transfer of orthographic learning and student literacy skills increase (Conrad, Kennedy, Saoud, Scallion, & Hanusiak, 2019; Shanahan, 2022).

Follow the same process from lesson 1 for dictating sentences. Incorporate a few words from the word-building lesson component with one or two sight words you've taught to create sentences containing five to seven words. Students can use the dotted lines at the bottom of the word mat to write the sentence, or they can write it in a writing journal. When you dictate the sentence for students to write, say them phrased, grouping three or four words at a time. To practice fluency, have students reread their sentences, grouping three to four words at a time when they read it. Follow the same steps from lesson 1 for dictating the sentence.

Once students are proficient in spelling words with each of the five short vowels within words with consonant clusters (a series of three consonants), they can begin constructing their own sentences. Use the discussion starter cards that you used for the comprehension discussion in lesson 2 so students have already orally rehearsed what they'll write. They can review and revisit their responses from lesson 2 to orally practice their phrases and sentences before writing them. Expect each phonics pattern and sight word that you've taught to be spelled correctly in students' writing. Students may need scaffolding with sound or spelling boxes when constructing their own sentences—this is expected and acceptable.

You may need to construct sound or spelling boxes on the lines for the words in the sentences to support students' segmenting and blending to write and read the words. Direct students to always say words out loud as they write the corresponding letters, making sure they slide from one sound into the next without pausing between and simultaneously write the letters that match the sounds coming out of their mouths to tightly integrate phoneme-grapheme connections. Differentiate the support you provide for students during writing based on their individual needs. Some students need more support with handwriting, while others need to focus on writing the correct letters for the sounds they represent.

Use the skills across the bottom of the lesson plan template as a progression for differentiating your instruction for each student. After students finish writing the sentence, choose a teaching or editing point as your focus for them to edit their sentences. The teaching points are in developmental order from left to right across the top row then from left to right across the bottom row on the lesson plan. Focus on one skill per lesson and don't move on to editing for the next skill until students master the writing skill you're currently teaching. A sample completed lesson plan for the full alphabetic phase is shown in figure 4.4.

Full Alphabetic Phase		
Lesson 1		
Word Building (4–5 minutes)	Scaffold: Sound boxes with magnetic letters	
Word List: 7	Phonics Skill: Consonant clusters	Patterns: scr, spl, spr
Sight Words (4–5 minutes)	does	goes
Complete Each Step:	Teach and map	Build	Write

Writing—Sentence Dictation or Sentence Starter (4–5 minutes)					
Flora goes to school with the insects.			She does rescue the spiders.		
Teaching Focus:	☐ Handwriting	☐ Spacing		☑ Phonetic spelling	☑ High-frequency words
☐ Noun-verb agreement	☐ Sentence structure	☐ Possessives	☐ Irregular plural nouns	☐ Irregular verbs	☐ Past-, future-, present-tense verbs

Notes for Next Lesson: Review *s* blends, then move on to *sh* and *th* blends (next two columns).

Lesson 2	
Text Title: *Fly to the Rescue!*	Phonics Skill: Consonant clusters, -ed endings

Reading (8–9 minutes)

Give Overview and Introduce Phonics Skill or Sight Words: Three sounds for -ed endings: /id/, /d/, /t/

Vocabulary:	swept (p. 9)	nimble (p. 11)	

Strategies and Actions for Decoding (Check box when used during the lesson):

☐ Stretch / blend the letter sounds.	☐ Dictate or make word via sounds → letters.
☐ Try this sound. . .	☐ You know this word. . . (write an analogy).
☐ Have student blend sounds aurally, then read.	☐ Does that make sense?
☐ Chunk the word or break it into syllables.	☐ Reread the sentence and tell me what it means.

Strategies and Actions for Fluency and Comprehension (Check box when used during the lesson):

☐ Swoop three to four words for student to practice fluency.	☐ What did you read? Tell me about it.
☐ Read along and then repeat after me.	☐ *What* happened to *who, where, when,* and *why*?

Teaching Decoding (2–3 minutes)	Skills: Consonant clusters, beginning and ending blends, -ed endings

Examples: screaming, swept, sticky; needed-wanted, liked-looked, tried-screamed

Discussing Text (2–3 minutes; use cards in appendix C, page 247)

Notes for Next Lesson: Practice fluency and strategic 1:1.

Lesson 3		
Word Building (3–4 minutes)	Scaffold: Sound boxes	
Word List: 7	Phonics Skill: Consonant clusters	Patterns: shr, thr
Review Sight Words (3–4 minutes)	does	goes
Complete Each Step:	Teach and map	Build	Write

FIGURE 4.4: Sample completed full alphabetic phase lesson plan.   continued ▶

Rereading (3–4 minutes)			
Reading Format:	☐ Independent read	☐ Echo read	☐ Choral read	☑ Partner read

Strategies and Actions for Fluency and Comprehension (Check box when used during the lesson):	
☐ Swoop three to four words for student to practice fluency. ☐ Try to sound like you're talking. ☐ Read to the punctuation before stopping. ☐ Make your voice go up for a question. ☐ Read it the way the character feels (exclamation).	☐ Read along then repeat after me. ☐ Were there any words or parts you didn't understand? ☐ What did you read? Tell me about it. ☐ What new information did you learn? ☐ Why do you think. . .?

Writing—Sentence Dictation or Sentence Starter (3–4 minutes) Problem and solution with sentence starters.

The problem in the story was. . . It was solved when. . .

Teaching or Editing Focus:	☐ Handwriting	☐ Spacing	☑ Phonetic spelling	☑ High-frequency words
☑ Noun-verb agreement	☐ Sentence structure	☐ Possessives	☐ Irregular plural nouns	☐ Irregular verbs	☐ Past-, future-, present-tense verbs

Notes for Next Lesson:

Source for text: Benjamin, 2012.

*Visit **go.SolutionTree.com/literacy** to download a free reproducible version of this figure.*

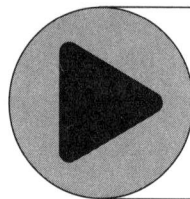

> Use the QR code to watch a video of a teacher conducting a full-alphabetic lesson 3.

Answering Common Questions About the Full Alphabetic Phase

Most of your focus for instruction during the full alphabetic phase will be on helping students to develop accurate and fluent decoding skills. These skills occur by providing a wealth of opportunities for students to read and write connected text. These opportunities facilitate the orthographic mapping process, connecting the spelling, sounds, and pronunciations of hundreds of new words. Differentiating your instruction during this phase of reading development is crucial for students. Students with strong and efficient decoding skills will move quickly through the full alphabetic phase, while you can provide students who need more repetition with extended practice until they master decoding new words.

What follows are the most common questions about the full alphabetic phase that may not have been addressed in this chapter.

Can't I Just Teach Sight Words, Since My Students Can Learn to Read So Much Faster That Way?

There are several problems with this approach to reading instruction. Words aren't islands in themselves. When students learn words in isolation as whole units, they're shut off from engaging in any self-teaching and learning of new words on their own. What students can learn from one word they can use to apply to many other unknown words. Your job isn't only to teach students to read—it's to teach students how to read new words when you aren't available to provide scaffolding for them. Teaching students to read only certain predetermined words eliminates opportunities to learn an abundance of new words. In addition, when students learn words in isolation, they don't practice transferring the knowledge of those words to authentic reading and writing experiences. In the long run, learning words through memorization and in isolation is the least efficient and slowest manner to teach students to read. This negates any positive effect that word learning may have had.

Research shows that words don't become sight words by learning them as whole units (Ehri, 2020). Sight words are simply any words that we recognize quickly and automatically, but the term can be misleading and result in teachers advocating for the visual memorization of words. The term *sight word* is often misrepresented and misused, leading to instruction that's not highly efficient. A good rule of thumb is to be aware of early readers who appear to read quickly and fluently but aren't skilled at learning new words by sounding them out. Many times, these readers have developed a coping mechanism and have learned to memorize what could be hundreds of words by sight.

You may be spending a considerable amount of time teaching phonics but aren't applying that instruction to teaching sight words. Instead, you may be teaching early readers to memorize words visually rather than teaching them to orthographically map those words through letter and sound instruction. Research suggests that is the wrong approach (Duke & Mesmer, 2018–2019). Although students can learn to read a small number of words via memorization, this instructional method will fail students later on. Students who learn to read words only through visual memorization will struggle to learn new words over time because the formation of the neural connections for orthographic mapping has been delayed. Students who learn words only through memorization early on actually learn fewer words over time, according to cognitive psychologist Stanislas Dehaene (2013). Students' orthographic memory should strengthen over time, and they should learn an increasing number of words each school year. Learning new words shouldn't stall or decrease over time—it should increase as students move through the phases of reading development. If the neurological connections for the orthographic mapping process have been properly established, students will learn a growing number of words over time.

Should I Teach the Six Syllable Types?

Teaching the six types of syllables can be helpful for students to learn if they're taught alongside morphology and etymology; however, teaching syllable types on their own as a strict, rigid set of rules to be memorized can be too restrictive. Wasowicz (2021) explains:

> While declarative knowledge about syllable division and spelling rules can be helpful, at least for some students, there is research evidence that calls into question whether

teaching memorization and application of these rules is a *necessary* and *most efficient* method of instruction. (p. 14)

In the research on teaching syllable types, when instruction focused on teaching syllabication as a rigid set of rules to adhere to, reading didn't improve (Shanahan, 2021b). Research studies where teaching practices included the six syllable types and focused on the flexible use of syllable division yielded significantly better results over instruction that didn't include teaching syllable types. The key to the positive research outcomes was that students acquired knowledge about syllables, then used that knowledge in a flexible manner when learning new words. There is definite value in teaching students how to break words apart in reading to decode and pronounce them. Knowing how to break words into syllables is also a very beneficial spelling strategy. There are several caveats to teaching syllable types that shouldn't be overlooked.

- Word pronunciation doesn't always equate to syllable division. For example, the word *cabinet* has three syllables (cab-i-net). Yet, we pronounce it "cab-nit" because we don't accentuate the *i* (schwa) syllable. This is a common occurrence among many words in the English language, such as *different, interest, several,* and *vegetable.*

- Syllables differ from morphemes. Syllables are based on pronunciation, and morphemes are based on the meanings of parts of words. The way we divide a word into syllables may differ from how we break it apart into its morphemes. For example, morphologically, in the word *baking,* the root is *bake,* with the inflected ending *-ing.* Through syllable instruction, the first syllable is *ba* and the second is *king.* Readers must ultimately know how to pronounce the word they are dividing into syllables. We know how to pronounce a word only if it's stored in our listening vocabulary. For example, phonetically reading the word *carrot* would produce the two syllables that should sound like the words *car* and *rot.* Yet, we pronounce it *carrot,* with a short *a,* not an *r*-controlled *a,* and with a schwa sound for the letter *o* rather than a short *o.* We know how to pronounce the word correctly only because it's in our listening vocabulary (we've heard the word before) and we know what it refers to. Not having access to this information shuts us off from reading and pronouncing the word properly, regardless of our knowledge of syllable division.

- The six types of syllables don't account for the schwa vowel sound—an unaccented vowel sound—which is the most common vowel sound in English.

Yes, syllabication rules can be helpful for students when they're taught alongside morphology and etymology and in relation to vocabulary. Like other skills associated with reading, familiarity with syllable types is helpful when they're taught in the context of authentic reading and writing but isn't helpful when taught as a set of rules to be memorized in isolation. Students can benefit from learning about the various types of syllables, but as with most reading concepts, they must learn to be flexible in their understanding and application of that knowledge. The six types of syllables are taught in the consolidated alphabetic phase because up to that phase, words with inflected endings taught in the full alphabetic phase should be taught via morphology—their word parts.

Transitioning Students to the Consolidated Alphabetic Phase

The full alphabetic phase is pivotal for reading development. During this phase, students learn to self-monitor and self-correct their decoding; accumulate hundreds, if not thousands, of words that they can read and write phonetically; and learn to teach themselves new words based on what they know about the decoding process, and they learn to self-correct based on how words are pronounced. The orthographic mapping process becomes fine-tuned during the full alphabetic reading phase. As students continue to read new words and reread known words, their orthographic memory expands exponentially. By the end of the full alphabetic phase, students should be able to:

- Consistently and quickly associate letters and sounds and letter-sound combinations (digraphs, blends, and so forth)

- Spell words based on letter-sound mappings

- Fluently read words with basic phonetic combinations

- Use systematic phonics rules for self-teaching

- Read an increasing number of irregularly and regularly spelled sight words

- Easily read commonly occurring phonetic words with digraphs, blends, consonant clusters, and common long vowels (without having to sound words out every time)

- Read text with increased fluency and expression

- Self-monitor to determine whether they've correctly decoded words and understand what they've read

- Self-correct (or attempt to) decoding errors

In addition to being proficient in the activities in the lesson plan components for the full alphabetic phase, you can use the decoding assessment to be sure that students are proficient in reading words with all the phonetic patterns from the full alphabetic word lists before they progress to the consolidated alphabetic phase.

Follow the directions for administering the decoding assessment in appendix C (page 241). Begin by having students read the list of words similar to those they read and wrote in the full alphabetic phase. The word list contains twenty words. Students will read each word as you point to it. Students have read the word correctly when they can read it within two to three seconds. The decoding assessment contains a teacher score sheet that you can use to record which words the student reads correctly. If the student correctly reads at least sixteen (80 percent) of the words, proceed to the next list. When the student isn't able to read at least sixteen words correctly, stop assessing at that list.

Students who can read fourteen to fifteen words correctly will need some additional lessons in the full alphabetic phase. Students who read fewer than fourteen words correctly will need several more lessons in the full alphabetic phase. Assess students again when they successfully complete the activities in the full alphabetic lessons with very little scaffolding.

Conclusion

The full alphabetic reading phase is arguably the most important reading phase. During this phase of reading, readers learn multiple letter and sound combinations, practice their decoding skills, and have the opportunity to learn to read and write hundreds of new words through self-teaching. Through explicit reading and writing instruction and a multitude of opportunities to apply decoding skills, full alphabetic students read an impressive number of familiar and new words and their reading fluency greatly increases. This growth builds a strong foundation for advanced literacy skills to develop during the consolidated alphabetic phase. Monitoring students' progress and providing ongoing differentiated small-group instruction should provide mastery in the full alphabetic reading phase for all students. Small-group instruction must be informed by ongoing observations, anecdotal notes, and assessments of students' word-reading skills. Providing responsive instruction with reading and writing at this pivotal point in students' reading development is critical.

CHAPTER 5

Turning the Corner: The Consolidated Alphabetic Phase

We do think in words, and the fewer words we know, the more restricted our thoughts. As our vocabulary expands, so does our power to think.

—Madeleine L'Engle

In this chapter, you'll learn how to teach students to decode words by using their bases and roots, morphemes, and other familiar word parts; determine the meanings of unknown words; and construct a basic understanding of the texts they read based on the language and sentence construction in the text. Next, I describe the characteristics of consolidated alphabetic readers and present the components of the consolidated alphabetic lesson plans. You'll learn how to assess and group your consolidated alphabetic readers. You'll then learn how to teach students to decode and determine the meanings of words with various morphemes. Students will learn to read and write the most common sight words used in reading and writing, and you'll learn how to teach students to write about what they've read by paraphrasing and using vocabulary words. Next, I answer common questions about the consolidated alphabetic phase. Finally, the chapter concludes with instructions on how to determine when students are ready to progress to the automatic reading phase. Appendix D (page 249) contains the resources to be used with the consolidated alphabetic lessons.

Characterizing Consolidated Alphabetic Readers

When readers have transitioned from the full alphabetic to the consolidated alphabetic phase, they decode words in chunks rather than letter by letter. Multiletter patterns like digraphs, blends, word families, and vowel teams are consolidated in their orthographic memory as chunks and recognized with little to no effort. This helps them to not only read but also spell with ease and flexibility. Consolidated alphabetic readers:

- Recognize common letter patterns and chunks that occur in words

- Make analogies to word families, onsets, rimes, and morphemes

- Retain words in their orthographic memory by chunking word parts rather than by individual letters and sounds

- Teach themselves words through connections to known words (self-teaching)

- Learn new words based on knowledge of phonetic spelling patterns (statistical learning)

- Require fewer connections to secure words in orthographic memory because orthographic mapping has become automatic

- Read with sufficient accuracy and expected fluency

During this transition from the full alphabetic to the consolidated alphabetic reading phase, you should witness the rapid development of fluency with reading and writing. This isn't the time to remain idle while students read and write independently. Students are expanding their word knowledge rapidly at this point in their reading development and need explicit vocabulary instruction and opportunities to learn new words in context. Adding new words to their lexicon will strengthen their comprehension abilities.

Teaching Your Consolidated Alphabetic Readers

The consolidated alphabetic reading phase marks a pivotal point in reading development, where the transfer of foundational decoding skills to proficient reading requires ongoing targeted instruction that elevates vocabulary and comprehension development. There's a strong reciprocal relationship between vocabulary and comprehension skills. Students who perform poorly in measures of comprehension also perform poorly in measures of vocabulary, and vice versa. By the time students enter high school, vocabulary and comprehension abilities are virtually impossible to separate.

During the consolidated alphabetic phase, you'll focus on teaching vocabulary and strategies for students to learn new vocabulary words on their own. Students are better served at this more advanced level of reading instruction if we strongly emphasize vocabulary alongside basic comprehension skills and strategies. As depicted in Scarborough's reading rope, language comprehension skills influence overall reading comprehension as much as word recognition does. Intentionally placing attention on vocabulary and language comprehension skills enables students to apply and be successful with reading comprehension strategies during the next reading phase.

Where to Focus Instruction During Small-Group Lessons

When readers enter the consolidated alphabetic phase, it marks a turning point in their reading development. They have built a strong foundation in phonemic awareness, phonics, and fluency to establish quick decoding skills and are turning the corner from "learning to read" to "reading to learn." When the basic reading skills of decoding and fluency have become smooth and accurate, it frees up working memory in the brain to focus on vocabulary and comprehension. Decoding words now requires less effort, which allows consolidated alphabetic readers to use all their mental energy to read and understand longer, more complex text. This advancement in reading development also marks a shift in your instructional focus. Your small-group lessons for consolidated alphabetic readers will contain each of the following essential pieces.

- Reading complex and engaging texts that offer readers opportunities to practice advanced decoding skills

- Breaking down syllables and morphemes in words to determine their meanings

- Providing explicit instruction on using context clues and word analysis strategies

- Writing words with advanced phonics patterns and vowel combinations

- Reinforcing advanced phonics skills through word-building activities

- Providing instruction and feedback in fluency and reading with expression, sufficient pacing, and intonation

- Teaching foundational reading comprehension strategies

For your small-group lessons, use texts that students can read with about 95 percent accuracy or text that's as close as you can get to your grade-level band where students can read with 95 percent accuracy or higher. Reading text that's closer to an independent reading range allows you to focus on teaching vocabulary and comprehension instead of decoding.

How to Assess Your Consolidated Alphabetic Readers

The decoding assessment in appendix D (page 259) is a quick and useful tool to utilize during the consolidated alphabetic reading phase because it will help you determine what letter-sound patterns students know and which ones they need to learn. Students during this reading phase may span a wide range, from students who are just learning to chunk simple words with basic long vowel patterns to those who are reading to learn morphological patterns and multisyllabic words. For students who are just exiting the full alphabetic phase, you can simply begin instruction with word list 1 of the consolidated alphabetic phase (page 123).

Using the decoding assessment will help you quickly identify gaps in phonics knowledge as well as purposefully group students for instruction. Knowing exactly where individuals are in their ability to decode advanced phonetic words will allow you to identify the focus for your small-group instruction. Note that the words students will read on the assessment contain cumulative phonics patterns. For example, a word that contains an *r*-controlled vowel (a vowel followed by an *r*) may contain a consonant digraph, or an initial blend. A word that contains the vowel pattern *eigh* may also contain an initial or final digraph or blend. Words with prefixes and suffixes will contain at least two syllables. These expectations align with common state literacy standards. Follow the directions on the decoding assessment carefully to ensure that you group your students and plan your lessons accordingly.

How to Group Your Consolidated Alphabetic Readers

Although the decoding assessment for consolidated alphabetic readers contains a variety of phonics spelling patterns, you can group students together with similar needs. For example, you can group students who need instruction in similar phonics patterns, such as *r*-controlled vowels or vowel digraphs, words with closed and *-le* syllables, or words with prefixes and suffixes. Grouping students of similar needs together will make your instruction efficient and effective. As long as you informally assess students' areas for growth during your small-group lessons and periodically reassess and regroup students as needed, skills-based phonics groups allow you to provide valuable, targeted, ability-appropriate instruction. This skills-based approach to differentiated instruction has been shown to be the most effective way to group students for small-group instruction (Conradi Smith et al., 2022; Diamond, n.d.; Hall & Burns, 2018; IES, 2016; Puzio et al., 2020; Vaughn et al., 2020; Young, 2023).

Planning Lessons for Consolidated Alphabetic Readers

The consolidated alphabetic lesson plan contains three separate lessons. The focus for lesson 1 is on word building and teaching sight words (if necessary), prereading or previewing the text students will read, and creating a graphic organizer based on what students already know about the text topic. The focus for lesson 2 is on students sharing their graphic organizers, reading the text and clarifying any misunderstandings, then learning vocabulary or discussing the text. Finally, lesson 3 focuses on incorporating new vocabulary into writing. The components within this series of lessons contains a variety of instructional strategies that will foster oral language and vocabulary development to provide a strong foundation for comprehension. Students will read the text when they're with you, and they'll reread the text outside of small-group instruction. For this phase, your students will need a notebook to use during small-group instruction. The structure and components for the consolidated alphabetic lessons are shown in table 5.1.

TABLE 5.1: Consolidated Alphabetic Lesson Plan Structure and Components

Lesson 1	Lesson 2	Lesson 3
Word Building and Sight Words	Discuss Graphic Organizers	Plan for Writing
Text Introduction, Preview, and Vocabulary	Reading and Clarifying	Oral Rehearsal and Writing
Graphic Organizer	Teaching Vocabulary or Discussing Text	Editing-Language Standards

As I previously suggested, it's best to choose texts as close to or within your grade-level Lexile band that students will be able to read with approximately 95 percent accuracy. This way, students aren't spending as much time and working memory decoding the text so they can use their mental energy to focus on interpreting the meanings of the words (vocabulary) and comprehension. Students should be reading texts that connect to prior knowledge or to concepts and topics you're teaching in other subjects throughout the school day. These connections create a springboard to build new domains of knowledge. By this phase of reading development, you should be using various genres of texts during small-group instruction, including the following.

- Poetry

- Historical fiction

- Biographies and autobiographies

- Folklore

- Mysteries

- Graphic novels

- Mythology

- Essays and speeches

- Informational texts and current event articles

- Realistic fiction

Planning and Teaching Lesson 1

Lesson 1 contains three components: (1) word building and teaching sight words (if necessary); (2) text introduction, preview, and vocabulary; and (3) building a graphic organizer. The word-building activities in lesson 1 are designed for students to manipulate phonemes in words with long vowels, *r*-controlled vowels, and abstract vowel patterns (vowel digraphs that make two sounds). The goal of the activities in the word-building lesson plan component is for students to simultaneously develop their reading and writing abilities with these phonics patterns using the scaffolds in figure 1.4 (page 28). If needed, throughout each set of lessons, students will learn to read and write any sight words they haven't yet mastered. Students will then preview the text, and you'll teach any new vocabulary that can be defined with a simple synonym. Students will then build a graphic organizer to make connections to prior knowledge, activate background knowledge, and provide a conceptual framework for integrating new information and setting a purpose for reading. For students needing more scaffolding to connect to familiar places, concepts, or proper nouns, provide photos, maps, diagrams, and other visuals. You can also incorporate short video clips and photos to aid in vocabulary and establishing a basic understanding of the text content. Lesson 1 is shown in figure 5.1.

Lesson 1				
Word Building (3–4 minutes)		Scaffold:		
Word List:	Skill:			Patterns:
Sight Words (2–3 minutes, if necessary)				
Complete Each Step:	Teach and map		Build	Write
Introduction, Preview Text, and Vocabulary (2–3 minutes)				
Text:				
Vocabulary:				
Graphic Organizer (5–6 minutes)				
Notes for Next Lesson:				

FIGURE 5.1: Consolidated alphabetic phase lesson 1.

*Visit **go.SolutionTree.com/literacy** to download a free reproducible version of this figure.*

Word Building and Sight Words

During the consolidated alphabetic phase, students will continue to develop their blending and segmenting skills with phonemes within words that have *r*-controlled vowels, vowel diphthongs, and syllable types. By completing the word-building activities, students will learn to read, spell, and write words that contain these phonics and spelling patterns. Connecting reading and writing through phoneme manipulation when reading, building, and spelling words will continue to promote the orthographic mapping process and increase students' orthographic memory.

Students in the consolidated alphabetic phase may need the word mat in appendix D (page 252) to complete the word-building activities. Follow the directions in tables 1.5 (page 26) and 1.6 (page 27) to complete the activities. The amount of support and scaffolding that you use for the word-building activities should decrease as students progress through the consolidated alphabetic phase. Use the scaffolds from figure 1.4 (page 28) when necessary, keeping in mind that the goal for mastery of the word-building activities is for students to be able to correctly write the words with little to no support or scaffolding.

In lesson plan 1, write the phonics pattern you'll begin with. The following are the categories of words you'll work with based on how students performed on the decoding assessment.

- *R*-controlled vowels
- Vowel digraphs
- Closed syllables
- Consonant -*le* syllables
- Open syllables
- Vowel combination syllables
- Syllables with silent *e*
- *R*-controlled syllables
- Words with common prefixes
- Words with common suffixes

For each word chain list (found across this chapter's three lessons), spend three to four minutes completing the word-building activities (both the reading and phonemic manipulation tasks) with each set of words, using the scaffolds from figure 1.4 (page 28) as needed. When students can quickly and easily write the words for a phonics pattern, move on to the next word list for that skill. If students haven't mastered the words after completing a word list, provide additional support using the supplemental lists in appendix D (page 254) until students have mastered the word list.

Table 5.2 contains the word list for phonics patterns with long vowel sounds. It consists of common words containing the long vowel patterns *ei, ie, igh, ow, ew, ui,* and short *e,* spelled *ea.*

Here are some helpful hints and rules for long vowel patterns.

- The spelling pattern *ei* is one of the least common spellings for the long *a* sound.
- The spelling pattern *ea* is the least common for the short *e* sound.
- Long *e* can be spelled *ie* in words, typically except after the letter *c.* After *c,* the spelling is *ei,* hence the saying "*I* before *e,* except after *c.*"

- Most words that have the long *i* sound spelled with *igh* end in the letter *t*. The only long *i* words spelled with *igh* that don't end in the letter *t* are *high*, *nigh*, *sigh*, and *thigh*.

- The spelling pattern *ow* is the most common when you hear the long *o* sound at the end of a word.

- The spelling pattern *ew* is the most common when you hear the long *u* sound at the end of a word.

- The spelling pattern *ui* is one of the least common spellings for the long *u* sound.

TABLE 5.2: Word List 1—Skill: Vowel Patterns

Word List 1						
Phonics and Spelling Patterns						
Long *a*, ei	**Short *e*, ea**	**Long *e*, ie**	**Long *i*, igh**	**Long *o*, ow**	**Long *u*, ew**	**Long *u*, ui**
rein	deaf	chief	high	low	few	suit
neigh	death	field	thigh	bowl	chew	fruit
eight	dread	grieve	might	growth	grew	juice
weight	health	shield	bright	known	strew	bruise
eighth	spread	shriek	slight	thrown	shrewd	cruise

Table 5.3 contains lists of common words containing the *r*-controlled spelling patterns *ar*, *er*, *ear*, *eer*, *ir*, *or*, and *ur*. When a vowel is followed by the letter *r*, the vowel and the *r* are pronounced as one sound. Complete both the reading and phonemic manipulation tasks with each set of words, using the scaffolds from figure 1.4 (page 28) as needed. When students can quickly and easily write the words for a phonics pattern, move on to the next word list for that skill.

Here are some helpful hints and rules for *r*-controlled vowels.

- *R*-controlled vowels spelled with *ar* and *or* make their own distinct sounds.

- *R*-controlled vowels spelled with *er*, *ir*, and *ur* sound similar. The spelling pattern *er* is the most common, followed by *ir*. The spelling pattern *ur* is the least common for the /er/ sound.

TABLE 5.3: Word List 2—Skill: *R*-Controlled Vowels

Word List 2						
Phonics and Spelling Patterns						
ar	**/or/, ar**	**or**	**/er/**		**ir**	**ur**
			er	**ear**		
arch	ward	force	germ	earn	dirt	burn
chart	warp	north	clerk	earth	birth	hurt
sharp	wart	scorch	perch	heard	chirp	blurt
snarl	dwarf	storm	verge	pearl	quirk	curve
starve	swarm	sworn	stern	search	swirl	splurge

Table 5.4 contains the word list for phonics patterns with vowel diphthong spelling patterns. A *vowel diphthong* is a combination of letters that make two vowel sounds within one syllable. The vowels sound as if the first one slides into the second sound. The spelling pattern *wa* is included because when the letter *a* is preceded by a *w*, the *a* makes a short *o* sound. Complete both the reading and phonemic manipulation tasks with each set of words, using the scaffolds from figure 1.4 (page 28) as needed. When students can quickly and easily write the words for a phonics pattern, move on to the next word list for that skill. You don't need to complete each set of words within a list for students who master writing the words more rapidly than others.

Here are some helpful hints and rules for vowel diphthongs and *wa*.

- The spelling pattern *oo* can have a long /oo/ sound, as in *hood*, or a short /oo/ sound, as in *book*.
- When the /oy/ sound appears at the end of a word or syllable, it's spelled with *oy*.
- When the /oy/ sound is at the start of or inside a syllable, it's spelled with *oi*.
- When the /ow/ sound is at the end of a word or syllable, or if it rhymes with *clown* or *howl*, it's spelled with *ow*.
- When the /ow/ sound is at the start of or inside a syllable, it's spelled with *ou*.
- The spelling pattern *au* never comes at the end of a word in English.
- The spelling pattern *au* usually is used at the end of a syllable.
- The spelling pattern *al* is used with words that rhyme with *all* or *walk*.
- When you hear the /ō/ sound at the beginning or in the middle of a syllable, it's usually spelled with *au*. When you hear the /ō/ sound at the end of a syllable, it's usually spelled with *aw*.
- If the letter *l*, *n*, or *k* follow the /ō/ sound at the end of a word, they use the *aw* spelling.
- When a *w* is followed by an *a*, it usually makes the short *o* sound.

TABLE 5.4: Word List 3—Skill: Vowel Diphthongs and *wa*

Word List 3								
Phonics and Spelling Patterns								
/oo/, Short o	**/oi/**		**/ou/**		**/ȯ/**			**/o/**
oo	**oy**	**oi**	**ou**	**ow**	**al**	**au**	**aw**	**wa**
hood	boy	boil	ouch	cow	bald	haul	paw	wad
hook	coy	join	shout	brow	balk	fault	raw	walk
wool	joy	broil	bound	fowl	halt	vault	bawl	swab
brook	soy	hoist	pouch	how	malt	cause	dawn	swan
stood	toy	point	ground	plow	salt	fraud	fawn	swap

After students have completed the word-building activities with vowel diphthongs, they're prepared to work with words with two or more syllables. Teaching students to break words into syllables is an invaluable skill for both reading and spelling. It improves both encoding and decoding skills by helping students break down words into manageable chunks as they read and write. It also helps them apply similar patterns when spelling words because they're able to learn reliable patterns that they can apply to many words.

There are generally six different types of categories for words with multiple syllables. Knowing these syllable types can help students increase their spelling skills and reading fluency. The six types of syllables aren't an absolute set of rules for all multisyllabic words—not every syllable fits into one of these six categories. The syllable types are categories for many, but not all, syllable formats. Equipping students with knowledge of the six types of syllables facilitates breaking down words into decodable chunks, applying reliable phonics rules, expanding vocabulary, and improving spelling skills.

Table 5.5 (page 126) contains the word list for phonics patterns with the six types of syllables. Complete both the reading and phonemic manipulation tasks with each set of words, using the scaffolds from figure 1.4 (page 28) as needed. When students can quickly and easily write the words for a phonics pattern, move on to the next word list for that skill. You don't need to complete each set of words within a list for students who master writing the words more rapidly than others.

Here are some helpful hints and rules for syllable types.

- A trick for remembering the spelling patterns for the six syllable types is to spell the acronym *CLOVER*. Each letter represents a syllable type.

    - The letter *C* represents *closed*. A closed syllable may start with a vowel or consonant, but it always ends with a consonant. Both syllables in the word *basket* (bas-ket) are closed.

    - The letter *L* represents *le*. An *le* syllable begins with a consonant and ends with the letters *le*. The second syllable in the word *juggle* (jug-gle) ends with an *le* syllable.

    - The letter *O* represents *open*. An open syllable ends with a single vowel, which makes the long sound. The word *menu* (men-u) ends with an open syllable.

    - The letter *V* represents *vowel*. A vowel syllable contains more than one letter representing the vowel sound. In the word *boating* (boat-ing), the syllable with *boat* is considered the vowel syllable.

    - The *E* represents *silent* e. A silent *e* syllable ends with a silent *e*, contains a vowel that makes a long sound, and has a consonant before the silent *e*. In the word *invade* (in-vade), the second syllable is a silent *e* syllable.

    - The *R* represents r-*controlled vowel*. An *r*-controlled vowel syllable contains at least one vowel (sometimes two) followed by the letter *r*. In the word *earring* (ear-ring), the first syllable is an *r*-controlled syllable.

As students progress through the consolidated alphabetic reading phase, they will turn the corner from "learning to read" to "reading to learn." Words they encounter will have two or more syllables and common prefixes and suffixes. The focus of reading will shift from phonemic awareness, phonics, and fluency to vocabulary and comprehension. Knowing the morphology of words is a critical skill that helps expand students' language and vocabulary knowledge. Learning common prefixes and suffixes helps students understand word meanings. Most prefixes and suffixes have consistent meanings, which can help students figure out the definitions of new words they encounter. Knowing common prefixes and suffixes helps students break down unfamiliar words and determine their meanings. This skill enables students to learn novel vocabulary words faster.

TABLE 5.5: Word List 4—Skill: Six Syllable Types

Word List 4					
Syllabication and Spelling Patterns					
Closed	Consonant and *le*	Open	Vowel Combinations	Silent *e*	*R*-Controlled
basket	babble	focus	breathing	complete	better
magnet	grumble	moment	destroy	debate	confirm
rotten	purple	protect	grounded	frustrate	plural
tablet	sprinkle	resist	shrieking	reptile	return
velvet	thimble	vacant	straighten	trapeze	termite

Table 5.6 contains the word list for phonics patterns with the most common prefixes. A *prefix* is a letter or group of letters that is added to the beginning of a word to form another word. A prefix changes the meaning of its base (or main) word.

Complete both the reading and phonemic manipulation tasks with each set of words, using the scaffolds from figure 1.4 (page 28) as needed. When students can quickly and easily write the words for a phonics pattern, move on to the next word list for that skill. You don't need to complete each set of words within a list for students who master writing the words more rapidly than others.

Here is a helpful hint and rule for prefixes.

• When we add a prefix to a word, the spelling for the word remains the same.

TABLE 5.6: Word List 5—Skill: Words With Common Prefixes

Word List 5		
Prefix Spelling Patterns		
dis-	re-	un-
disable	recharge	unclear
disgrace	reform	uncoil
disjoint	remark	unheard
disprove	resign	unkempt
distrust	revise	unnerve

Table 5.7 contains the word list for phonics patterns with the most common suffixes. A *suffix* is a letter or group of letters that's added to the end of a word to form another word. A suffix changes the meaning of a root word, the number or quantity of something, or the word's part of speech.

Complete both the reading and phonemic manipulation tasks with each set of words, using the scaffolds from figure 1.4 (page 28) as needed. When students can quickly and easily write the words for a phonics pattern, move on to the next word list for that skill. You don't need to complete each set of words within a list for students who master writing the words more rapidly than others.

Here are some helpful hints and rules for suffixes.

- The suffix *-es* is added to the end of a singular noun that ends in the sound /s/, /z/, /sh/, or /ch/.

- The suffix *-ed* is added to the end of a word to change the verb to past tense.
  - If the base word already ends in the letter *e*, we drop the *e* before adding *-ed*—for example, in the word liked.
  - If the base word ends in a short vowel with one consonant, we double the consonant before adding *-ed*—for example, in the word *clapped*.

- The suffix *-ing* is added to the end of a word to change the verb to present tense.
  - If the base word already ends in the letter *e*, we drop the *e* before adding *-ing*—for example, in the word *hiking*.
  - If the base word ends in a short vowel with one consonant, we double the consonant before adding *-ing*—for example, in the word *tapping*.

- The suffix *-ly* is added to the end of a word to mean *like*. It can be added to an adjective to form an adverb. For example, *quick* becomes *quickly*.
  - If the base word ends in *y*, change the *y* to *i*, then add the *-ly*. For example, *happy* becomes *happily*.
  - If the base word ends in *le*, just change the final *e* to *y*. For example, *gentle* becomes *gently*.

TABLE 5.7: Word List 6—Skill: Words With Common Suffixes

Word List 6			
Suffix Spelling Patterns			
-es	**-ed**	**-ing**	**-ly**
classes	advanced	building	costly
clothes	detached	glancing	frankly
failures	finished	striking	lovely
pictures	involved	trimming	smoothly
shambles	unharmed	yielding	sparkly

Table 5.8 (page 128) contains the sight words recommended for teaching during the full and consolidated alphabetic phases. These are words that contain phonics patterns not taught during the full alphabetic reading phase and that have irregular spelling patterns. First, be sure that students can read and write the sight words from the full alphabetic phase before turning your attention to teaching the sight words for the consolidated alphabetic phase. You can quickly administer an informal assessment to determine whether you still need to teach any words from the full alphabetic stage, and which words those are.

The sight words for the consolidated alphabetic phase contain phonics patterns that students haven't yet learned or are irregular due to their morphology or etymology. The words are in alphabetical order and grouped according to sound or spelling pattern. Focus on teaching one or two sight words per lesson. In lesson plan 1, there are spaces for you to write up to two sight words to teach. Spend three or four minutes of lesson 1 teaching sight words using the steps in the High-Frequency and Sight Words section in chapter 1 (page 7).

TABLE 5.8: Sight Words for the Full and Consolidated Alphabetic Reading Phases

Full Alphabetic Sight Words			Consolidated Alphabetic Sight Words	
about, round	even	of, off	again	people
after	very, every	only, open, over	always	pretty
said, again	far	our, out	another	their
also	first	one	around	thought
are	or, for, four	own	before	through
any, many	found, round	put	better	today
away	from	they	brought	together
been	full, pull	too, two	different	used
by, my, try, why	good, look	use	funny	were
come, done, some	grow, know, show	saw, draw	laugh	where
could, would, should	her	want	number	words
do, to	here, where, there	was	other	years
does, goes	little	what, who		
how, down	new	you, your		

Irregular sight words are usually only irregular by one or two sounds. Most of the word is still usually phonetically regular. Teach these common sight words by either explaining their morphology or pointing out the part of the word that's different or unexpected and then relating it to other similar words. For example, I don't explain the morphology or etymology of the word *through* to students; I simply explain to them that the letters *ou* in *through* represent the *ew* sound. This spelling pattern occurs in the words *group*, *wound*, *coupon*, and a few other common words students will recognize. This demystifies the spelling and phonetic patterns of these irregular sight words and helps students to understand and learn about how words are similar to other words. There are very few words that are true sight words, so learning about morphology becomes extremely important in vocabulary development.

Text Introduction, Preview, and Vocabulary

The second component in lesson 1 is the text introduction. Students will also preview the text, and you will provide synonyms for vocabulary words in the text. Introduce the text with a one-sentence summary by telling students what they'll read to learn about. For any words in the text that are names or proper nouns, simply point them out and demonstrate how to pronounce them. Have students spend a few minutes previewing, skimming and scanning through the text, and attending to text features. Next, quickly preteach any vocabulary words that are easy to define. Don't preteach all the vocabulary words during this lesson component. Students need to learn vocabulary before, during, and after they read. Learning too many new words prior to reading a text does little good, as students don't yet have context for connecting the words to memory. Words taught prior to reading the text should be words that students will quickly and easily relate to with a short definition or a simple, familiar synonym. Learning synonyms helps students quickly anchor the new term into memory for easy storage and retrieval and is an effective way for them to use new terminology for commonly known words.

Vocabulary words are considered to fall within three tiers.

- **Tier 1:** Words we use in everyday speech, understood by most students beginning at a young age

- **Tier 2:** General academic words that appear in textbooks, literature, and other instructional materials used in school (usually more specific and advanced than tier 1 words)

- **Tier 3:** Words that are highly technical and specific to a certain area of study

Tier 2 words that you can define with a simple tier 1 synonym are the words you should introduce to students prior to reading. Take a few minutes to sketch a simple T-chart on your whiteboard and on the left side, list the words you'll introduce. Quickly refer to the text and point out each word on the list, associate it with a common synonym, and write the synonym on the T-chart. Remind students that in the future, they'll use the new vocabulary word instead of the simpler word.

Graphic Organizers

During the third component of lesson 1, you'll introduce a graphic organizer that students will spend five to six minutes completing in their notebooks. There are five types of graphic organizers to choose from for this lesson plan component. The graphic organizer you choose will depend on which one you feel is most appropriate for that text. These graphic organizers lend themselves to whatever genre of text you'll be using. Examine the text you'll be using ahead of time to determine which graphic organizer is best to complete. If you have younger students in this phase (kindergarten through second grade), complete the graphic organizer together on a whiteboard. Students can write on sticky notes that you can place on the graphic organizer on the whiteboard.

Completing this graphic organizer will help students build the necessary schema to understand new topics and concepts. If you activate their existing knowledge, the schema that students built during lesson 1 will provide a foundation to which you can add new information. In this way, you'll improve their learning and comprehension, as the research of educator Ranulfo Friolo Cala (2019) confirms. Graphic organizers help students approach the text with a clearer sense of what to expect and what to focus on for their learning. The five graphic organizer choices follow.

Figure 5.2 (page 130) shows the I Know, I Wonder graphic organizer. This graphic organizer can be used with any genre of text and is useful when the text is on a topic students are only somewhat familiar with.

"I know. . ."	"I wonder. . ."

FIGURE 5.2: I Know, I Wonder graphic organizer.

*Visit **go.SolutionTree.com/literacy** to download a free reproducible version of this figure.*

Figure 5.3 shows the From Clues to Predictions graphic organizer. This graphic organizer can be used with any genre of text, but it lends itself more to fiction texts because the students will be making predictions about events in the text.

Clues from the title:	
Clues from the front and back covers:	
Clues from the table of contents:	
I predict. . . because. . .	

FIGURE 5.3: From Clues to Predictions graphic organizer.

*Visit **go.SolutionTree.com/literacy** to download a free reproducible version of this figure.*

Figure 5.4 shows the Questions I Have graphic organizer. This graphic organizer can be used with any genre of text, but it lends itself more to nonfiction because students will have questions that probably pertain to the photographs or text features.

Questions I Have

FIGURE 5.4: Questions I Have graphic organizer.

*Visit **go.SolutionTree.com/literacy** to download a free reproducible version of this figure.*

Figure 5.5 shows the K-W graphic organizer, which is adapted from Donna M. Ogle's (1986) K-W-L chart. This graphic organizer can be used with any genre of text, but it lends itself more to nonfiction because the chapters and sections tend to be organized by topic. Students can complete one pair of statements for each topic covered in the text they'll read.

What I Know	What I Want to Know

FIGURE 5.5: K-W graphic organizer.

*Visit **go.SolutionTree.com/literacy** to download a free reproducible version of this figure.*

Figure 5.6 shows the Making Connections graphic organizer. This graphic organizer can be used with any genre of text. Students must be familiar with the comprehension strategy of making connections. They should be proficient in practicing and explaining each type of connection to be made.

Text to Self What does this remind me of or make me think of?	
Text to Text What other text is this similar to? How?	
Text to World What does this text seem to have in common with the real world?	

FIGURE 5.6: Making Connections graphic organizer.

*Visit **go.SolutionTree.com/literacy** to download a free reproducible version of this figure.*

After lesson 1, students can read the text outside of small-group time. Have them continue to use a sticky note or slip of paper to jot down words or phrases they may not understand or need clarified. When students can identify words that they didn't understand or couldn't read, they are developing a self-monitoring process for comprehending. Self-monitoring is a critical process in reading that greatly affects vocabulary understanding and overall comprehension of the text. Students can also write down any questions they may have about what they have read. This is another self-monitoring strategy that helps readers think about what they do and don't know and understand while reading.

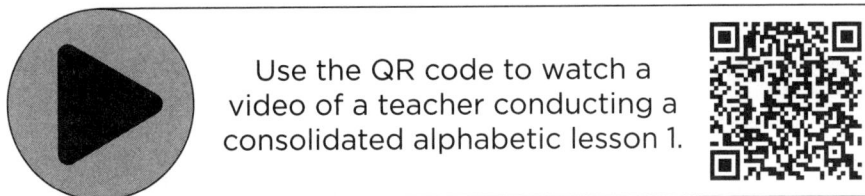

Use the QR code to watch a video of a teacher conducting a consolidated alphabetic lesson 1.

Planning and Teaching Lesson 2

Lesson 2 consists of three components that involve discussing students' graphic organizers, reading the text, and either teaching additional vocabulary through context clues or discussing the text. Before you can expect students to adequately comprehend the text they're reading, they must understand the words, phrases, and sentences in the context of that particular reading. These are all the strands in Scarborough's reading rope that are woven together to make reading comprehension possible. Comprehension is more about how students process language, or vocabulary, as they read (Nation, 2017). Unknown vocabulary hampers sentence comprehension, and when this accumulates throughout a passage or text, overall comprehension is negatively affected. Lesson 2 is shown in figure 5.7 (page 132).

Discuss Graphic Organizers

Begin lesson 2 by facilitating a discussion based on what students wrote about in their graphic organizers. This is also the opportune time for students to seek clarification about confusing or challenging parts of the text that they encountered, minimizing misunderstanding and maximizing potential for increasing

Lesson 2
Discuss Graphic Organizers (3–4 minutes)
Reading and Clarifying (5–6 minutes)

Strategies and Actions for Decoding and Self-Monitoring (Check box when used during the lesson):

☐ Chunk the word or break it into syllables.	☐ Were there any words you didn't understand?
☐ Find the root or base word.	☐ Is there a context clue you can use?
☐ Let's break it into parts.	☐ Reread the sentence and tell me what it means.
☐ This word is pronounced _____. It means _____.	☐ Does that make sense?

Strategies and Actions for Fluency and Comprehension (Check box when used during the lesson):

☐ Swoop or frame three- or four-word phrases for student to practice fluency.	☐ Read it the way the character feels (exclamation).
☐ Read along and then repeat after me.	☐ Try to sound like you're talking.
☐ Read to the _____ before stopping.	☐ Tell me about this paragraph, page . . .
☐ Make your voice go up at the end for a question.	☐ What is something new you learned? Tell me about it.

Teaching Vocabulary (4–5 minutes)						

OR: Discussing Text (4–5 minutes)	**Strategy:**
☐ Paraphrasing	☐ Summarizing with vocabulary
☐ Paraphrasing with vocabulary	☐ Paragraph shrinking

Notes for Next Lesson:

FIGURE 5.7: Consolidated alphabetic phase lesson 2.

*Visit **go.SolutionTree.com/literacy** to download a free reproducible version of this figure.*

understanding of the text. Students should discuss the text and anything that seems familiar about it or that they can relate and connect to in it. This familiarizes students with the text structure, complexity, length, and organization, which contribute to building schema. Encourage students to answer and respond to one another to co-construct their understanding of the text. Guide students in their discussion to help them clarify confusing words or phrases and answer each other's questions.

Reading and Clarifying

Spend the next five to six minutes listening to each student read. Provide students with a sticky note or a slip of paper when they begin reading and explain that it's for them to write down any words they don't understand or are unsure of as they're reading. This may occur while you listen to another student as they read. Students can whisper-read independently as you spend time listening to each one read. Take anecdotal notes or an informal reading record on the back of the lesson plan. When you listen to students read individually, you can help clarify their understanding of the words or phrases they wrote down. Provide strategies and actions for students for decoding first, then for self-monitoring.

If students read words incorrectly, teach the following decoding strategies and actions. They are in the lesson plan in two columns in order from the most support (left-hand column for decoding) to the least support (right-hand column for self-monitoring).

1. Divide, or chunk, the word at the onset and rime, at the syllable break, or between two morphemes.

2. Find the root or base word.

3. Break it into parts. Use the following prompt if the student can't decode the word and doesn't know how to break it apart.

    a. "The word is pronounced _____. It means _____." Use this prompt after showing the student how to break the word apart.

4. Ask the student if there are any words they didn't understand.

Once students are able to monitor their understanding of the text, you may need to prompt them to use context clues to figure out what an unknown word means. Teaching students to be proactive with determining the meanings of unfamiliar words enables them to add new words to their vocabulary independently without relying on you to define every unknown word. The process of rereading and searching for clues to a word's meaning requires and promotes text analysis skills. Students become more independent in figuring out the meanings of unknown words, which allows them to develop confidence in tackling difficult text on their own. Prompt students to use context clues to learn word meanings once you have explicitly taught this vocabulary strategy.

1. Provide a clue or a context clue for the student to determine the word's meaning.

2. Have the student reread the sentence and explain to you what it means.

3. Ask the student whether the sentence or part makes sense now.

If a student decodes each word correctly but lacks fluency, provide strategies and actions to increase fluency. The fluency responses are in the Strategies and Actions for Fluency and Comprehension section (see figure 5.7, page 132). The following responses require students to practice fluency.

1. Drag or swoop your fingers underneath three to four words at a time for students to practice phrased reading.

2. Read a page and have student reread and repeat after you.

3. Direct the student to read a phrase up to a certain point before stopping.

4. Demonstrate to the student how to raise or lower your voice or read with energy, depending on if the punctuation is a question mark, period, or exclamation mark.

5. Have the student read the sentence or phrase to you as if they were talking.

Be sure the student can read the text fluently, using appropriate phrasing, and understand what they have read before asking any comprehension questions. Choose one comprehension question to ask from the bottom right of the Strategies and Actions for Fluency and Comprehension columns of the lesson plan.

1. "Tell me about this paragraph, page . . ." This gives the student the opportunity to paraphrase what they read, the foundation of basic comprehension.

2. "What is something new you learned? Tell me about it." This allows the student to connect with new information they've read.

Teaching Vocabulary

Spend the next four to five minutes of lesson 2 teaching context clues and strategies to learn new vocabulary words. Unknown vocabulary slows reading rates and taxes working memory, which then hampers ability to critically analyze and synthesize text. As much as you would like to swiftly shift instruction to comprehension once students have solidified the decoding process, you cannot overlook the crucial importance of students acquiring vocabulary skills. To fully comprehend and extract the author's message, students must know and understand the words in the text—from the simplest to the most complex.

Vocabulary is the glue that enables students to connect and learn new information, and it is strongly associated with comprehension (Nation, 2017). When students have a limited vocabulary, it's harder for them to make sense of words and sentences, which negatively impacts their comprehension. Teaching students strategies to learn new vocabulary is as important—if not more important—than teaching comprehension strategies, yet teachers typically devote little reading time to vocabulary instruction (LD Center, 2023). Students learn vocabulary in only a few ways—by engaging in conversations with others, listening to others read to them, reading extensively on their own, and through direct instruction. You play an extremely critical role in helping your students increase their own vocabulary usage and their ability to learn new vocabulary words through reading.

When you're planning lesson 2, if students aren't adept at using context clues to determine the meanings of words, choose words you'll need to explicitly teach students to use from the text they read that they can't determine using a synonym, as in lesson 1. Choose tier 2 words that:

- Are essential to understanding the main idea of the text

- Are used frequently or repeatedly, or are used in different forms across various contexts

- Are not part of students' prior knowledge

- Follow general patterns of language—have base or root words, morphemes, common syllables

- Will improve language and comprehension and can be used again in writing

If you haven't yet thoroughly taught the concept of using context clues, that will be the strategy you'll teach. There are several types of context clues. Students will need ample time to learn how to search for and identify each one. Spend two or three sets of lessons teaching three or four types of context clues during each lesson 2. Choose texts that contain vocabulary that lends itself to teaching types of context clues. Table 5.9 contains the steps for teaching students how to determine the meanings of words using context clues.

TABLE 5.9: Steps to Teaching Context Clues

Step 1	Choose words to teach that fall into one of the following general categories of context clues. • Definition • Word parts • Inference • Example • Synonym or antonym • Figurative language • Text feature
Step 2	After students have read, write the vocabulary word you'll be teaching on a small whiteboard, show the word to students, and direct them to the page or section of the text where the word is located.
Step 3	Teach the type of context clue contained in the text for that word. Follow the list in step 1, as the types of context clues are in order from easiest to most complex.

Once you've thoroughly taught students how to use context clues, and they've had ample time to practice the rereading and self-monitoring skills necessary to effectively determine word meanings from context, they'll need to use these strategies while they read independently and reread during small-group lessons. Students can use the Context Clues bookmark in appendix D (page 258) as a reminder of how to determine the meanings of unknown words when they encounter them. Figure 5.8 contains several types of context clues to teach students. They are in order from the least to the most difficult.

If the text contains words that can't be determined through context or that require a great amount of inference to determine their meanings, you can explicitly teach those word meanings. Use one of the three strategies for teaching vocabulary after reading. The procedures for teaching these strategies are in table 1.7 (page 31).

1.   Morpheme analysis

2.   Examples and nonexamples

3.   Situations

Definition: The meaning of the word is stated in the sentence or a nearby phrase.	Example: <u>Target</u>, a store that sells men's clothing, is where we'll shop for your brother.
Example: An example of the word is given in the sentence or a nearby phrase.	Example: Be careful around my mother's new vase. It's so <u>delicate</u> it could easily break.
Text feature: A text feature either defines the word or shows an example of it with a photo, picture, or diagram.	Example: The cat and mouse made a <u>deal</u> that they wouldn't bother each other anymore.
Word parts: The meaning of the word can be determined from the base or root, prefix or suffix, or part of speech.	Example: Your parents can park their car in our <u>circular</u> driveway. (circle = round shaped)
Synonym or antonym: A word with the same meaning or a word with the opposite meaning is used in or near the sentence.	Examples: I was surprised and <u>shocked</u> to hear that I had won the contest. My brother is usually <u>sympathetic</u>, but this time he didn't feel bad for me when I got in trouble.
Inference: There are no explicit context clues, and the reader must read between the lines to determine the meaning of the word.	Example: I'm <u>determined</u> to study all afternoon so I can get a good grade on the test tomorrow.
Figurative language: Nonliteral language is used, such as idioms.	Example: My stomach was in <u>knots</u>.

FIGURE 5.8: Context clues.

Discussing Text

Once students are skilled in using context clues to determine the meanings of unknown words, you'll instead spend these four to five minutes of lesson 2 facilitating a basic discussion of the text with a focus on using the vocabulary words from the text. Students must use new vocabulary words several times before you can expect those words to become part of their *lexicon*, or speaking vocabulary.

Understanding and using vocabulary to paraphrase what they have read builds students' language comprehension skills. In addition to word recognition skills, language comprehension abilities comprise a large portion of Scarborough's reading rope. Language comprehension is one of the most overlooked aspects of reading comprehension. For students to successfully meet grade-level comprehension standards, they need to develop and refine their overall language comprehension—the ability to understand the meanings of words within the context of the sentences.

Five domains of language come together to form language comprehension, with vocabulary contributing the most. The other four language comprehension skills are background knowledge, language structure, verbal reasoning, and literacy knowledge. Language comprehension is the most basic level of comprehension, often referred to as *surface* or *literal comprehension*—the level at which students attend and connect to the basic message in the text with the language and vocabulary used in each sentence.

Successful reading comprehension in its totality often depends on basic sentence understanding of the text. The more background knowledge and familiarity with the topic and the language in the text, the stronger students' comprehension will be. On measures of overall comprehension, students who have strong language skills outperform students with weak language skills. Once students can decode the words in text, they extract its meaning using their:

- Overall knowledge and experiences (background knowledge)

- Knowledge of the words and their meanings (vocabulary)

- Understanding of the vocabulary within the context of the phrases and sentences (language structure)

- Ability to infer the meaning of the sentences in text (verbal reasoning)

- Understanding of the purpose, features, and conventions of text (literacy knowledge)

Because of the substantial impact that language comprehension skills have on overall reading comprehension, your text discussion should require students to use vocabulary to paraphrase the text. Just as babies learn to talk by parsing their thoughts and putting words together over and over as they increase their phrase and sentence construction, students in this reading phase need to do the same type of language practice to process what they're reading. You'll need to plan and facilitate discussions during your small-group lessons and allow as much time as possible for students to explain and expand on their thoughts using vocabulary from the text. This will promote a deeper understanding of the text by allowing them time to flesh out their thoughts and increase vocabulary usage and language structures.

Your purpose during this lesson plan component is to guide the discussion among students as opposed to teaching a comprehension strategy or creating worksheets and tasks for students to complete. Interactive discussion plays a critical role in reading comprehension because it requires students to actively process and interact with the text before they can begin to analyze it and critically comprehend it with their peers. Through this dialogue with each other, students learn to interpret the text more deeply, which leads to enhanced comprehension.

The four discussion strategies require students to paraphrase what they've read by putting it into their own words. Paraphrasing demonstrates that a student has understood the spoken or written phrases and sentences. If students can't paraphrase what they read, then they haven't understood it. Too often, this basic comprehension strategy is passed over in favor of teaching more difficult comprehension, such as main idea and details, cause and effect, or making inferences. We must devote ample time to developing speaking and oral language skills so students can coherently discuss text on a surface level before we turn our attention to more complex comprehension. Choose one of the four discussion strategies in table 5.10. They are in order from the most basic (paraphrasing) to the most advanced (paragraph shrinking). Continue to use a discussion strategy in each of your consolidated alphabetic lessons until students are proficient in that strategy, then move on to using the next one, and so on.

TABLE 5.10: Lesson 2 Discussion Strategies

Paraphrasing Use this strategy for students who need to build their oral language discussion skills before they can incorporate new vocabulary into the discussion.	1. Students reread a paragraph, page, or section of the text. 2. As a group, students take turns orally paraphrasing the portion of the text they just read. 3. Students may reread the portion of text as many times as they need to. The goal is for them to be able to cover their portion of the text and explain to others in the group what the part was about. 4. Students should be proficient in paraphrasing before you move on to paraphrasing with vocabulary.
Paraphrasing With Vocabulary	1. Write each vocabulary word on an index card and distribute so each student has at least one word. 2. Students take turns explaining to the other students what the vocabulary word on their index card means, then how the author used it in the text.
Summarizing With Vocabulary	1. Write each vocabulary word on an index card and distribute so each student has at least one word. 2. Students reread the portion of the text containing their vocabulary word. 3. Students take turns using the vocabulary word and summarizing the paragraph or portion in which it is used. 4. Follow the order that each word appeared in the text to create a cohesive and sequential summary of the text.
Paragraph Shrinking*	1. Students work in partners to reread the text. 2. After each paragraph or portion of text, students use a sticky note to jot down the *who* or *what* for that paragraph. 3. Students discuss the most important thing about the *who* or *what*—what happened or what someone did. 4. Students use another sticky note to summarize the *who* or *what* of that paragraph in ten or fewer words. This is the main idea of the paragraph. 5. Students can also complete this activity using a certain number of vocabulary or multisyllabic words.

Source: McMaster & Fuchs, 2016.

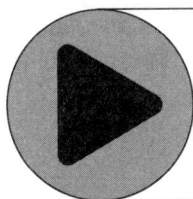

Use the QR code to watch a video of a teacher conducting a consolidated alphabetic lesson 2.

After you have completed lesson 2, allow students to reread the text independently, with a partner, or in a small group on their own. They can discuss the text and clarify any misunderstandings they may have had while reading. Students taking responsibility for their own understanding of the text builds their metacognitive skills so they can fully grasp key words, information, and concepts. Metacognition builds the essential reflective abilities that strengthen comprehension by promoting self-correcting one's understanding of the text. By leveraging metacognitive processes, students will become more actively attuned to their understanding of the text and accountable for their own reading success.

Planning and Teaching Lesson 3

The benefits of spending time to teach how to write well are endless. Writing instruction reinforces the reciprocal relationship of reading and writing. The act of writing allows students to reach a deeper level of reading comprehension. Research shows that well-planned writing lessons allow students to apply phonemic awareness, phonics, and handwriting skills, which strengthen and increase overall reading achievement (Ramirez-Avila & Barreiro, 2021; Sinambela, Manik, & Pangaribuan, 2015). Educators Steve Graham and Tanya Santangelo (2014) confirm that writing is a vehicle for improving reading instruction, but writing practice must be frequent and writing instruction must be explicit to positively affect reading comprehension. Writing about reading has proven to be better than reading alone, rereading, studying, discussing texts, and solely receiving reading instruction.

The process of connecting the practice of reading a text to writing about a text isn't as easy as it may seem. We have a limited processing capacity in our brains that makes it difficult to simultaneously attend to all steps or aspects of a task. Breaking down writing tasks into digestible steps is vital to helping students learn about the writing process in an organized fashion. In lesson 3, you'll plan for writing, guide students through writing, and complete the editing process with students. Lesson 3 is shown in figure 5.9.

Lesson 3			
Plan for Writing (1 minute)	Writing Format:		
Oral Rehearsal and Writing (10–12 minutes)			
1. Rehearse orally. 2. Repeat sentence in phrases and write. 3. Reread to self-monitor. 4. Repeat process for each sentence.			
Editing—Language Standards (1–2 minutes)			
☐ Conventions	☐ Parts of speech	☐ Sentence structure	☐ Verb tenses
☐ Conjunctions	☐ Compound sentences	☐ Commas	☐ Quotation marks
Notes for Next Lesson:			

FIGURE 5.9: Consolidated alphabetic phase lesson 3.

*Visit **go.SolutionTree.com/literacy** to download a free reproducible version of this figure.*

Plan for Writing

The strategy you chose for the comprehension discussion in lesson 2 will guide your plan for writing during lesson 3. Planning for writing will help students determine the purpose for writing and organize their ideas. Table 5.11 contains the writing format students will use based on the discussion strategy you chose for lesson 2. For lesson 3, write the writing format on the lesson plan that you'll use. Spend a minute explaining to students what the format and plan for the writing activity will be.

TABLE 5.11: Writing Formats for Discussion Strategies

Discussion Strategy	Writing Format
Paraphrasing	Students will explain in their own words what they've read.
Paraphrasing with vocabulary	Using the vocabulary words, students will explain how the author used them in the text.
Summarizing with vocabulary	Students will use vocabulary to summarize, write the main idea and details, or sequence the text.
Paragraph shrinking	Students follow explicit steps to summarize parts of the text, write the main idea and details, or sequence a portion of the text at a time.

Oral Rehearsal and Writing

Oral rehearsal is a critical step not to be overlooked. Oral rehearsal helps students organize their thoughts, flesh out ideas, and determine a logical structure for what they will write. It makes writing flow more smoothly by allowing students to build familiarity with the material before they write about it. Orally rehearsing before writing puts the key ideas into words so the act of writing becomes one of transcription rather than formulation. It's important to increase opportunities for students to reinforce the language structures they'll use when they transition from oral rehearsal to writing.

Students who have opportunities for oral rehearsal prior to writing are more equipped to produce high-quality writing than students who have fewer opportunities to interact with others before they write. Allow students to go back and reread the text as many times as they need to until they can read and either close, turn over, or cover up what they've read and put it in their own words. This may require lots of practice for students who are accustomed to copying from the text as a coping mechanism—a habit that they'll need to break. Begin using paraphrasing or paraphrasing with vocabulary as the writing format with the goal of students being able to summarize using vocabulary and use paragraph shrinking by the end of the consolidated alphabetic phase.

Table 5.12 (page 140) contains the oral rehearsal prompts students will use based on the discussion strategy and writing format you chose for lesson 2. Spend the next ten to twelve minutes having students orally rehearse and write their sentences one at a time.

If students need the sentence starters, write them on a small whiteboard or on a sentence strip, using only one at a time. Begin by having students use one phrase at a time and in partners or by practicing saying the entire phrase aloud and completing the sentence. After all students have been able to practice their sentences, they then write them in their notebooks. In the beginning, students' sentences may be similar to one another's, which isn't uncommon. As they progress through the prompts and increase their oral language skills, their writing will begin to differ and become individualized.

TABLE 5.12: Oral Rehearsal Prompts

Writing Format	Oral Rehearsal Prompts
Paraphrasing	• Students tell in one or two sentences what each portion of the text was about.
Paraphrasing with vocabulary Write vocabulary on whiteboard or index cards.	• The boys **descended** down the stairs in the back of the museum. The water was **cascading** down the fountain in the plaza.
Summarizing with vocabulary Use transitional phrases for sequencing.	• In the beginning, the boys **descended** down the stairs in the back side of the museum. • Then they suddenly noticed that the water was still **cascading** down the fountain.
Paragraph shrinking	• The most important piece of information that I learned was. . . • Another matter the author wrote about was. . . • The author explained that. . . • I was able to infer that. . . • The author wanted the reader to learn. . . Or, combine the vocabulary or multisyllabic words in phrases to summarize parts of the text.

Have students repeat their sentences in three- or four-word phrases at a time as they write them. Repeat this process for each word or sentence that the students will be writing. As students write each phrase or sentence, prompt them to reread to ensure that they're using proper sentence structure and semantics. This way, they can edit their writing responses as they work without having to go back and erase large amounts of text. Refer to the lesson plan template for the steps to complete the writing.

Editing—Language Standards

For the final one or two minutes of your lesson, decide what you'd like to teach for an editing or writing skill. Punctuation, grammar, mechanics, and conventions are considered editing skills. Students should be proficient in these skills before you attend to writing skills that focus on content. Refer to your grade-level language and writing standards to determine the expected and developmentally appropriate skills you should integrate into the editing process. Practice teaching and editing one or two items until students master them. Next, I list some general editing items—focus on one or two at a time at the end of each lesson 3. Once you've taught an editing skill, expect that from that point forward, students will correctly incorporate that skill in their writing. As students transfer each skill into their writing, move on to teaching and editing for the next skill. Following are some basic editing skills listed at the bottom of lesson 3 and after

- Rereading writing and self-correcting conventions
- Using correct subject-verb agreement and parts of speech
- Writing complete ideas—sentence structure
- Using correct verb tenses
- Using conjunctions

- Writing compound sentences
- Using commas and quotation marks correctly

When students have finished lesson 3, they should have a complete, cohesive writing response that's well organized and well written and contains a number of descriptive and tier 2 vocabulary words that are now in their speaking and writing lexicons. A sample completed lesson plan for the consolidated alphabetic phase is shown in figure 5.10.

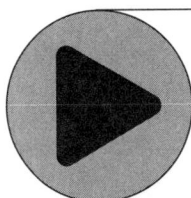

Use the QR code to watch a video of a teacher conducting a consolidated alphabetic lesson 3.

Consolidated Alphabetic Phase			
Lesson 1			
Word Building (3–4 minutes)		Scaffold: Word sort—dictation	
Word List: 4	Skill: Syllable types		Patterns: Closed / open
Sight Words (2–3 minutes)	through		though
Complete Each Step:	Teach and map	Build	Write
Introduction, Preview Text, and Vocabulary (2–3 minutes)			
Text: "The Speed of Light and Sound"			
Vocabulary:	light-years (p. 1) years for light to travel	galaxies (p. 1) solar system	speak of (p. 1) talk about	Mach 1 (p. 3) speed of sound
Graphic Organizer (5–6 minutes) I Know, I Wonder			
Notes for Next Lesson:			
Lesson 2			
Discuss Graphic Organizers (3–4 minutes)			
Reading and Clarifying (5–6 minutes)			
Strategies and Actions for Decoding and Self-Monitoring (Check box when used during the lesson):			
☐ Chunk the word or break it into syllables. ☐ Find the root or base word. ☐ Let's break it into parts. ☐ This word is pronounced _____. It means _____.		☐ Were there any words you didn't understand? ☐ Is there a context clue you can use? ☐ Reread the sentence and tell me what it means. ☐ Does that make sense?	

FIGURE 5.10: Sample completed consolidated alphabetic phase lesson plan.   continued ▶

Strategies and Actions for Fluency and Comprehension (Check box when used during the lesson):	
☐ Swoop or frame three- or four-word phrases for student to practice fluency.	☐ Read it the way the character feels (exclamation).
☐ Read along and then repeat after me.	☐ Try to sound like you're talking.
☐ Read to the _____ before stopping.	☐ Tell me about this paragraph, page [and so on].
☐ Make your voice go up at the end for a question.	☐ What is something new you learned? Tell me about it.

Teaching Vocabulary (4–5 minutes)				
light-years	explosion	barrier	speed of light	speed of sound / Mach 1

OR: Discussing Text (4–5 minutes)	
☐ Paraphrasing	☐ Summarizing with vocabulary
☑ Paraphrasing with vocabulary	☐ Paragraph shrinking

Notes for Next Lesson:

Lesson 3	
Plan for Writing (1 minute)	Writing Format: Paraphrasing with vocabulary
Oral Rehearsal and Writing (10–12 minutes)	

1. Rehearse orally.
2. Repeat sentence in phrases and write.
3. Reread to self-monitor.
4. Repeat process for each sentence.

Editing—Language Standards (1–2 minutes)			
☐ Conventions	☐ Parts of speech	☑ Sentence structure	☐ Verb tenses
☐ Conjunctions	☐ Compound sentences	☐ Commas	☐ Quotation marks

Notes for Next Lesson:

Visit **go.SolutionTree.com/literacy** *to download a free reproducible version of this figure.*

Answering Common Questions About the Consolidated Alphabetic Phase

When students reach the consolidated alphabetic phase, they've developed a deep orthographic memory for reading and remembering words that allows their knowledge to flourish as they greatly increase their amount of reading. Over time, by increasing the amount of new words that students solidify in their orthographic memory, their speed and fluency increase because they've leveraged these new contexts to teach themselves new words as they read. This advancement in reading ability marks a turning point for consolidated alphabetic readers, as they now focus their attention to reading to learn new vocabulary and deeply understand the text they read. What follows are the most common questions about the full alphabetic phase that may not have been addressed in this chapter.

Can I Teach Strategy Groups and Work on My Grade-Level Comprehension Standards?

This is a tricky question because the focus of your small-group instruction depends on your students' literacy needs. Properly determining your students' needs is crucial to ensuring that the instruction you provide in your small groups is worthwhile and effective. Before you teach comprehension standards, your students must be able to read texts within their grade-level band. When looking at the hierarchy of reading skills in figure 1.1 (page 8), you need to first address whether students are proficient in the skills at the base of the triangle—phonemic awareness, phonics, and fluency speed—before you can turn the focus of your instruction to teaching grade-level comprehension standards. In addition, the ever-important skill of vocabulary is a bridge between the foundational skills and comprehension. Students must be able to decode and understand most words in grade-level text in order for you to teach complex and challenging grade-level comprehension standards.

When looking at the hierarchy of reading skills, approximately 80 to 90 percent of students who struggle with reading on measures of comprehension display decoding difficulties; however, only 10 percent of students, approximately, are considered poor comprehenders (Nation, 2017). A very small percentage of students display difficulties in both decoding and comprehension. The great majority of students who display difficulties in reading really struggle with decoding. Of course, this impacts vocabulary learning and the ability to deeply and critically comprehend complex text on their grade level. In 2018, Barbara R. Foorman, Yaacov Petscher, and Sarah Herrera concluded that the variance in students' reading abilities in grades 1–10 was due to either decoding and language (mainly vocabulary) skills or solely language skills—the majority of which depend on students' understanding of vocabulary. Adequate reading comprehension depends on the reader knowing at least 90 percent of the words in a text (Foorman et al., 2018).

Before being able to determine whether teaching grade-level standards in comprehension strategy groups is appropriate to meet your students' needs, you'll need to determine whether students are proficient in the foundational skills at the base of the triangle. To address phonemic awareness and phonics, administer the decoding assessment for consolidated alphabetic readers in appendix D (page 259). Follow the decision-making flowchart in figure 5.11 (page 144) to determine whether your students have acquired the basic foundational literacy skills that will enable them to critically analyze and synthesize text, make inferences, and draw conclusions, as with your grade-level comprehension standards. Refer to table 1.1 (page 19) for the links to the referenced assessments.

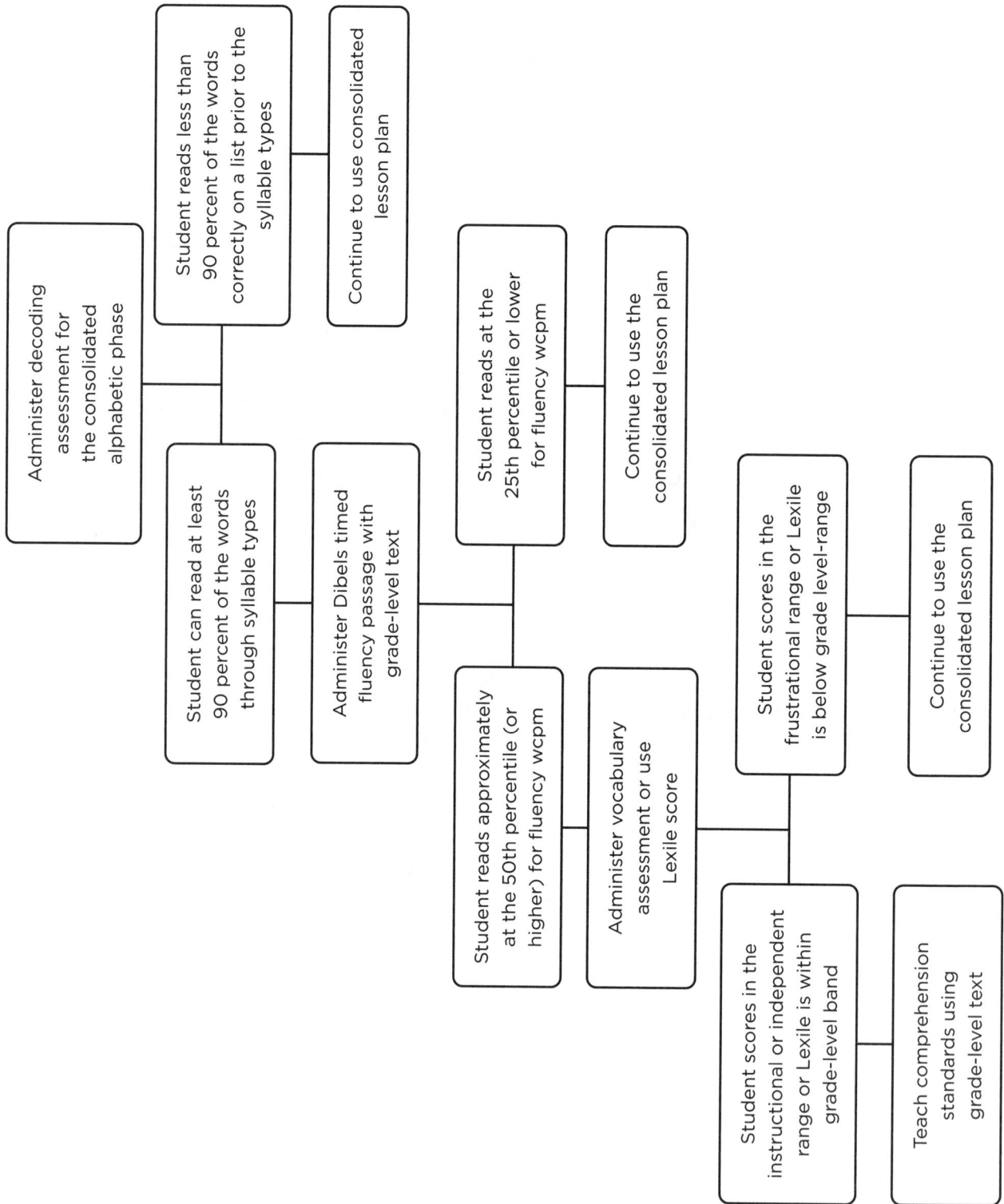

FIGURE 5.11: Decision-making flowchart.

Administer decoding assessment for the consolidated alphabetic phase

Student reads less than 90 percent of the words correctly on a list prior to the syllable types

Continue to use consolidated lesson plan

Student can read at least 90 percent of the words through syllable types

Administer Dibels timed fluency passage with grade-level text

Student reads at the 25th percentile or lower for fluency wcpm

Continue to use the consolidated lesson plan

Student reads approximately at the 50th percentile (or higher) for fluency wcpm

Administer vocabulary assessment or use Lexile score

Student scores in the frustrational range or Lexile is below grade level-range

Continue to use the consolidated lesson plan

Student scores in the instructional or independent range or Lexile is within grade-level band

Teach comprehension standards using grade-level text

What if Students Read the Words on the Decoding Assessment, but They Can't Have a Comprehension Discussion After They Read a Text?

After you've determined which decoding and phonics pattern the student needs instruction with, choose a text that contains words with those phonics patterns that the student hasn't read before. After the student reads, rate the individual's fluency using the rubric in table 5.13.

TABLE 5.13: Fluency Rubric

Fluency Rubric	
Score	Characteristics
1	Student reads with no phrasing or expression, word by word, and in a monotone voice. Student hesitates frequently, sounds out words, and reads slowly and laboriously.
2	Student reads with little phrasing or expression. Student reads moderately slowly, in two- or three-word phrases, not adhering to all punctuation.
3	Student reads with some phrasing and expression, but not ideally. Student reads with a bit of choppiness and may have difficulty with specific words or phrases, so reading is both fast and slow throughout.
4	Student reads with good phrasing and expression, paying attention to punctuation. Student reads smoothly with pauses and breaks.

The higher a student scores in fluency, the better the student tends to comprehend. For small-group instruction, a fluency score of 2 or 3 is ideal to leave room for improvement during lessons.

After you've listened to the student read, rate them using a retelling scale. Ask the student to tell you about what they've read. The student may reread the text and use the pictures for the retelling—this won't lower the student's score on the retelling rubric. You're trying to gauge the best the student can perform using as many scaffolds as you would provide for them during instruction. Use one of the two rubrics in table 5.14 to determine your student's retelling score.

TABLE 5.14: Fiction and Nonfiction Retelling Rubrics

Score	Retelling Rubric—Fiction	Retelling Rubric—Nonfiction
1	Provides little to no summary of the text—excludes most characters, setting, problem, events, or the solution	Gives little to no summary, main idea, or details about the text
2	Provides a minimal and nonsequential summary of the text—includes random information about characters, setting, problem, events, and the solution	Gives a minimal summary of the text with random details
3	Provides a partial summary of the text—includes characters, setting, problem, events, and the solution	Gives a partial summary of the text—includes the main idea and some details
4	Provides a sequential summary of the text—includes characters, setting, problem, events, and the solution	Gives a complete summary of the text—includes the main idea and important details

You would ideally need to instruct the student with the most difficult phonics pattern that they can still read with about 90 to 95 percent accuracy, score a 2 or 3 in fluency, and score a 2 or 3 in retelling. This way, there's some decoding, fluency, and comprehension to be taught within a book where the phonics pattern is challenging enough to foster the orthographic mapping of new words, but not so difficult that it causes the student frustration. If the student can read the text with ease and scores a 3 or 4 in fluency and a 3 or 4 in retelling, the text is too easy, and the student won't need much instruction. If the student reads with less than 90 percent accuracy and scores a 1 or 2 in fluency and a 1 or 2 in retelling, the text is too difficult and requires too much instruction in decoding, fluency, and comprehension.

The general rule of thumb for students who read below the expected level is to use text for instruction that's as close as possible to grade-level expectancy that the student can read with at least 90 percent accuracy and score a 2 or 3 on the fluency rubric.

For students who meet or exceed grade-level reading expectations, use text for instruction that's at grade level expectancy or up to a year above that the student can read with at least 95 percent accuracy.

With some practice listening to your students read and noting their decoding abilities and difficulties, you'll be able to arrange your groups so all students can be challenged while improving their reading, which will close any gaps in phonics and decoding and continue to develop their fluency, vocabulary, and comprehension.

Transitioning Students to the Automatic Reading Phase

To read text fluently, students should be able to decode about 95 percent of words correctly within a reasonable amount of time for their grade-level expectancy and with grade-level text. This ability to automatically decode almost all the words they read enables them to focus their mental energy on determining the meanings of words and, crucially, understanding the text. When students achieve this, they have completed the consolidated alphabetic phase of reading development and can transition to the automatic reading phase. By the end of the consolidated alphabetic reading phase, students should be able to:

- Consistently and quickly relate letters and sounds and letter-sound combinations in syllables, morphemes, and inflected endings

- Recognize roots and bases in words with syllables and morphemes

- Extract and understand the meanings of the morphemes in words and associate them with the word's meaning

- Spell words in chunks based on strong letter-sound mappings

- Fluently read words with at least two syllables

- Use systematic phonics and morphological rules for self-teaching and statistical learning

- Utilize the orthographic mapping process to quickly turn unknown words into sight words

- Correctly decode about 95 percent of words in grade-level text

- Read grade-level text with increased fluency, expression, and understanding

Conclusion

The end of the consolidated alphabetic reading phase marks the transition to fully reading to comprehend complex, grade-level text, which students can interact with because they've constructed a strong foundation in phonemic awareness, phonics, fluency, and vocabulary skills. Students can take ownership of decoding and unlocking the meanings of unknown words without relying on the teacher's help, support, and scaffolding. Students can strategize to decipher the meanings of most words that they encounter, and their comprehension flourishes. These skills transfer widely—students will utilize them across various subjects and contexts. Vocabulary learning and reading comprehension will now form a reciprocal relationship, strengthening each other in cycles—comprehension enables more vocabulary and knowledge learning, which then enable greater comprehension. These two anchors—vocabulary and comprehension skills—are the hallmarks of reading proficiency.

CHAPTER 6

Reaching the Pinnacle: The Automatic Reading Phase

The end of reading development doesn't exist; the unending story of reading moves ever forward, leaving the eye, the tongue, the word, the author for a new place from which the "truth breaks forth, fresh and green," changing the brain and the reader every time.

—Maryanne Wolf

In this chapter, you'll learn how to teach students to comprehend complex text using a variety of vocabulary and standards-based comprehension strategies. I describe the characteristics of automatic readers and present the components of the automatic lesson plans. You'll learn how to assess and group your automatic phase readers, then how to teach students to decode larger words by units or morphemes. Students will also learn to simultaneously process the meanings, spellings, and pronunciations of words. Then, you'll learn how to plan lessons that incorporate vocabulary and comprehension into written responses. Finally, I answer common questions about the automatic phase. Appendix E (page 273) contains the resources to be used with the automatic reading phase lessons.

Characterizing Automatic Phase Readers

Once students have reached the automatic reading phase, they decode words by reading them in parts, or units (unitization). This is the final phase of reading development. During this phase, students will read and analyze, synthesize, and evaluate a variety of texts using comprehension strategies. Decoding for readers in the automatic phase is relatively quick and effortless. Students read with a high degree of accuracy (approximately 95 percent or higher) and can read complex grade-level text. At this phase, students can center their attention on using vocabulary and comprehension strategies to focus entirely on the meaning of the text. Automatic phase readers:

- Use morphology to decode unknown words
- Display highly developed automaticity and speed in identifying familiar and unfamiliar words

- Read most words effortlessly in or out of context
- Decode words and determine their meanings without expending much effort
- Simultaneously decode and process the meanings of unknown words
- Fluently read text using appropriate phrasing and prosody
- Focus on extracting meaning from the text
- Know when they have to reread to clarify unknown words
- Apply metacognitive reading strategies, such as noticing when they don't understand text, using context clues to determine the meanings of unknown words, and rereading to reinforce their understanding of the text

The comprehension process expands greatly during the automatic reading phase as students connect prior knowledge with new knowledge and form a more comprehensive understanding of a wide range of topics and concepts. Comprehension during this reading phase transforms into a tool that students use to fully interpret and internalize authors' intended messages.

Teaching Your Automatic Phase Readers

The automatic reading phase marks the pinnacle of reading proficiency. Yet, simply providing opportunities for students to read won't necessarily ensure that they'll adequately and completely comprehend text. Individual readers bring their own interests, background knowledge, metacognitive abilities, language- and vocabulary-processing abilities, and reasoning abilities to construct an understanding of the author's message in a text. How readers interpret the texts you read during the automatic reading phase will depend on these factors. As teachers, we can engage students in a supportive learning environment that encourages them to improve and apply reading comprehension strategies. To achieve this environment requires us to provide students with learning experiences where we can model comprehension strategies for them, give guidance and feedback while they apply these strategies, and then gradually release control so they can move to applying comprehension strategies independently across a variety of texts.

Comprehension typically develops in a progression—from a literal level to an inferential level to an evaluative level. Another way to conceptualize this progression is from a surface (or literal) understanding; then to a deeper understanding, where students begin making inferences; and, finally, to the ability to apply and transfer their understanding to new and different learning experiences. When students are able to generalize the application of reading strategies that improve their critical understanding of texts, we have imparted the ability to truly comprehend text on their own.

Figure 6.1 contains some of the more common standards-based reading strategies that you can use to plan for your instruction. Based on how you use them, and how much cognitive demand you place on the reader, they may be interchangeable within each level of comprehension. For example, if you teach summarizing as a basic concept by having students use some important words from the text to discuss what they've read, that's a literal comprehension strategy. But if you teach summarizing by having students use main ideas and integrate details to arrive at the author's purpose and then determine the text's theme based on their inferences, that's an evaluative comprehension strategy.

Literal	Inferential	Evaluative
Clarifying and understanding vocabulary	Making inferences and drawing conclusions	Summarizing
Making connections	Describing and interpreting how text features and illustrations contribute to understanding text	Evaluating how authors support their points
Asking and answering questions	Determining the main idea and details	Establishing point of view
Paraphrasing and retelling	Comparing and contrasting	Supporting and concluding the theme of a text
Using vocabulary	Distinguishing the relationship between causes and effects	Determining text structure

FIGURE 6.1: Organization of comprehension skills.

Once students become proficient decoders and can rapidly and automatically identify words and connect them to meanings, the role of language comprehension becomes increasingly important, as students shift from paying attention to the words in a text to paying attention to the meanings of those words. At the most literal level of comprehension is language comprehension. Teaching students basic, literal comprehension strategies will be the foundation of automatic reading small-group lessons. With each new bit of content knowledge, each vocabulary word, and each understanding of the language used in text, students strategically integrate this knowledge to comprehend text. From there, they'll transition to making inferences about the text, or "reading between the lines." Students will also synthesize and evaluate texts, or more deeply understand complex ideas and integrate that new understanding into their knowledge base. Each set of small-group lessons will follow this progression. Co-constructing an integrated understanding of complex text through rich discussion, text analysis, and text synthesis will be central to your small-group lessons for automatic phase readers.

Comprehension improves knowledge and knowledge improves comprehension, so it's imperative to choose high-quality texts for small-group instruction that build students' vocabulary and content-area knowledge. Students need to read texts from a variety of genres, which include the following.

- Texts on various somewhat-unknown topics
- Rich, challenging vocabulary
- Grammatically complex phrases and sentences
- Varied writing styles—poetry and prose, articles, and speeches

Choose texts that students can connect with and are an extension of knowledge they may already have. For example, if students are familiar with westward expansion, choose texts about well-known explorers from and battles during the late 1800s. Texts that students can connect with provide a springboard for integrating new knowledge into current knowledge. Students more readily learn new knowledge when it's supported by and meaningfully connected to what they already know.

Small-group instruction is critical for advanced readers in the automatic reading phase. The discussions that occur in a small-group format are more likely to engage active participation from all members when compared to larger groups (Dew, Swanto, & Pang, 2021). Research results indicate significant gains in reading comprehension scores when students were arranged in small groups when compared to whole-class and one-on-one instruction. In small reading groups, students can actively engage with one another while the teacher facilitates a higher quality of interaction by purposefully guiding conversations.

Small-group instructional time is the ideal opportunity to utilize the gradual release model while guiding students to a higher level of critical thinking. During small-group lessons, you'll keep the lesson focused and guide instruction while students work together to co-construct a deeper, more meaningful understanding of texts. This gradual release of responsibility is shown in figure 6.2.

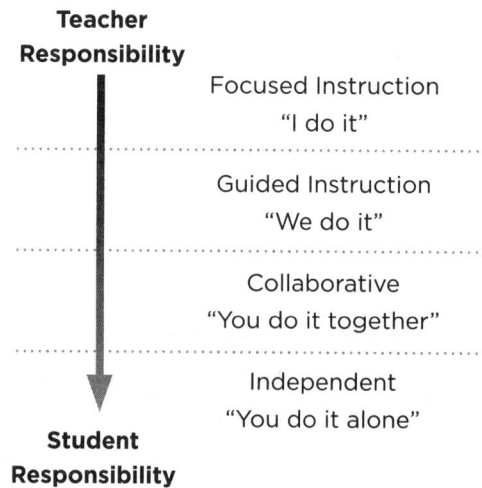

Teacher Responsibility

Focused Instruction
"I do it"

Guided Instruction
"We do it"

Collaborative
"You do it together"

Independent
"You do it alone"

Student Responsibility

Figure 6.2: The gradual release model.

How to Assess Your Automatic Phase Readers

Readers bring a skill set to the task of reading, and they vary considerably in these factors, which impacts their proficiency in comprehension. Reading comprehension isn't a single construct that can be measured with one test or improved with short-term intervention (Catts, 2021–2022). The ability to comprehend text depends on a wide range of knowledge and skills. Assessing automatic phase readers can be tricky because once you can rule out difficulty with decoding, most of the variance in students' reading abilities mainly hinges on their background knowledge and their oral language and vocabulary skills (Foorman et al., 2018; Foorman et al., 2020; O'Reilly, Wang, & Sabatini, 2019). By the time students enter high school, language and comprehension proficiency are virtually one and the same (Foorman et al., 2020). Knowledge accumulates over weeks, months, and years, and language skills strengthen over time as well, so trying to capture a measure of those two skills in one snapshot can be a difficult feat.

Students in the automatic reading phase should be able to read the word lists on the consolidated decoding assessment in appendix D (page 259) with sufficient speed and accuracy. They should correctly read at least 90 percent of the words within a few seconds. Students should also read close to the average number of words correct per minute on a grade-level text using the fluency norms in table 1.2 (page 20).

Once students are successful with these two assessment measures, you can turn your attention to any assessment that gives you a measure of the student's Lexile score. Lexile measurement tools accompany typical computerized reading assessment programs and are most readily available to all students. A Lexile score should contain a number range of 150 points between BR (Beginning Reader) and 2000.

A Lexile measure predicts a text's difficulty based on the word and sentence difficulty of a six-hundred-word sample from a text. The word and sentence difficulty tend to align with students' language and vocabulary skills. It gives a range of a text's language complexity. This Lexile point range or band predicts the appropriate level of text difficulty for the student.

How to Group Your Automatic Phase Readers

A Lexile measure is an appropriate way to arrange students for small-group instruction *only* once you can rule out decoding difficulties contributing to any comprehension difficulties. When you view a computerized report that contains a student's Lexile score, it's typically a range of 150 Lexile points. This is an average—it estimates that the student's reading ability is 100 points from the low end of the range and 50 points from the high end of the range (NWEA Connection, 2022). For example, if a student's Lexile range is 300–450, their approximate Lexile measure is 400. Lexile measures refer only to the difficulty of a text, not the subject or its content.

A Lexile range is a good starting point for forming small groups in the automatic reading phase. Group students within about a 100- or 150-point Lexile range and then use your professional judgment to group and regroup your students. You can also take an informal reading record to ensure that students' reading accuracy is approximately 95 percent in text within your grade-level band. At this point in students' reading comprehension abilities, accuracy and Lexile range won't fluctuate greatly in short amounts of time, since advanced readers' comprehension abilities develop incrementally over long periods of time. Lexile ranges for each grade level are shown in table 6.1.

TABLE 6.1: Average Reader Measures by Grade

Grade	Student Lexile Measures (50th percentile) Beginning of Year–End of Year
K	BR 345L–BR 160L
1	10L–165L
2	290L–425L
3	530L–645L
4	735L–850L
5	900L–950L
6	990L–1030L
7	1060L–1095L
8	1125L–1155L

Source: LEXILE® is the trademark of MetaMetrics, Inc., and is registered in the United States and abroad. Copyright © 2024 MetaMetrics, Inc. All rights reserved. Reprinted with permission.

Planning Lessons for Automatic Phase Readers

During the automatic reading phase, students will read the text independently, during and outside of their small-group instruction. When you choose texts that students can read with a high degree of accuracy (approximately 95 percent), the text is considered to be at their independent reading level. They won't need you for assistance with word-attack skills and have developed the metacognitive strategies to recognize when they don't understand something in the text. When this does occur, you can clarify those misunderstandings during their small-group lesson.

During the small-group instructional time, you'll be facilitating discussions that require students to think critically about the text and teaching specific reading comprehension strategies. Research on reading comprehension reveals that approaches to discussion-based comprehension had particularly strong effects on students' high-level comprehension of text (Duke, Ward, & Pearson, 2021). In addition to guiding thought-provoking discussions, you'll choose texts for students to read that combine knowledge acquisition with literacy instruction. Using this integrated approach ensures that students build knowledge while refining and increasing their ability to think critically about a text or topic.

After each of your small-group lessons, students will reread the text you've chosen for instruction. Rereading allows them to clarify any confusions, address misconceptions, understand the vocabulary within the sentences and context, and ensure a more accurate understanding of the material. It also enhances comprehension because, as students become more familiar with the content, they grasp relationships between ideas and concepts more effectively. Spaced repetition or rereading in intervals enhances students' long-term retention of material. When students review material at increasing intervals over time, it reinforces memory and prevents learning loss.

This rereading is referred to as *scaffolded silent reading*—when students are able to read the text without teacher support. In this way, the teacher is able to scaffold comprehension instruction during small-group lesson time. After students learn a comprehension strategy, they practice applying it when they read independently. When compared to traditional silent reading, students make much more progress when the teacher guides their silent reading by teaching comprehension strategies and setting goals for them (Proepper, 2016).

The automatic reader lesson plan contains three separate lessons. For lesson 1, choose a literal comprehension strategy. This will ensure that your students can paraphrase and retell and are able to use and understand the vocabulary contained in the text. For lesson 2, you'll teach an inferential or an evaluative comprehension strategy. You can choose a book because you have a comprehension strategy in mind that you'd like to teach, or you can select a book and teach a comprehension strategy appropriate for it, depending on how it's written and organized.

The focus for lesson 1 is on word building and clarifying vocabulary, and students will read while applying a literal, surface-level comprehension strategy. During lesson 2, you'll introduce the comprehension strategy you've chosen and facilitate a discussion about the text. Students will then apply the inferential or evaluative comprehension strategy you've chosen while they reread the text and build a graphic organizer. The focus of lesson 3 is on composing a writing piece in response to the reading.

This series of lessons integrates text discussions with applying comprehension strategies that require students to think more critically about the text each time they read it. The rich vocabulary and focus on oral language provide a strong foundation for students to reach an evaluative level of comprehension with the text. Your students will need a notebook to use during small-group instruction that should be divided into two sections: (1) graphic organizers and (2) writing. Students will use their notebooks and sticky notes for each small-group lesson. The structure and components for the automatic reading phase lessons are shown in table 6.2.

TABLE 6.2: Automatic Lesson Plan Structure and Components

Lesson 1	Lesson 2 Choose one inferential or evaluative comprehension strategy.	Lesson 3
Word Building	Introduce Strategy	Provide a Prompt
Clarifying and Vocabulary	Discussing Text	Plan for Writing
Literal Comprehension	Graphic Organizer	Writing and Editing

Planning and Teaching Lesson 1

Prior to your first lesson, students can preview and preread the text. They can use a sticky note to jot down any words or phrases they don't understand or have questions about or use a sticky flag to mark any spots where they need clarification. During this first read, they're reading to gain a basic, literal understanding of the text; to note any places in the text that they need clarification on; and to write down any questions they have about concepts they may not understand. This first reading of a text allows students to grasp the new vocabulary, activate background knowledge, and build a schema for the topic or material in the text.

During lesson 1, students will complete word-building activities. After word building, students will have the opportunity to clarify any information and vocabulary they're uncertain about. You'll then teach them a literal comprehension strategy so they gain a surface-level understanding of the text. After you complete lesson 1, students can reread the text independently, in partners, or their small groups before lesson 2. This will help reinforce new concepts so students can gain a deeper, more nuanced understanding of the reading. Lesson 1 is shown in figure 6.3.

Automatic Phase		
Lesson 1		
Word Building (3–4 minutes)	Word List:	Text:
Skill:	Pattern:	**Literal Comprehension (6–7 minutes)**
Scaffold:		Choose Strategy:
Clarifying and Vocabulary (3–4 minutes)		☐ Clarifying and understanding vocabulary
		☐ Making connections
		☐ Asking and answering questions
Notes for Next Lesson:		☐ Paraphrasing and retelling
		☐ Using vocabulary to retell

FIGURE 6.3: Automatic reading phase lesson 1.

*Visit **go.SolutionTree.com/literacy** to download a free reproducible version of this figure.*

Word Building

The first component of lesson 1 is word building. The activities in this component are designed for students to manipulate word units—prefixes, suffixes, and base and root words—and morphemes. The goal of the activities in the word-building lesson plan component is for students to develop their reading and writing abilities with these morphological patterns simultaneously while they also learn the meanings of them. By understanding common morphemes in words, readers can break down unfamiliar words and determine their meanings. This improves vocabulary, language skills, and overall comprehension.

The word lists contain meanings and examples of all the morphemes. Familiarize yourself with these morphemes before you begin word-building instruction. During the automatic reading phase, students will continue to develop their word-solving and vocabulary skills. In addition, they'll determine and explain the word meanings, provide examples of how the words are used, and relate the words to any of the texts they're reading. By completing the word-building activities, students will learn to read, spell, and write words that contain these morphological patterns. Learning words with a variety of common morphemes is beneficial for readers in many ways.

- Understanding the meanings of these word units allows students to decipher the meanings of complex words.

- Knowing morphological units expands students' speaking and writing vocabulary.

- Learning morphological units enhances spelling skills.

- Breaking down words into their parts aids in comprehension because students can more easily understand words and their meanings.

- Knowing morphemes develops students' skills in analyzing words, which transfers to other contexts and subject areas.

- Learning morphology helps students understand more subject-specific vocabulary, such as tier 3 vocabulary terms.

For the word-building activities, begin with word list 1 and spend three to four minutes working with the words by having students read, make, and write them, paying particular attention to their morphological units and meanings. If you have students who need more support for the word-building activities, you can continue to use the scaffolds in figure 1.4 (page 28). Follow these four steps for students to read each word.

1. Write the word on your small whiteboard.

2. Have students write the word on their word mat (appendix E, page 276), dividing it into morpheme or syllable units.

3. Have students read the word.

4. Have students determine the meaning of each part of the word, then the word itself when the morphemes or syllables are combined.

If you have students who are advanced learners, you can dictate the words and complete step 4. Next, have students make each word using letters or letter tiles. Follow the preceding steps 2–4, using the word in a sentence in step 4. After students have made each word, they'll put their letters or tiles away. Dictate each word for students to write, instructing them to use the spaces at the top of the word mat if they need to divide the words into morphemes or syllables. Students should also practice using the words in the context of sentences. If you're teaching advanced students, you can jump to this step after you've dictated the words. They can use an online sentence generator to create a sentence if necessary. They'll need to use the word and paraphrase the sentence to ensure that they understand the sentence.

There are three levels of word lists for the word-building activities—(1) beginner, (2) intermediate, and (3) advanced. These words align with the expectation for common state literacy standards. The word lists contain words with prefixes, suffixes, and Greek and Latin roots. Students will progress through the word-building lists gradually while mastering the reading, spelling, and meaning of each word. Students can determine the meanings of the words by using either a thesaurus or dictionary. When students can connect to one or more of the synonyms for a word, they can easily and efficiently add the new word to their vocabulary.

On the planning template for lesson 1, you'll begin by writing the number of the word list you'll use. Word lists 1 and 2 contain words for beginning students, grades 3 and 4. Word lists 3 and 4 contain words for intermediate students, grades 4 and 5. Word lists 5 and 6 contain words for advanced students, grades 5 or higher. If you're not sure which list to begin using, start with word list 1. On the next line of the lesson plan, write the skill—prefixes, suffixes, or Greek and Latin roots. On the next line, write the morpheme pattern or patterns you'll work with—such as *re-*, *dis-*, *contra-*, or *-less*. If students need to use any scaffolds from figure 1.4 (page 28), write it on the next line on the lesson plan.

During the word-building component, complete the preceding steps 1–4 with reading, making, and writing the set of words for that skill and pattern. When the text you're reading contains words with the morphemes on the word lists, teach those morphemes and create a list of similar words to teach along with them. This way, students can relate similar words to those in the text and will be able to witness the transfer between word building, reading, and writing. Refer to the word lists in tables 5.6 (page 126) and 5.7 (page 127) in chapter 5 if you haven't taught the seven most common prefixes and suffixes, and teach those before beginning word list 1. Appendix E (page 278) contains supplemental word lists for students who need extra practice with the word-building activities. You can also repeat rotating through the word lists at the level in which students need more practice, gradually using less scaffolding.

Here are some helpful hints and rules for morphemes.

- Prefixes don't change the spelling of the base or root word.
- Greek roots usually contain vowel combinations like *ae* and *oe*.
- Greek uses alternate spelling patterns, like *ph* for the /f/ sound and *ch* for the /k/ sound.
- The *p* is silent in Greek roots.
- Latin roots generally follow predictable vowel patterns, like *ie*.
- Latin roots use double consonants at times.
- Latin roots often end in suffixes or spelling combinations like *ology* or *ic*.

Table 6.3 (page 158) contains the two word lists for the word-building activities for beginners. Word list 1 contains the words with prefixes and suffixes for students just beginning the automatic reading phase. Start teaching the words in the first column of the chart—words that contain prefixes and suffixes. Continue in this manner with each pattern, working across the chart. After you've completed the word list for prefixes and suffixes, continue to word list 2 and teach the words with Greek and Latin roots across the chart from left to right. When students can read, make, and write each word in word lists 1 and 2, move on to word lists 3 and 4. Be sure to help students determine and be able to explain the meaning of each word. They should also be able to use them orally in sentences. Review each word

TABLE 6.3: Beginner Word Lists for Word Building

Word List 1: Beginner Prefixes and Suffixes

Prefixes

il-, im-, in- ir- (not)	en-, em- (within, in)	non- (not)	in-, im- (in, onto, on, toward)	de- (away from)	mis- (wrong, incorrect)	sub- (underneath, lower)
illegal	embody	nonfiction	infield	devalue	misjudge	submerge
impossible	embrace	nontoxic	inlay	detract	misdirect	subtitle
indirect	empower	nonsense	inseam	destruct	misplace	subset
irregular	enable	nonstop	insole	describe	mislead	subside
immobile	enamor	nonvocal	impart	defer	misspeak	subscribe

Suffixes

-er, -or (one who)	-en (made up of)	-able, -ible (can be done)	-al (having characteristics of)
promoter	earthen	amicable	arrival
commuter	glisten	capable	medical
editor	stolen	audible	musical
instructor	sweeten	visible	removal
builder	thicken	possible	renewal

Word List 2: Beginner Greek and Latin Roots

dict (say)	form (shape)	port (carry)	sect (cut apart)	struct (build)	vac (empty)
dictate	conform	porter	dissect	construct	vacate
predict	uniform	passport	intersect	deconstruct	evacuate
verdict	reform	transport	sectional	obstruction	vacancy
dictation	transform	export	sector	structure	medivac
contradiction	informant	deport	midsection	restructure	vacation

first to familiarize yourself with its pronunciation and meaning. After you've completed word lists 3 and 4, teach the advanced words on word lists 5 and 6.

Table 6.4 (page 160) contains the two intermediate word lists for the word-building activities. Word list 3 contains the words with prefixes and suffixes for students who are progressing through the automatic reading phase or are at the intermediate level of word building. Begin on the left side of the chart and continue working through each pattern. When students can read, make, and write each word in word list 3, move on to word list 4.

Table 6.5 (page 161) contains the two advanced word lists for the word-building activities. Word list 5 contains the words with prefixes and suffixes for students who are in an advanced level of the automatic reading phase or are at the advanced level of word building. Begin on the left side of the chart continue working through each pattern. When students can read, make, and write each word in word list 5, move on to word list 6.

Additional tables containing prefixes, suffixes, and Greek and Latin roots can be found at **go.SolutionTree.com/literacy**. Use these lists if you'd like to continue to teach the most common affixes found in texts for automatic phase readers.

Clarifying and Vocabulary

The next lesson plan component is clarifying information and teaching vocabulary. Students should come to the small-group lesson with their sticky notes containing the words or phrases they need clarified. This is the first comprehension strategy shown in figure 6.1 (page 151). Spend three to four minutes helping students clarify their understanding of unknown vocabulary words. If there's context in the text to determine the meaning of a word, direct them to use a context clue to approximate the meaning of each word (see figure 5.8, page 135). If there's no context for the word, provide a synonym or a quick definition of the word. Since the students are working with texts that they can read with a high degree of accuracy, you shouldn't have to define or clarify more than a few words or phrases. If you need to explicitly teach the meanings of unknown words that don't have any context, follow the steps in table 1.7 (page 31). After you've clarified any misunderstandings and defined any necessary words, have students paraphrase and explain what the word means in the context of what they read. Note the vocabulary words in the boxes of lesson 1 so you can revisit them in the subsequent lessons to review their meanings.

Literal Comprehension

During the third component of lesson 1, students will use a basic comprehension strategy to gain a surface-level, literal understanding of the text. Literal comprehension is important for several reasons. It's the foundation of being able to verbalize and understand any piece of information. It involves grasping an explicit, basic-level understanding of the text and being able to translate that into oral language through paraphrasing. Literal comprehension is fundamental for students to acquire new knowledge and information in various contexts. Having a literal understanding of text is a prerequisite to being able to analyze, evaluate, or synthesize any information. Readers need to be able to understand the literal meaning of any reading material to set the stage for deeper cognitive processes to occur.

If we refer back to Scarborough's reading rope, most surface-level comprehension strategies involve students' proficiency in language comprehension. When students struggle with reading comprehension, their difficulties usually lie within the context of language comprehension (Nation, 2019). Reading comprehension can be enhanced through rich and varied oral language dialogue. These types of

TABLE 6.4: Intermediate Words for Word Building

Word List 3: Intermediate Prefixes and Suffixes

Prefixes

pre- (before)	inter- (among, between)	fore- (before, front)	over- (too much)	trans- (across, beyond)	bi- (two)	semi- (half, partial)
predict	interact	forego	overcome	transmit	bifocals	semicircle
preshow	interject	forecast	overcrowd	transfuse	biweekly	semicolon
prejudge	interlocking	foresee	overprice	transpire	biceps	semiformal
preclude	interchange	foretell	overbook	transplant	binoculars	semilunar
preoccupy	intermission	forefront	overheat	transport	bilingual	semipro

Suffixes

-y (characterized by)	-ness (state or condition of)	-ity, -ty (state of)	-ment (action or process)	-ic (having characteristics of)
grouchy	stillness	activity	argument	economic
filthy	thickness	infinity	enrollment	metallic
accuracy	willingness	maturity	judgment	problematic
boundary	wishfulness	serenity	movement	horrific
recovery	loneliness	severity	testament	artistic

Word List 4: Intermediate Greek and Latin Roots

auto (self)	co (with, together)	meter (measure)	micro (small)	graph, gram (write)	multi (many)	tele (from afar)
automatic	coexist	diameter	microphone	diagram	multitask	teleport
autopilot	cohort	millimeter	microcosm	telegram	multimedia	telescope
autopsy	cohesive	centimeter	micronize	telegraph	multigrain	telephone
autograph	coincide	speedometer	microscopic	autograph	multipack	televise
automotive	cooperate	meterstick	microimaging	pictograph	multifamily	telepathic

TABLE 6.5: Advanced Words for Word Building

Word List 5: Advanced Prefixes and Suffixes

Prefixes

anti- (against)	bene- (good)	ex- (without, not, out of, from)	mid- (middle)	super- (above, beyond)	under- (less, lower)	uni- (one)	up- (higher, toward the top)
antibody	benefit	exclude	middleman	superior	undercut	uniformity	upperclass
antidote	benefactor	execute	midrange	superficial	undergo	unify	upgrade
antipolar	beneficial	expend	midsection	supernatural	underwhelm	unionize	upheaval
antirust	beneficiary	export	midtown	supersede	underlie	unitarian	uprooted
antiwar	benevolent	extract	midterm	supervise	undertake	universal	upscale

Suffixes

-eous, -ious, -ous (possessing qualities of)	-tion, -sion, -ition, -ation (act or process)	-ive, -isive, -ative (adjectival form of a noun)	-ful (full of)	-less (without)
contagious	election	adaptive	flavorful	heartless
facetious	erosion	cumulative	masterful	merciless
rebellious	decision	divisive	plentiful	pointless
previous	nutrition	implosive	ungrateful	priceless
disingenuous	limitation	impassive	wasteful	worthless

Word List 6: Advanced Greek and Latin Roots

astro, aster (star)	aud (hear)	cred (believe)	hydr (water)	liter (letter)	pend (hang)	therm (heat)
astrodome	applaud	credible	hydration	literary	pendulum	exothermal
astrology	audible	accredited	dehydrated	literal	pending	hydrothermal
asteroid	audition	discredit	hydraulic	alliterate	suspend	hypothermia
astronomer	auditorium	credentials	hydroplane	nonliteral	appendage	thermalize
astronomic	auditory	incredible	hydrogen	literally	expend	thermodynamic

conversations are central to facilitating a basic understanding of the text using the literal comprehension strategy you choose. You should embed sophisticated vocabulary and terminology in the conversations that you construct and guide students through rather than use simplified words. Have students utilize the technical and advanced vocabulary from the text.

Choose one of the comprehension strategies described in figure 6.4 that you think is appropriate and check it off on the lesson plan. Using the bookmarks in appendix E (page 273), have students reread the text, then facilitate a discussion so, as a group, they can co-construct a surface-level understanding of the text. The bookmarks provide sentence stems for students to guide their discussion.

Your facilitation of the discussion during this component plays a crucial role in enhancing the comprehension process in several ways. Discussion involves students developing their own general understanding of the text through active participation and paraphrasing what they read. This provides an opportunity for them to contribute additional information, share perspectives, and gain insights from the other students, which leads to a clearer understanding of the text. Students' usage of these metacognitive strategies will strengthen their ability to reflect on their own thought processes. This provides a foundation for students to then increase their text comprehension and gain a wider understanding of the material they read.

After lesson 1, students will reread the text independently, with a partner, or as an independent group. This revisit with the text is a powerful tool for memory retention; rereading helps commit information to long-term memory, making it more likely that students will be able to recall the information when they need it. When students reread text, they continue to gain an increased understanding of the material, and this allows you to teach higher-level analytical and synthetical comprehension skills in your small-group lessons that will follow.

Use the QR code to watch a video of a teacher conducting an automatic phase lesson 1.

Planning and Teaching Lesson 2

The first component of lesson 2 is to introduce an inferential or evaluative comprehension strategy. During the second component of the lesson, students will discuss and cite examples of how this strategy applies to the text they read. For the third component, students will construct a graphic organizer for one of the inferential or evaluative comprehension strategies that you choose to use. Comprehension builds incrementally throughout the lessons as students construct an understanding of the text and the author's intended message. Lesson 2 is shown in figure 6.5 (page 164).

Strategy	Explanation and Procedures
Clarifying and understanding vocabulary	Similar to the clarifications that were made earlier with vocabulary words, these clarifications include ideas, phrases, or sentences presented in the text that students may not understand or need you to clarify. Sometimes, they need this clarification because the text may be grammatically complex—for example: *The majority of the students voted in favor of the lunch choice, while there were a few that still voted against it.* Ensure that students understand who and what the pronouns in the sentence refer to. Does "there were a few" refer to the lunch choices or the students? What is meant by "voted against it"? Facilitate a discussion so students share information and assist one another in better understanding any literal information in the text. The Clarifying bookmark for students is in appendix E (page 281). Another option is for students to create a graphic organizer containing the vocabulary from the text and an explanation of how that word was used in the text (by paraphrasing or summarizing). <table><thead><tr><th>Word</th><th>Page</th><th>How It Was Used</th></tr></thead><tbody><tr><td>majority</td><td>7</td><td>The author wrote about how the majority of the students were late for school that day because of the storm.</td></tr><tr><td></td><td></td><td></td></tr><tr><td></td><td></td><td></td></tr></tbody></table>
Making connections	Making connections to text helps students relate new information or concepts to existing knowledge. This creates a schema of how this information will add to the knowledge they already have. These connections create a springboard for learning new information. There are three types of connections we make with the texts we read. **Text Connections** <table><thead><tr><th>Text–Self</th><th>Text–Text</th><th>Text–World</th></tr></thead><tbody><tr><td>• What does this remind me of in my life? • Is this similar to or different from something I've experienced? • Has something like this ever happened to me? • How does this relate to my life?</td><td>• How does this remind me of something else I've read? • How is this text different from other books or articles I've read? • How is this text similar to others that I have read? • Have I read any other texts on a similar topic?</td><td>• How does this remind me of something in the real world? • How is this text similar to or different from things that happen or have happened in the real world? • How did that part relate to the world around me?</td></tr></tbody></table> Distribute sticky flags to students and have them place them in the text next to the connections they can make when they read that part or section of the text. Then, have them explain their connections to the group. The Making Connections bookmark for students is in appendix E (page 282).

FIGURE 6.4: Literal comprehension strategies.

continued ▶

Asking and answering questions	Asking questions requires students to use their oral language skills to develop questions about the text that other students can then answer. When students reflect on the questions they generate and the answers they provide, it promotes metacognition—students become aware of their own understanding and thought processes. This metacognition contributes to students being able to thoroughly understand what they're reading. The Questioning bookmark in appendix E (page 283) provides question stems for students.
Paraphrasing and retelling	Paraphrasing is an essential comprehension skill for students as well as one of the first indicators of whether students are understanding what they read. That is, students must be able to explain in their own words what they read, or they haven't understood the text. Paraphrasing helps students actively process new information and express it in a new way. This helps students expand their vocabulary, improve oral language skills and sentence structure, and refine their ability to speak about a text. Provide students with sticky notes to use throughout the reading. Have them write one word on their sticky note that will help them paraphrase that paragraph, page, or section. Their word must be two or more syllables. This restricts students to using more complex vocabulary words and language when they discuss what they've read.
Using vocabulary to paraphrase and retell	Decide on six, eight, or nine vocabulary words for students to use to describe, paraphrase, and retell what they read. Have students make a 2 × 3, 2 × 4, or 3 × 3 grid with one of the vocabulary words at the bottom of each square. Have them draw a simple picture to represent each word, then have them use the vocabulary words to explain what the author wrote by paraphrasing, retelling, or describing.

Lesson 2	
Introduce Strategy (2–3 minutes)	
Discussing Text (4–5 minutes)	
Graphic Organizer (6–7 minutes)	**Choose Inferential Comprehension Strategy:**
Sketch Graphic Organizer:	☐ Making inferences and drawing conclusions
	☐ Text features and illustrations
	☐ Main idea and details
	☐ Compare and contrast
	☐ Cause and effect
	OR Choose Evaluative Comprehension Strategy:
	☐ Summarizing
	☐ Evaluating author's points
	☐ Point of view
	☐ Theme
	☐ Text structure
Notes for Next Lesson:	

FIGURE 6.5: Automatic reading phase lesson 2.

*Visit **go.SolutionTree.com/literacy** to download a free reproducible version of this figure.*

Introduce Strategy: Inferential Comprehension

For the first component of lesson 2, you'll spend two or three minutes introducing an inferential or evaluative comprehension strategy. *Inferential comprehension* refers to the ability to form interpretations based on information that's not explicitly stated in the text. It involves using background knowledge, reasoning skills, and vocabulary to understand and analyze implied meanings throughout the text. This level of comprehension requires readers to critically engage with the text to derive deeper meanings. Students must think about what they read, analyze the information, and consider multiple perspectives on topics or events in the text. These are essential components of being able to make inferences after reading. If you've chosen one of the inferential comprehension strategies described in figure 6.6, sketch a quick model of it on a small whiteboard.

Comprehension Strategy	Explanation and Procedures
Making inferences and drawing conclusions	Making inferences is one of the main reasons authors write text and we enjoy reading it. Being able to "read between the lines" makes reading feel like a mystery-solving accomplishment. Making inferences involves students evaluating their thoughts, connecting to prior knowledge, asking questions, and analyzing information to make inferences about what they have read. Distribute sticky flags to each student. Have students flag places in the text where they had questions or could make a prediction about events, actions, or dialogue in the text. Have them develop questions to ask the other students that require them to state evidence from the text and, using their prior knowledge, make an inference. Use the graphic organizer that follows and the Making Inferences bookmark in appendix E (page 284) to guide the discussion.

Question or Prediction	Evidence From the Text	Background Knowledge	Inference
I wonder if the Rough-Face Girl can really see the Invisible Being, or is he something they picture in their minds?	When the author describes what he is like, there are illustrations that show him, but he is up in the clouds.	Native Americans use a lot of what is in nature to represent their beliefs.	I think the Invisible Being represents the strength and character that he has. The Rough-Face Girl has imagined what he would be like.

FIGURE 6.6: Inferential comprehension strategies.

continued ▶

Describing and interpreting text features and illustrations	Authors use illustrations and text features to add details so the reader can make connections and inferences while they're reading. Illustrations and text features do the following.
	• Show what's happening in the text
	• Contribute to the mood the author sets for the text
	• Give the reader discrete details that aren't in the words of the text
	• Help the reader understand the story elements, vocabulary, or concepts in the text
	• Provide the reader with a better overall understanding of the text
	• Provide the reader with a visual example of a vocabulary word that was used on that page or in that section

The Text Features and Illustrations bookmark for students is in appendix E (page 285). Two possible examples of graphic organizers are shown here.

Page	How the Illustration or Text Feature Contributes to a Better Understanding of the Text
6	The illustration shows. . . This is how we know. . .

Page	Word	What the Illustration Shows
9	fashioned	The illustration shows the clouds that the dragons fashioned (made).

Determining the main idea and details	Determining the main idea in the text can be difficult for students because it requires them to see the forest for the trees. Students tend to think every detail in a text is crucial, so when teaching the main idea and details, it can be easier to start by identifying the details in the text before moving to the main idea. Many times, when students are required to determine the main idea, they include every piece of information they can remember from what they've read, hoping that one of those is the main idea.

Students can first list the details from the text, then group them into main ideas. Students can design a graphic organizer, like the one that follows, to help them. Students can group the main ideas to determine the topic.

Details	Main Ideas	Topic
List all the important details you can find.	Group details together into similar ideas.	Determine what all the main ideas have in common.

For the details, direct students to look for key words—usually those with two, three, or more syllables; vocabulary words; and words from the index. Put these words together into phrases.

For the main ideas, direct students to group similar details together. Color coding works best for this. Students highlight similar details in one color. The main idea is a phrase describing what they all have in common.

For the topic, direct students to determine what the main ideas have in common. The topic is one, two, or three words that main ideas have in common.

continued ▶

Comparing and contrasting	Have students construct a Venn diagram.

Students then discuss the items in their Venn diagrams using the language associated with each.

Compare (Similar)		Contrast (Different)	
alike	similar to	although	on the contrary, in contrast
like, likewise	similarly	different from	on the other hand
as well as	not only, but also	however	unless
compared with, in comparison	the same as	in contrast	more than, less than
in common	in addition to	instead of	nevertheless
also	in the same way	as opposed to	whereas
		but not	

Distinguishing the relationship between causes and effects

Teach students to build a two-column graphic organizer to sort causes and effects.

Causes	Effects

Because effects can create causes that result in additional effects, teach students to build a domino-type graphic organizer.

Students can discuss their graphic organizers using the language associated with causes and effects.

accordingly	for this reason	thus
as a consequence	if. . . then. . .	but
consequently	nevertheless	reason why
as a result	since	may be due to
because	so that	for this reason
due to	therefore	is caused by
effect of	this led to	

If you've chosen to teach an evaluative comprehension strategy, continue to follow the steps in the next section.

Introduce Strategy: Evaluative Comprehension

If you prefer, or if a text lends itself to using one, you may teach an evaluative comprehension strategy instead of an inferential one. Like the inferential comprehension strategies, students will design a graphic organizer to show their understanding of the text. When students have reached the level of being able to evaluate a text, they can critically assess and consider information, ideas, or arguments presented in a text. Doing so involves making judgments, forming opinions, and evaluating the validity or credibility of the information presented. This higher-order cognitive skill requires readers to synthesize and apply their knowledge by engaging in a thorough examination (or evaluation) of the content in the text. Choose one of the five evaluative comprehension strategies in figure 6.7.

Comprehension Strategy	Explanation and Procedures
Summarizing	Summarizing a text involves condensing the main ideas, key points, and essential details of the original content into a concise and coherent format. The goal of summarization is to capture the core meaning of the text while eliminating unnecessary details and retaining the most important information. Summarizing is not reiterating everything a student can remember about a text. Being able to summarize involves efficiently being able to convey the main points of a text, capture the essential details, and concisely communicate how the details support the main ideas. For an informational text, students must be able to differentiate between the main ideas and details and focus on the most crucial information in the text. They then have to be able to present the information in a logical and coherent order and ensure that they follow a clear structure that mirrors the organization of the original text. The Summarizing bookmarks in appendix E (page 286) will assist students in designing graphic organizers that will help them effectively and efficiently summarize both informational and literary texts. Turn the main idea into a topic sentence and combine the signal words for either type of text with the details to summarize the text. For an informational text, the Summarizing bookmark in appendix E (page 286) will guide students through summarizing the text. Use the signal words for determining text structure to summarize the text. For a literary text, sequencing or transitional words help to signal the progression of the story. The Summarizing bookmark in appendix E will guide students through summarizing the main events.

FIGURE 6.7: Evaluative comprehension strategies. continued ▶

Evaluating how authors support their points	Many times, authors make their points by writing a persuasive text. Students will need to identify the major points the author makes and then state the reasons the author presents that support their position on the topic. The author's position is what the author writes about the topic, stresses, or emphasizes as important information. This strategy is very similar to determining the main idea.
	Show students a place in the text where the author presents their position or opinion on a topic or idea. Have students place sticky flags in the text where the author uses persuasive language to signal their opinion to the reader. Students can design a graphic organizer like the one that follows and use the How Authors Support Their Points bookmark in appendix E (page 287) to assist them in looking for words that signal how the author feels about a topic.
	Author's Point _____ _____ Reason Reason Reason _____ _____ _____ _____ _____ _____
Establishing point of view	Teach students how to determine the point of view from which the story is told (see the Point of View bookmark in appendix E, page 288). Choose three short texts told from different points of view as examples. Demonstrate how to focus on the opinions made and the pronouns used in each text to determine from whose point of view the story is told. Students determine the differences among them by creating a chart or graphic organizer like the following.

Title: *Ricardo's Dilemma*	
Point of View: Third-Person Omniscient	
Character	**How the Point of View Affected the Story**
Ricardo	He feels negatively toward Cinderella and the ballet. It makes the reader think the ballet won't be a good experience.
Mrs. Periwinkle	She has a positive attitude about seeing the ballet and wants students to enjoy the field trip.
Max	Max is excited about his job at the theater. He's friendly and welcoming to the students on the field trip. This makes them feel like they can enjoy the trip.
Zach	Zach only cares about soccer and winning the championship, so he isn't interested in any other activities at school.

Supporting and concluding the theme	The theme of a text is the central, unifying idea that the author wants to convey. For students to fully grasp text theme, you'll need to demonstrate how to decipher the differences among the main idea, moral, and theme. Use the figure that follows to explain the differences between the concepts. Use the table of common themes in appendix E (page 290) to familiarize students with the most common themes depending on their grade level.

	Definition	**Example**
Main Idea	The main idea tells what the story is generally about. It's usually a one-sentence summary using the topic.	Goldilocks gets lost in the woods and visits a house owned by the three bears.
Moral, Lesson, Central Message	The moral, lesson, or central message teaches the reader about a principle.	It's important to respect the property of others and to think about how your actions could cause damage.
Theme	The theme of a story is usually a one-word principle that encompasses the theme and topic.	Responsibility

Begin by practicing how to identify the theme of a text with stories that students are familiar with so they can quickly gain an understanding of the differences among the main idea, moral, and theme before moving on to new or more complex texts. Students should be able to justify the theme they chose and provide examples that support their reasoning. Use the graphic organizer that follows to show students how to determine the theme of a story.

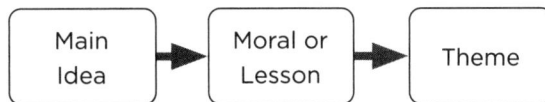

Main Idea ➤ Moral or Lesson ➤ Theme

Here is a more advanced organizer for theme.

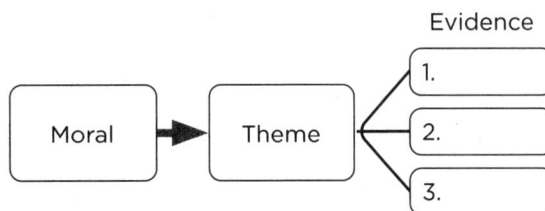

Evidence

Moral ➤ Theme
1.
2.
3.

Students in grades 3 and higher: Identify details from the text as evidence of how a theme is conveyed by the character's actions, dialogue, thoughts, or beliefs using the graphic organizer that follows.

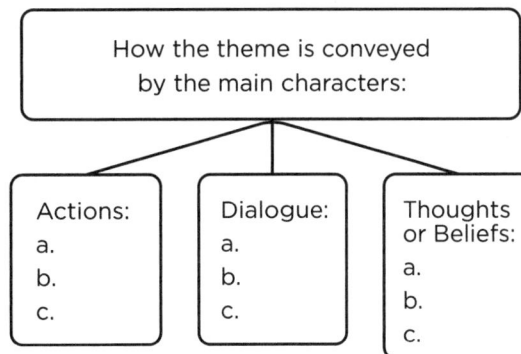

How the theme is conveyed by the main characters:

Actions:
a.
b.
c.

Dialogue:
a.
b.
c.

Thoughts or Beliefs:
a.
b.
c.

continued ▶

Determining text structure	Determining the structure of a text aids in comprehension because it provides an organizational scaffold for critically understanding the text. Teaching informational text structures and the clue words associated with them helps draw students' attention to the most important information in the text.
	Graphic organizers for text structure help students organize the critical information they read. Some texts contain a combination of two or three types of structures. It's important for students to become flexible with integrating these various text structures. Use the Text Structure bookmark in appendix E (page 289) to assist students in identifying text structure by using clue (or signal) words. When students can determine the structure of a text, they can create an accompanying graphic organizer that arranges the material in a manner that matches the text structure. The Text Structure bookmark in appendix E (page 289) provides a graphic organizer for each type of text structure.

Source for text: Henderson Megard, n.d.

Discussing Text

Spend four to five minutes having students discuss the text as it pertains to the comprehension strategy that you chose. You can sketch the graphic organizer on your whiteboard, and students can share the information they plan to write in their graphic organizers as well as their thoughts, opinions, and ideas about the text. This will help them rehearse discussing the information they'll write in their graphic organizers. At the root of comprehension is language, and building an understanding of text revolving around a cooperative discussion is invaluable. This collaborative, cooperative learning style of conversation promotes students piggybacking on one another's ideas.

Engaging in these discussions builds communication skills, such as how to articulate thoughts clearly, express ideas purposefully, and listen actively. Student discussions encourage critical thinking by analyzing and evaluating arguments and creating connections between ideas. These ongoing group discussions provide motivation and accountability among students as they learn to prepare to thoroughly discuss what they've read. This fosters a sense of responsibility for their own learning. Critically discussing a text encourages students to articulate their thoughts and ideas. The verbal expression helps improve language skills like vocabulary, syntax, and semantics, which are integral to comprehension and also help to refine writing skills.

When discussing a text, it's important for students to learn how to support their arguments with evidence from the text and reason through any conclusions and generalizations they may be making. Students bring their own experiences and knowledge to the discussion and build on their collective prior knowledge, making connections and enhancing their overall understanding of the text. When students actively engage in a discussion where they build on one another's statements, they become more involved in the learning process and thus process the text more deeply. Students may notice different aspects of the text, so sharing ideas and insights allows for a more well-rounded understanding of the material. Synthesizing information through this critical-thinking process deepens their comprehension and provides the oral rehearsal that will transfer their new knowledge from reading and discussing to discussing and writing in lesson 3.

Using Graphic Organizers

Students will use the next blank page in the Graphic Organizer section of their notebook to sketch out and then complete their graphic organizers. Plan for students to spend about six to seven minutes completing their graphic organizers. Teaching students about how graphic organizers help them develop self-efficacy and metacognition allows them to gradually take over learning tasks more independently. Graphic organizers aren't designed for students to "fill in"—they aren't worksheets. Graphic organizers encourage students to arrange their own thoughts in a manner that's understandable to them. The goal of graphic organizers is for students to create a visual model of how they can connect to and construct a better understanding of the text. This enables them to have easier access to information to analyze and synthesize.

When designing their own graphic organizers, students can group the information in a manner that makes sense to them—it may not be in the same format as your model. The graphic organizers in figure 6.6 (page 165) are suggestions for you to sketch out on a small whiteboard, and students can either use that design in their notebooks or create their own graphic organizer design. For graphic organizers to be effective, it's important that students organize the text material in a way that makes sense to them. If students need additional time to complete their graphic organizers, they can work together or independently outside of your small-group instruction to do so.

If time permits, after students design and build their graphic organizers, facilitate a discussion so that they can show and explain the information they wrote. They can discuss how the information in the text aligns with or challenges their own thinking, beliefs, values, and prior knowledge. Ask students if they agree or disagree, and why. Ask them what more they can add or how their thinking differed. This reflective aspect of comprehension contributes to the students' evaluation of the text and the material they read. It's valuable for students to apply their own knowledge and critical-thinking skills to assess and apply this new information in real-world contexts.

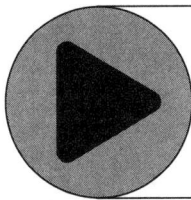

Use the QR code to watch a video of a teacher conducting an automatic phase lesson 2.

Planning and Teaching Lesson 3

Lesson 3 will be a culmination of an extensive analysis and synthesis of the text students read. You'll provide students with a writing prompt and support them in planning and completing their written responses. Writing is closely tied to reading comprehension and signifies students' extensive understanding of what they've read. Engaging students in extended writing activities improves their reading comprehension (Duke et al., 2021). Writing in response to reading prompts students to reflect on what they've read by engaging with the text more deeply, leading to a reciprocal relationship that increases comprehension. Coherently organizing their own information through writing helps students internalize the logical structure of the texts they read, which also aids and reinforces comprehension. When students are aware of their own cognitive processes, it improves comprehension—turning reading and writing into connected, active, and reciprocal processes that strengthen each other.

Lesson 3 is shown in figure 6.8 (page 174).

Lesson 3	
Provide a Prompt (1–2 minutes)	
Plan for Writing (3–4 minutes)	**Writing and Editing (8–10 minutes)**
Writing Type:	Edit for:
Graphic Organizer:	☐ Oral rehearsal
	☐ Spelling
	☐ Conventions and grammar
	☐ Sentence construction and syntax
	☐ Punctuation, commas, quotation marks
	☐ Sentence variety and presentation of ideas
	☐ Sentence combining
	☐ Complex sentences
Notes for Next Lesson:	

FIGURE 6.8: Automatic reading phase lesson 3.

*Visit **go.SolutionTree.com/literacy** to download a free reproducible version of this figure.*

Provide a Prompt

During the first component of the lesson, you'll present a writing prompt to students. Your writing prompt will introduce the writing topic and provide a focus for students' responses. The purpose of this lesson plan component is to encourage student interest in responding to the topic based on the knowledge they've gained from the previous reading lessons. Your prompt will need to provide the writing task with clear instructions. When developing a writing prompt, you'll need to consider the text structure of the reading material from your previous lessons, what type of writing students will complete, and how you'll guide them to complete it.

If you'd like to integrate a general reading response to a prompt, you can choose from the following suggestions for literary texts.

- Describe the characters, setting, events, or details.

- Summarize the major events in the beginning, middle, and end.

- Describe how a character responded to a problem, another character's action, or an event in the story.

- Contrast two characters and their points of view or how they respond to the problem.

- Write a poem from the character's point of view.

- Write an alternative ending to the story.

- Write a letter from one character in the story to another and include the character's thoughts and feelings from the story.

If you'd like to respond to a prompt that's suitable for informational text, you can choose from the following options.

- Explain a topic or expand on the main idea using examples or evidence from the text.

- Describe the main idea and include details to support it.

- Write about the author's purpose and include details to support it.

- Describe the author's reasons and support them with text evidence.

- Write an opinion in response to the text and support it with evidence from the text.

- Describe a cause-and-effect relationship from the text.

- Compare and contrast two ideas or events from the text.

If you'd like for students to complete a more advanced writing piece in response to what they've read, continue by following the process explained next.

An effective writing prompt includes two main parts: (1) a situation and (2) directions. The situation presents the topic to students and refers their attention back to the text they read so they know exactly what they'll write about. The directions will contain the purpose for the students' writing and detail the task the students will complete, using a verb that will require them to, for example, *describe, analyze,* or *compare*. When you develop a writing prompt, first consider whether it aligns with the topics and material in the text students read. The text should include enough information, examples, and evidence for students to use in their writing. Develop your prompts so students use a variety of writing types and styles.

Table 6.6 (page 176) contains signal words to use in your prompt that will inform students of the purpose for the writing piece. It also provides you with what the students will do when they write for each purpose. Before creating your writing prompt, think about the purpose for the writing. Use a signal word from table 6.6 to craft an appropriate prompt for students. For example, if students read a text that presents information on different types of bees and how they're a necessary part of food chains, your prompt might be one of the following.

- **Second and third grade:** Contrast the differences between honey bees and carpenter bees. Describe how each one is an essential part of a food chain.

- **Fourth and fifth grade:** Contrast the differences between honey bees and carpenter bees. Argue which bee is more of an asset for the environment.

Develop your prompt ahead of time when you read the text and plan your lessons. During this lesson component, take a minute or two to write the prompt on a small whiteboard or print it out on a sheet of paper to present it to students. Ask students to reiterate to you what they'll need to do for the writing piece so you can be sure they understand the topic and writing task. Here are some tips to help you develop your writing prompts.

- Use text features or illustrations to generate ideas.

- Prompt students to use the vocabulary.

- Choose a line of text or quote from the reading material.

- Ask students to expand on an idea presented in the text.

- Require students to reflect on a point of view.

- Use the signal words from text structures (see the Text Structure Bookmark in appendix E, page 289).

TABLE 6.6: Setting the Purpose for Writing

Purpose for Writing	Students will. . .
analyze	Break the topic into parts and explain the various parts.
argue	State a claim on an issue and support it with reasons and evidence from sources, while also countering possible statements or arguments from individuals who have different positions.
compare	Show how two things are similar, including details and examples.
contrast	Show how two things are different, including details and examples.
critique	Point out both the positive and negative points about the topic.
describe	Write about the subject so the reader can easily visualize it and tell how it looks or what happened, including details about *who, what, when, where, how,* and *why.*
discuss	Present a complete and detailed response, including important details and main points.
evaluate	Give their opinion on the topic and discuss its strengths and weaknesses.
explain	Provide the meaning of something and present facts and details that make the topic easy to understand.
interpret	Explain the meaning of a text, statement, photo, or graphic aid. Discuss what it means to the reader and how it makes the reader think or develop an opinion.
justify	Give convincing reasons and evidence from the readings to support a claim.
persuade	Present convincing reasons to get someone to do or believe something, or to agree with your position.
respond	State your overall reaction to the content, then support your opinion or claim with reasons, examples, and evidence from the text.
state	Summarize the main points in a brief, clear format.
summarize	Provide an objective overview of the topic and important details from a text using paragraph form, key topic words, and no personal opinions about the content.
synthesize	Combine ideas in a single response, providing reasons and examples.
trace	Describe an event or process in chronological order.

Plan for Writing

The second component of lesson 3 will require students to plan their writing. Planning is a critical step for students to develop a well-organized writing response after reading. Planning helps students clarify what they want to write and how they want to write it, reducing the likelihood of a disorganized, unclear piece of writing. A well-thought-out plan provides structure for students' writing and ensures a logical flow of information in the writing piece. As they did for reading, students will continue to use their graphic organizers for their writing, or they may design a new one based on the suggestions in figure 6.9. Their graphic organizers will help them plan for the overall structure of their writing by providing a framework for responding to the prompt in a logical progression. The graphic organizers students create will help them maintain clarity and focus in their writing. This planning stage will help students think critically about the relationship among ideas, supporting evidence, and the overall communication of their ideas.

You'll spend these three to four minutes of lesson 3 allowing students time to think about their ideas and how to effectively present them. This will result in high-quality writing because students will have considered what ideas to include and how to support them in a concise and coherent way. This contributes to the overall effectiveness and quality of students' work. There are three possible types of informational writing responses you'll use during lesson 3.

1. **Persuasive (to persuade):** When the writer tries to convince the reader to agree with their opinion or position on a topic or subject

2. **Expository (to inform):** When the writer shares knowledge and ideas by explaining, using examples and evidence, and quoting the author

3. **Descriptive (to explain):** When the writer focuses on communicating the details of a character, event, or place

The purposes for writing shown in figure 6.9 can also signal the type of informational writing for students to consider when composing their writing responses. Reflect on the prompt to decide what type of expository text structure is best to address it. Students can use the Text Structure Bookmark in appendix E (page 289) to decide on a graphic organizer that best fits the purpose and type of response they'll write. They can also use one of the graphic organizers in figure 6.9 to plan their writing.

Type of Writing	Possible Graphic Organizers
Persuasive	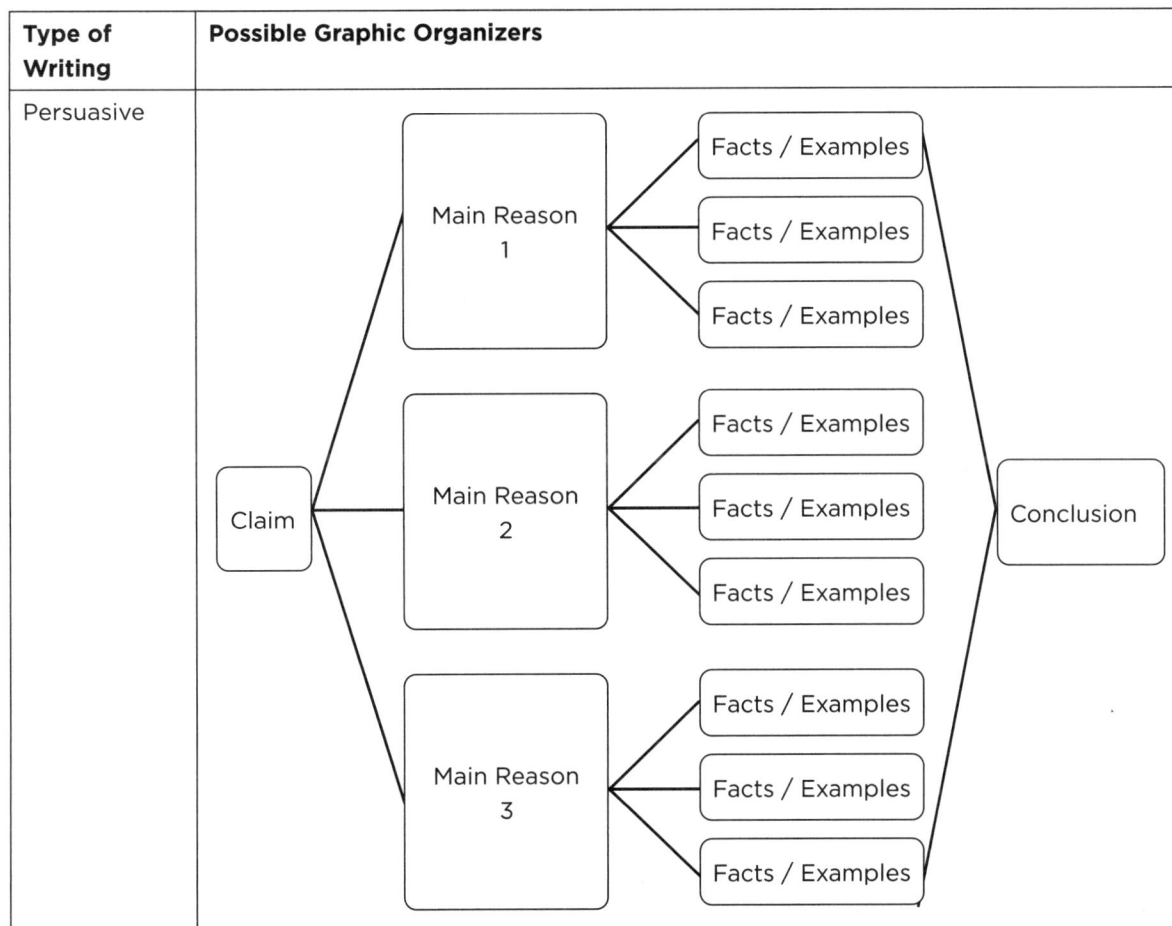

FIGURE 6.9: Writing types and graphic organizers.   continued ▶

Persuasive—opinion	Opinion:	
	Pros:	Cons:
	Conclusion:	

Opinion:

Reason:

Examples:

1.

2.

3.

4.

5.

Topic Sentence:

I think you should _____

_____

Reason 1:	Reason 2:	Reason 3:
First, _____	First, _____	First, _____
_____	_____	_____
_____	_____	_____
_____	_____	_____
_____	_____	_____
Evidence sentence:	Evidence sentence:	Evidence sentence:
_____	_____	_____
_____	_____	_____
_____	_____	_____
_____	_____	_____

Concluding Sentence:

Now you know why I think you should _____

_____

_____

Expository or descriptive (main idea and details, summarizing, theme)	Topic Sentence:
	Details or Examples: 1. 2. 3. 4. 5.
	Conclusion Sentence:

Main Idea:

Detail:	Detail:	Detail:

Summary

Theme:

Examples:

1.

2.

3.

4.

5.

continued ▶

Expository or descriptive

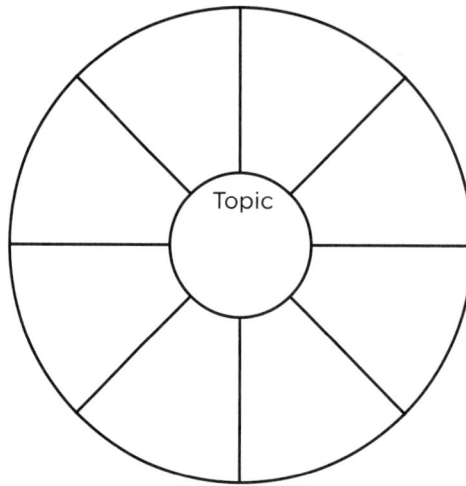

Topic

Topic Sentence:

Examples and Support:

1.

2.

3.

4.

5.

Conclusion:

Expository—
Compare and
contrast

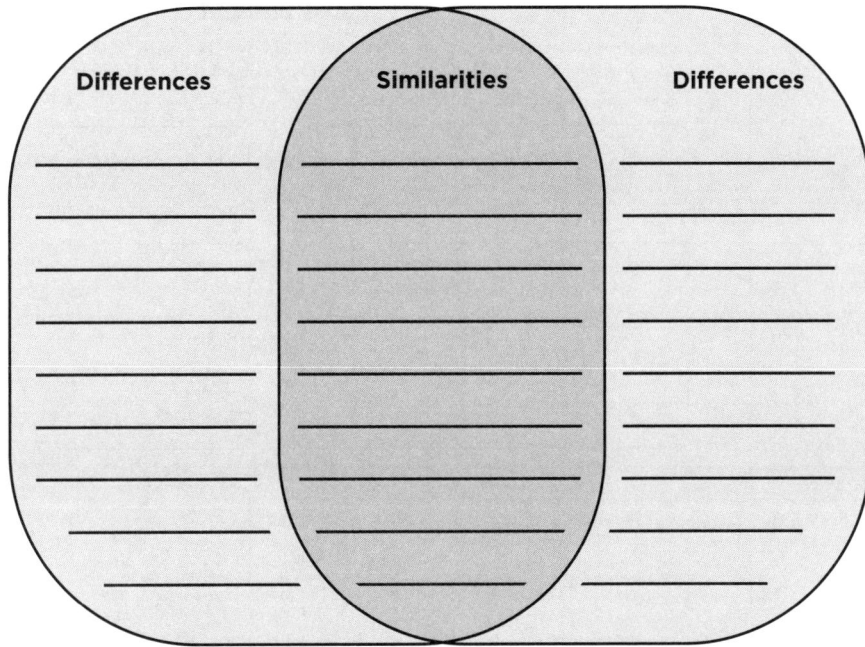

Differences   **Similarities**   **Differences**

_____   _____   _____

_____   _____   _____

_____   _____   _____

_____   _____   _____

_____   _____   _____

_____   _____   _____

_____   _____   _____

Compare and Contrast

Problem / Solution

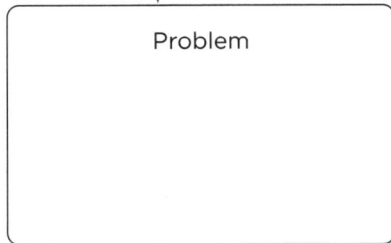

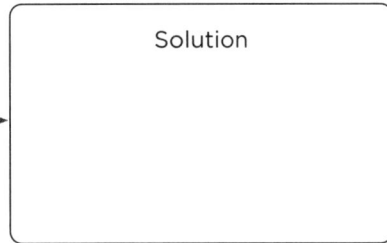

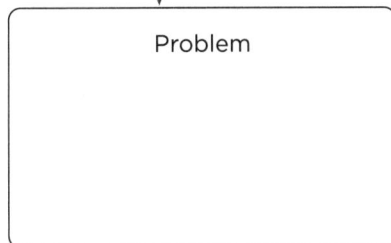

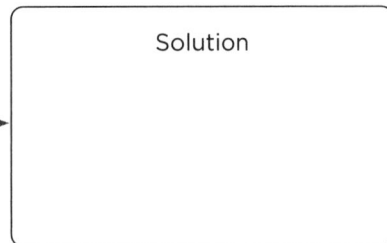

Text 1

Problem		Solution

Text 2

Problem		Solution

continued ▶

Expository—Cause and effect	**Cause and Effect**
	Write what happened (cause) and why it happened (effect).

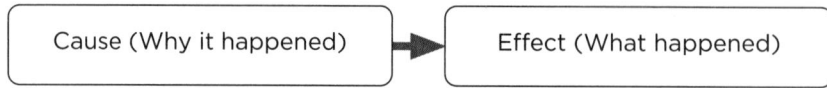

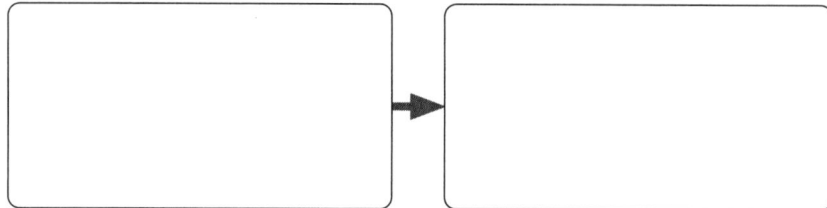

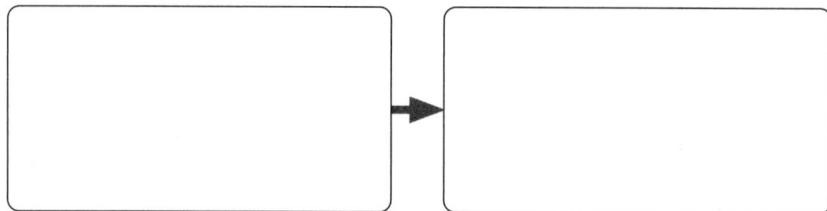

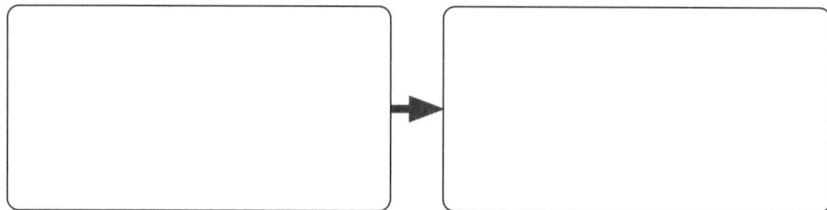

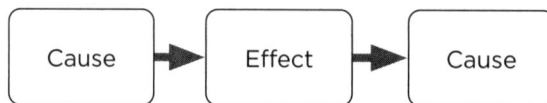

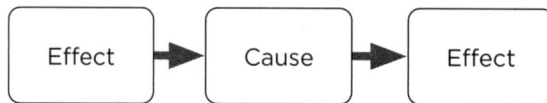

Cause (Why it happened)	→	Effect (What happened)
	→	
	→	
	→	

Cause	→	Effect	→	Cause

Effect	→	Cause	→	Effect

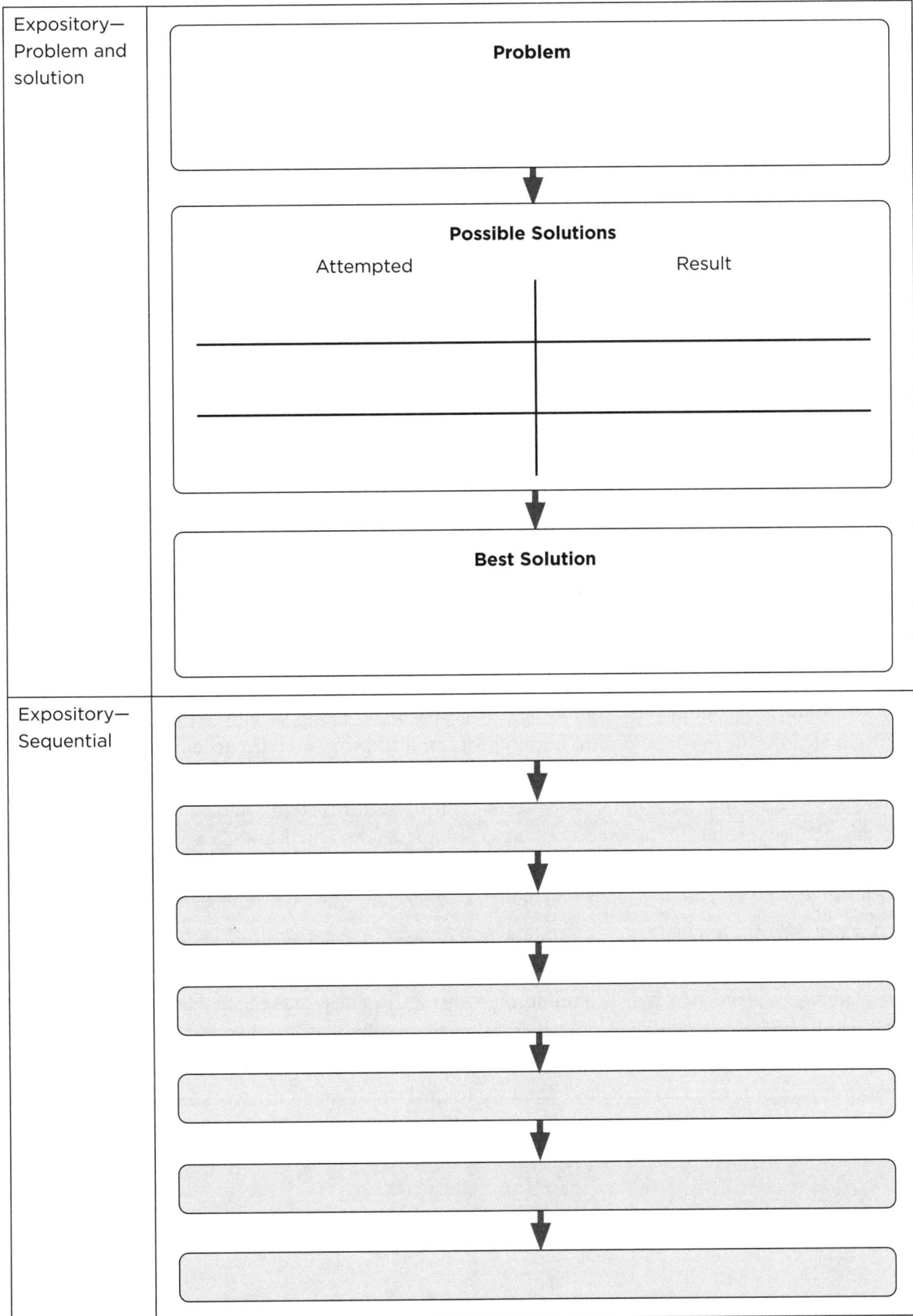

Expository—Problem and solution	**Problem**
	↓
	Possible Solutions
	Attempted Result
	↓
	Best Solution

| Expository—Sequential | |
| | ↓ ↓ ↓ ↓ ↓ ↓ |

Writing and Editing

For the next eight to ten minutes, students will compose and edit their writing pieces. When students write in response to what they've read, they articulate ideas in their own words, use new vocabulary, and connect their own evaluative ideas to the ideas presented in the text. You'll prompt students to orally rehearse each phrase or sentence, apply writing conventions, reread and self-monitor when writing from sentence to sentence, and reread their writing to ensure they've fully expressed their intended ideas. I recommend that students write one sentence at a time and follow this process after writing each sentence.

During this time, students should be able to draft a well-organized paragraph or more. Instruction aimed at helping students construct a well-organized paragraph is essential to helping them learn how texts are effectively organized. This includes instruction and scaffolding in writing a topic sentence, elaborating on their ideas, using logical transition statements and signal words, and writing an impactful concluding sentence. Using their graphic organizers helps students visualize and follow the typical structure of paragraphs and understand the reciprocal relationship between analyzing material from reading and synthesizing information for writing. The use of a graphic organizer will aid students in transitioning from the prewriting process to the writing process; their ideas will already be organized and compiled in a format that lends itself to paragraph writing.

If students haven't learned how to write a simple, grammatically correct sentence, they'll need to learn this first. Sentence-level activities should include applying basic editing skills (see lesson 3 in chapters 4 and 5), writing sentences in standard English form, and using proper subject-verb agreement and tense. If students aren't familiar with orally rehearsing phrases and sentences before they write them, they'll need instruction and practice with this. Before constructing these more complex writing pieces, students should also be familiar with basic punctuation, phonetic spelling, and self-monitoring by rereading their sentences. Students' writing should mirror the language used during the comprehension discussions that you facilitated for the previous lessons. Use students' oral language and discussion skills from lessons 1 and 2 as preparation, sentence examples, and rehearsal for writing. When students are able to write individual sentences that are grammatically correct, turn your instructional and editing focus to meaning, semantics, and syntax of the sentences students compose. This will help students vary their sentence structure and include conjunctions and advanced vocabulary from the texts they've read. This will aid students in writing varied, interesting, and complex sentences in their writing pieces.

Table 6.7 contains signal words and phrases for students to use depending on the type of prompt they're responding to and what type of writing piece they'll compose. These signal words serve as transitional phrases and are incredibly helpful during writing. They help maintain students' coherence and flow within a writing piece by signaling the relationship between ideas. They assist students in organizing and structuring their ideas logically. Signal words guide the reader smoothly from one point to the next, making the text easy to follow. The use of signal words shows mastery of language skills and demonstrates students' ability to express the nuanced relationships between ideas.

TABLE 6.7: Signal Words for Text Types

Text Type	Signal Words to Include			
Persuasive or opinion	**Introductory Phrases**	**Transitions**		**Opinion Clues**
	I believe	first of all		always / never
	I feel	to begin with		awful / wonderful
	in my opinion	in addition		beautiful / heinous
	I feel strongly that	equally important		better / best / worst
	from my perspective	besides		delicious / disgusting
	it is my belief	furthermore		definitely
	I am convinced	clearly		enjoyable / horrible
	based on what I know / learned	obviously		favorite
	I think that you will agree that	for all these reasons		all for / against
	I am confident that	finally		superior / inferior
	oppose / support	terrible / worthwhile		fair / unfair
Descriptive	for example	contains		including
	for instance	is made up of		is like
	specifically	to illustrate		identified as
	in addition	another		is a feature of
	described as	such as		characteristics
	defined as	first, second, third		
Compare and contrast	**Compare (Similar)**		**Contrast (Different)**	
	alike	similar to	although	on the contrary, in contrast
	like, likewise	similarly	different from	on the other hand
	as well as	not only, but also	however	unless
	compared with, in comparison	the same as	in contrast	more than / less than
	in common	in addition to	instead of	nevertheless
	also	in the same way	as opposed to	whereas
			but not	
Cause and effect	accordingly	for this reason		thus
	as a consequence	if. . . then. . .		but
	consequently	nevertheless		reason why
	as a result	since		may be due to
	because	so that		for this reason
	due to	therefore		is caused by
	effect of	this led to		

continued ▶

Problem and solution	problem, to fix the problem	attempt	however
	issue	because of	therefore
	dilemma	since	solved
	difficulty	so that	solution, to solve this
	trouble	nevertheless	as a result
	try to		
Sequential	first, second, next, then, after that, finally	during	later
	before	eventually	meanwhile
	at last, lastly	first of all	not long after
	previously	following	previously
	in conclusion	immediately	recently
	afterward	in the first place	soon
	at the same time as	initially	when, whenever

After students have completed their writing pieces, choose one topic from the checklist on lesson 3 as your teaching point or editing focus. For more specific editing skills, refer to your grade-level language and writing standards to determine what expected and developmentally appropriate skills you should integrate into the editing process. Practice teaching and having students edit one or two items until they master them. Then, move on to editing for the next set of items. If you prefer to use the checklist on the lesson plan, it contains a generalized list of editing topics. They're listed on the lesson plan in developmental order from the least to the most complex. If you'd like students to edit and revise their writing pieces, they can do that as an extension after you've completed lesson 3. You can add on an additional lesson before moving on if you need to revisit any of the instruction you provided during lesson 3, or if you'd like to allow students time to share their writing pieces with the group.

When students are able to edit their writing for basic conventions and grammar, turn your instructional attention to helping them improve the content of their writing. Expanding sentence length to include more descriptive words is an important first writing strategy. Students can expand on the words in their sentences by including more adjectives and adverbs and using more vocabulary words from the text they read. They can include more words to:

- Describe the subject
- Describe the verb with -*ly* words
- Describe the direct object
- Tell *when*, *how*, and *why*
- Tell what happened as a result
- Explain what the author meant

Using these phrases as cues for students after they write each sentence will help them write robust sentences one by one as they complete their writing responses. A sample completed lesson plan for the automatic reading phase is shown in figure 6.10.

Use the QR code to watch a video of a teacher conducting an automatic phase lesson 3.

Automatic Phase		
Lesson 1		
Word Building (3–4 minutes)	Word List: 1	Text: *Daphne Dragon*
Skill: Prefixes	Pattern: il, im, in, ir, and innumerable	**Literal Comprehension (6–7 minutes)**
Clarifying and Vocabulary (3–4 minutes) demonstrate (p. 3) dissolved (p. 5) illuminate (p. 8) fashioned (p. 11)	Choose Strategy: ☐ Clarifying and understanding vocabulary ☐ Making connections ☐ Asking and answering questions ☑ Paraphrasing and retelling ☐ Using vocabulary to retell	
Notes for Next Lesson:		
Lesson 2		
Introduce Strategy (2–3 minutes): Lesson → moral → theme		
Discussing Text (4–5 minutes): Narrow down theme to one word (see theme card in appendix E, page 290)		
Graphic Organizer (6–7 minutes)	Choose Inferential Comprehension Strategy:	
Sketch Graphic Organizer: Moral → Theme → Evidence 1. 2. 3.	☐ Making inferences and drawing conclusions ☐ Text features and illustrations ☐ Main idea and details ☐ Compare and contrast ☐ Cause and effect	
	OR Choose Evaluate and Comprehension Strategy:	
	☐ Summarizing ☐ Evaluating author's points ☐ Point of view ☑ Theme ☐ Text structure	

FIGURE 6.10: Sample completed automatic reading lesson plan.

continued ▶

Lesson 3
Provide a Prompt (1–2 minutes)
Identify the theme you chose and justify why you chose that theme using evidence from the story.
Plan for Writing (3–4 minutes)

Writing Type: Expository	**Writing and Editing (8–10 minutes)**
Possible Graphic Organizer (or use graphic organizer from Lesson 2): Topic Sentence: Examples / Support: 1. 2. 3. Conclusion:	Edit for: ☑ Oral rehearsal ☐ Spelling ☐ Conventions and grammar ☑ Sentence construction and syntax ☐ Punctuation, commas, quotation marks ☐ Sentence variety and presentation of ideas ☐ Sentence combining ☐ Complex sentences
Notes for Next Lesson:	

Source for text: DiGilio, 2022.

Answering Common Questions About the Automatic Reading Phase

To comprehend is the reason we read, and there are many factors that contribute to how well students comprehend text. The comprehension strategies in this chapter combine various instructional techniques and scaffolds that maximize the gradual release model to help students build their language skills, vocabulary knowledge, content-area knowledge, critical understanding of complex text, and writing skills. From this variety of reading and writing strategies, students will develop the ability to analyze and synthesize texts; make judgments about them; apply reasoning skills to interpret authors' intentions and viewpoints; and compose organized, well-written, and focused reading-response pieces of writing. What follows are the most common questions about the automatic reading phase that may not have been addressed in this chapter.

What if My Students Can Read, but They Have Difficulty Discussing a Text?

Usually when students are struggling to articulate themselves and have a conversation about texts they've read, they're experiencing difficulties not so much with comprehension but with putting their thoughts into words. Before you begin using the five literal comprehension strategies for lesson 1, use the Conversation Starter Comprehension Cards in appendix C (page 247). These conversation cards provide a more basic structure and additional scaffolding for students to discuss the text they've read because they are more open-ended than the literal comprehension strategies for lesson 1.

Guide the comprehension discussions among students so they become used to expressing their thoughts and ideas as they participate in discussions that hold them accountable for their reading. Knowing that they'll have to contribute to the discussion encourages them to think metacognitively while they're reading. Offer support by providing sentence starters, modeling sentence frames, and guiding students in expressing their thoughts. Foster a collaborative learning environment by encouraging participation among all students equally. This allows students to share their interpretations and learn from one another. Gradually reduce the scaffolding, and their conversational and language skills will improve over time. When students are able to use the Conversation Starter Comprehension Cards more comfortably while reflecting on what they've read, return to using the literal comprehension strategies presented in lesson 1.

Once students are more comfortable and confident with participating in text-based discussions, consider implementing a reciprocal teaching format to develop both oral language and comprehension skills. The reciprocal teaching format can be used with any text, genre, and subject or content area, and with students who are in either the consolidated alphabetic or the automatic reading phase. Developed in 1984 by Annemarie Sullivan Palincsar and Ann L. Brown, *reciprocal teaching* involves teaching students to use specific reading strategies that are associated with both improving reading comprehension and self-monitoring of comprehension while they read. The comprehension strategies used for reciprocal teaching are as follows.

1. Clarifying

2. Generating questions

3. Summarizing

4. Predicting

Reciprocal teaching may also include the reading strategies of making connections and visualizing. Cards for teaching the six types of reading strategies for reciprocal teaching are in appendix E (page 273). You'll need to thoroughly teach students each reciprocal teaching role before they can fully utilize and benefit from these strategies.

During reciprocal teaching lessons, students each read the same text and then participate in a group conversation where they construct a better understanding of the text. During the postreading discussion, the teacher guides students while they each express how they applied one of the reciprocal teaching strategies as they read. This is similar to a think-aloud, where the students discuss how they thought about and interpreted the text. Applying these oral language and discussion skills with metacognitive reading skills enhances students' overall reading comprehension.

When you begin implementing a reciprocal teaching format, first teach students the same role and allow them time to practice their discussions like you would in your small-group lesson format. Be sure that students learn each reciprocal teaching role while reading the same text. Use the role cards and discussion starters on **go.SolutionTree.com/literacy** to help students get accustomed to sharing their thinking and strategies with the group. Guide students through their discussions by only facilitating their conversations.

Once all students are familiar and comfortable with each reciprocal teaching role, they can switch roles so for one section of text, or day of reading, they each have a different job. After they read, each student uses their sentence starters and frames to discuss the text using that reading strategy. The concerted efforts of the reciprocal teaching format ensure the improvement in students' ability to resolve any comprehension difficulties or misunderstandings. This enables them to internalize new knowledge and develop their reading potential (Dew et al., 2021). If you'd like students to take notes as part of their reading strategy application, there's a template on **go.SolutionTree.com/literacy.**

Remember to be patient and supportive as students develop and improve their comprehension skills. Reading comprehension is a construct that improves over time with intentional instruction and the application of strategic reading, along with teacher scaffolding. Increasing reading proficiency is a gradual and incremental process, and students will progress at different rates.

How Do I Teach Poetry?

Teaching poetry can be challenging for several reasons, and we face various complexities in the process. The main factor that contributes to the difficulty of teaching poetry is the amount of abstract language and linguistic complexity in poetry. Poets use heightened, complex language structures, obscure vocabulary, wordplay, and linguistic structures that students aren't familiar with. Poetry often employs literary devices such as metaphor, symbolism, and imagery. Teaching students to recognize and analyze these devices requires a deep understanding and ability on the teacher's part to scaffold the learning for students when studying poetry.

The ambiguity inherent in poetry can be intimidating for both students and teachers. Poetry comes in a wide range of forms and styles, including sonnets, haikus, free verse, and many more. Each form has its own set of conventions, making it challenging for teachers to comprehensively address each format. Some teachers may feel more comfortable with clear-cut prose because the open-ended nature of poetry can lead to uncertainty. Poetry is subjective to how the reader interprets it, and different readers may interpret a poem in diverse ways. It can be challenging to address and evaluate student interpretations objectively.

Teaching the background knowledge and context of a poem is essential for comprehension, and this can be time-consuming when students aren't familiar with a wide range of poetry. Some students have limited exposure to poetry outside of the classroom, making it unfamiliar territory. This makes it harder for teachers to create interest and engagement when guiding students to understand and appreciate the intended meanings in poetry.

It's essential and expected that students study poetry at every grade level, beginning in kindergarten. Teaching poetry demands more time for additional readings, discussions, and reflection. When poetry is taught at every grade level as it should be, teachers are afforded the time and opportunity for in-depth exploration and examination of individual poems. Despite these challenges, effective instructional strategies that incorporate multimedia, facilitate discussions, and provide diverse examples can enhance the teaching of poetry. Encouraging a supportive and open environment while teaching poetry can help overcome the difficulties associated with it.

Teaching poetry involves understanding and learning about the elements and types of poetry that are appropriate and pertain to various grade levels. There is common vocabulary that students must learn that's associated with poetic elements and several types of poems. First, teach students the characteristics and elements of poetry appropriate for their grade level. Choose several types of poems to point out the elements and characteristics of poetry that students at every grade level should know. Additional information for teaching poetry at every grade level is available at **go.SolutionTree.com/literacy**.

Conclusion

The automatic reading phase is the pinnacle of reading development. Yet just because a reader can fluently read the words doesn't mean that they'll infer the author's intent. True reading comprehension also requires a broad range of knowledge, language skills, and reading strategies. Proficient comprehenders engage in specific mental activities to support their understanding of what they're reading (Duke et al., 2021). Some students learn comprehension strategies naturally, which enables them to seamlessly interpret the author's message within a text, but the overwhelming majority of students benefit from explicit instruction in how to think metacognitively while they're reading and processing the author's message. Learning how to connect to the text, how to understand all the words the author uses, and how to analyze and synthesize the author's message are challenging endeavors that we, as teachers, must continue to strive for in our reading instruction.

Conclusion

One child, one teacher, one book, and one pen can change the world.

—Malala Yousafzai

Teaching students to read is arguably one of the most difficult jobs we have as teachers. Although all students need structured, explicit, and systematic instruction in phonemic awareness, phonics, fluency, vocabulary, and comprehension, who needs what, when, and how much can be a difficult endeavor to undertake.

The reading process is a moving target depending on students' ages, grade levels, and degrees of proficiency with each reading skill. This book has provided you with the *what*, *when*, and *how much* so you now have a scientifically based small-group model that ensures that you provide the highest-quality reading instruction. Your next responsibility is to act on the knowledge you've gained from reading this book about differentiating small-group instruction.

Small-group literacy instruction can maximize learning outcomes for all students. It can counter negative circumstances by helping you manage student learning diversity effectively (Dubé, Dorval, & Bessette, 2013). Students who consistently receive individualized reading instruction from year to year have shown the strongest reading achievement scores by the end of the third grade (Connor et al., 2013). In striving toward equitable student learning, you can't afford to overlook the impact that a skills-based method of small-group instruction can have on your students. The targeted, responsive, and focused small-group instruction presented to you in this book can help you to meet that challenge.

Glossary

Term	Definition
alliteration	When the same letters occur at the beginning of several words in a phrase—for example, "Brian bounced the ball at the backyard barbecue."
alphabetic principle	The understanding that letters represent sounds in the words we speak and that those letters and sounds can be combined to form the words we read and write.
background knowledge	Topic knowledge—speaking, reading, listening, and learning about science, social studies, art, music, geography, and so forth contribute to students' background knowledge.
base word	A word whose spelling doesn't change when a morpheme is added.
blend	A group of two or three consonants that retain their own sounds.
bound morpheme	Word part that can't stand alone.
consonant (C)	Letters that represent a speech sound where breath is partly obstructed (by teeth, lips, or tongue).
consonant cluster	A blend of three consonants is usually called a cluster.
consonant digraph	Two consonants that combine to make one sound.
decoding	The act of reading a word, or segmenting the phonemes to blend them together to read unknown words.
evaluative comprehension	Being able to relate the text to one's own opinions and existing thoughts or beliefs, and understanding different aspects of the text, like motivations and author's intent.
fluency	The ability to read words with acceptable speed and prosody.
free morpheme	A word that can stand alone.
grapheme	A letter used to represent sounds.
inflectional ending	A morpheme added to the end of a word that changes the word's quantity or verb tense.
interpretive comprehension	Being able to infer meaning from text and "read between the lines."
language comprehension	The ability to understand the meanings of words within the context of the sentences to comprehend written or spoken language.
language structure	The arrangement and order of the words in sentences that impact their meanings.
literacy knowledge	The understanding of the purposes, features, and conventions of texts. When teachers provide students with a variety of genres of texts to read, students learn to attend to certain text features. This helps improve comprehension by providing a contextual framework for students.
literal comprehension	The foundational, or simplest, meaning of written text.

long vowel	A vowel sound that's the same as its letter name. Each vowel can make a long sound.
morpheme	The smallest unit of speech that carries meaning.
onset	The first phonological unit of a word before the vowel—for example, the *cr* in the word *crab* is the onset.
oral language area of the brain	The area of the brain associated with speech production and pronunciation.
orthographic mapping	The process by which readers use the oral language processing part of the brain to connect the sounds of the words they know to a word's spelling.
phoneme	An individual sound in a word.
phonemic awareness	The ability to understand the individual sounds (phonemes) in spoken words. This includes the forty-four English phonemes.
phonics	The skill that allows a reader to associate the letters in words to the sounds they represent.
phonological awareness	The ability to understand the parts in spoken words. This includes compound words, syllables, onsets and rimes, rhyming words, and words that start with the same letter.
prosody	The expression that a student uses when reading words.
reading comprehension	The understanding and interpretation of written text.
rhyming words	Words that have the same or similar ending sounds.
rime	The ending of a one-syllable word starting with a vowel—for example, the *ab* in the word *crab* is the rime.
root word	A word whose spelling changes when a morpheme is added.
self-monitoring	A strategy used to check the pronunciation and understanding of the words we've read.
set for variability	A reader's ability to self-correct or fix any mismatch between a word's pronunciation when it is read using common decoding rules versus how it is actually pronounced.
speed	The rate at which a reader decodes words.
statistical learning	Learning that occurs implicitly when students are taught words' spelling rules and properties, enhancing their reading ability.
substituting phonemes	The ability to segment, delete, and then add a phoneme to make a new word.
syllable	A segment of speech containing a vowel sound. It may or may not contain consonant sounds.
verbal reasoning	The ability to draw conclusions and make inferences from the information in the text and to develop an understanding of text.
visual area of the brain	The primary region of the brain that receives visual images relayed from the eyes.
vocabulary	The knowledge of words and their meanings.
vowel (V)	A letter that represents a speech sound where air leaves the mouth without any obstructions (by teeth, lips, or tongue).
vowel digraph (VV)	Two vowels that combine to make one sound.

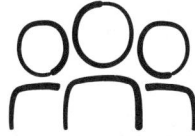

APPENDIX A

Teacher Resources for the Pre-Alphabetic Phase

Lesson Plan Template (Pre-Alphabetic Phase)

Pre-Alphabetic Phase	
Lesson 1	**Lesson 2**
Phonological Awareness (2–3 minutes)	**Phonemic Awareness (2–3 minutes)**

Lesson 1 — Phonological Awareness (2–3 minutes)

Word List:
- ☐ Rhyming words
- ☐ Compound words
- ☐ Syllables
- ☐ Rimes

- ☐ Isolating
- ☐ Blending
- ☐ Segmenting
- ☐ Adding
- ☐ Deleting
- ☐ Substituting

Notes:

Lesson 2 — Phonemic Awareness (2–3 minutes)

Word List:
- ☐ Initial sounds
- ☐ Final sounds
- ☐ Medial sounds

- ☐ Isolating
- ☐ Blending
- ☐ Segmenting
- ☐ Adding
- ☐ Deleting
- ☐ Substituting

Notes:

Letter and Sound Learning (3–5 minutes) *(Lesson 1)*

Trace and Name Letters or Sounds:

Handwriting and Letter Formation:

Notes:

Letter and Sound Learning (3–5 minutes) *(Lesson 2)*

Trace and Name Letters or Sounds:

Handwriting and Letter Formation:

Notes:

Reading and Concepts of Print (5 minutes) *(Lesson 1)*

Text:

Reading Format: ☐ Echo read ☐ Choral read

Teach a Concept of Print:

Notes:

Reading and Concepts of Print (5 minutes) *(Lesson 2)*

Text:

Reading Format: ☐ Echo read ☐ Choral read

Teach a Concept of Print:

Notes:

Writing (3–5 minutes) *(Lesson 1)*

Sentence From Text:

Teaching Focus:
- ☐ Letter names and formation
- ☐ Letter sounds
- ☐ Beginning sounds
- ☐ Final sounds

Notes for Next Lesson:

Writing (3–5 minutes) *(Lesson 2)*

Sentence From Text:

Teaching Focus:
- ☐ Letter names and formation
- ☐ Letter sounds
- ☐ Beginning sounds
- ☐ Final sounds

Notes for Next Lesson:

Supplemental Word Lists (Pre-Alphabetic Phase)

COMPOUND WORDS

Isolating (First Then Last Word)	Blending	Segmenting	Adding (Before Then After)	Deleting (First Then Second Word)	Substituting
eyesore	key + board	sandbox	add *hand* before *bag*	passport – port	makeup – make + mark
gumdrop	book + mark	himself	add *high* before *way*	hilltop – top	sunset – sun + in
leapfrog	make + up	herself	add *nick* before *name*	necktie – tie	moonlight – moon + sun
earlobe	cross + walk	teapot	add *lap* before *top*	textbook – book	hedgehog – hedge + ground

SYLLABLES

Isolating	Blending	Segmenting	Adding	Deleting	Substituting
octopus	in + vent + or	envelope	add *wall* before *paper*	fable – ble	baker – ba + pick
violin	dang + er + ous	telephone	add *left* before *over*	little – le	shoulder – shoul + bol
marshmallow	beau + ti + ful	curious	add *fresh* before *water*	napkin – kin	inner – inn + out
raspberry	fav + or + ite	pineapple	add *salt* before *water*	danger – ger	circus – cir + fo

RIMES

Isolating	Blending	Segmenting	Adding	Deleting	Substituting
jip	l + ip	nip	add *wh* before *-ip*	much – m	big – ig + ug
kit	p + it	lit	add *b* before *-ath*	sour – s	pin – in + ot
mob	r + ob	sob	add *m* before *-op*	fizz – f	cop – op + up
log	h + og	wog	add *b* before *-ot*	thin – th	dot – ot + ug

Page 1 of 2

Isolating	Blending	Segmenting	Adding	Deleting	Substituting
top	b + op	pop	add *h* before *-ot*	has – h	cob – ob + ut
rot	t + ot	cot	add *j* before *-ob*	fake – f	dog – og + en
cub	h + ub	nub	add *l* before *-ug*	boil – b	sun – un + ad
bug	d + ug	tug	add *n* before *-ut*	face – f	rut – ut + un
fun	w + ith	nun	add *r* before *-ich*	five – f	cub – ub + at
gut	h + ut	shut	add *t* before *-ub*	dice – d	rug – ug + ich

INITIAL SOUNDS

Isolating	Blending	Segmenting	Adding	Deleting	Substituting
Dan	l + a + p	chat	add *p* before *-ath*	hen – h	get – g + j
fig	k + i + n	jip	add *h* before *-it*	job – j	chip – ch + sh
chop	g + o + t	nub	add *l* before *-ed*	sun – s	gut – g + n
gab	h + a + d	jag	add *h* before *-og*	fish – f	map – m + g

FINAL SOUNDS

Isolating	Blending	Segmenting	Adding	Deleting	Substituting
pop	h + a + sh	cash	add *n* after *va*	chat – t	kit – t + d =
buck	p + u + p	fun	add *t* after *me*	ten – n	job – b + t =
wow	r + o + t	tag	add *m* after *hi*	fish – sh	sham – m + ck =
yam	b + i + b	hutch	add *d* after *ri*	wig – g	hem – m + n =

MEDIAL SOUNDS

Isolating	Blending	Segmenting	Adding	Deleting	Substituting
fox	l + a + g	sick	z + a + p	set – e	sub – u + o =
yam	th + i + s	lug	r + i + p	lot – o	man – a + e =
zip	c + a + sh	box	th + a + t	him – i	dish – i + a =
sick	b + u + n	peg	p + i + n	math – a	max – a + i =

Additional Compound Words for Phonological Awareness (Pre-Alphabetic Phase)

surfboard	steamboat	daydream	snowman	raincoat
sunlight	seashell	hallway	earthquake	snowflake
roadside	airline	password	raindrop	driveway
shortstop	windshield	quicksand	touchdown	upstairs
drumstick	catfish	eggplant	network	scrapbook
headphone	skateboard	outline	weekday	grapefruit
shipwreck	rainfall	scarecrow	toolbox	sideways
rainfall	eyelash	someday	groundhog	downtown
sunburn	notebook	toothpaste	outfield	cartwheel
toothpick	cupcake	classroom	hedgehog	haircut

Additional Multisyllabic Words for Phonological Awareness (Pre-Alphabetic Phase)

Words With Two Syllables				
cactus	baker	penguin	furry	Saturn
invent	marble	candle	ignite	monkey
perfect	neighbor	corner	yellow	uncle
danger	circus	silver	fabric	water
pencil	donkey	super	laughter	window
early	problem	dancing	under	purple
napkin	ignore	center	Venus	jumbo
ocean	candy	wanted	marble	mother
turtle	shoulder	balloon	orange	million
jumbo	monster	hundred	tiny	powder

Words With Three Syllables				
lumberjack	otherwise	pocketbook	submarine	thunderstorm
blueberry	everyday	handwriting	strawberry	skyscraper
overboard	firefly	whatever	anyway	fisherman
everywhere	waterfall	understand	overlap	volleyball
Superman	grandparent	grasshopper	firewood	fireplace
piggyback	candlestick	sunflower	underline	honeybee
bulldozer	anything	waterproof	pineapple	grandmother
bumblebee	firework	dragonfly	afternoon	honeycomb
afterward	leftover	sunglasses	ladybug	rattlesnake
tablespoon	firehouse	overheard	butterfly	hardworking

Additional Rime Unit Words for Phonological Awareness (Pre-Alphabetic Phase)

Rime Unit	Possible Words
-ab	jab, lab, nab, tab
-ad	lad, mad, pad, rad, sad, Chad, Thad
-ash	bash, cash, dash, gash, lash, mash, rash, sash
-ath	bath, math, path
-ag	bag, lag, nag, rag, sag, tag
-am	ram, Sam, yam, sham
-an	man, Nan, pan, ran, tan, van, than
-ap	cap, map, nap, rap, sap, tap, zap, chap
-at	hat, mat, pat, rat, sat, vat, chat, that
-ed	Ned, red, Ted, wed, shed
-en	Ken, men, pen, ten, then, when
-et	let, met, net, pet, set, yet
-esh	mesh
-eth	Seth
-ig	gig, jig, pig, rig, wig
-in	pin, tin, win, chin, shin
-ip	lip, nip, pip, rip, sip, tip, chip, ship, whip, quip
-it	kit, lit, pit, sit, wit, quit
-ish	dish, fish, wish
-ith	with
-ob	lob, mob, rob, sob
-og	hog, jog, log, nog
-op	cop, lop, mop, pop, top, chop
-ot	hot, jot, lot, not, pot, rot, tot, shot
-oth	moth
-ub	hub, pub, rub, sub, tub, chub
-ug	jug, lug, mug, pug, rug, tug, chug, thug
-un	nun, pun, run, sun, shun
-ut	hut, jut, mut, rut, shut
-uch	much, such
-ush	mush

Letter-Sound Assessment: Student Copy (Pre-Alphabetic Phase)

UPPERCASE LETTERS

F	B	M	U	R	G
A	K	P	X		E
V	Q	H	D		N
Z	T	I	W		O
Y	S	J	C		L

LOWERCASE LETTERS AND SOUNDS

f	b	m	u	r	g
a	k	p	x		e
v	q	h	d		n
z	t	i	w		o
y	s	j	c		l

Letter-Sound Assessment: Teacher Score Sheet (Pre-Alphabetic Phase)

Student Name _____ Date _____

UPPERCASE LETTERS

F	B	M	U	R	G
A	K	P	X		E
V	Q	H	D		N
Z	T	I	W		O
Y	S	J	C		L

LOWERCASE LETTERS

f	b	m	u	r	g
a	k	p	x		e
v	q	h	d		n
z	t	i	w		o
y	s	j	c		l

SOUNDS

f	b	m	u	r	g
a	k	p	x		e
v	q	h	d		n
z	t	i	w		o
y	s	j	c		l

Assessment Record (Pre-Alphabetic Phase)

Assessment Record for Grouping Pre-Alphabetic Students		# Uppercase Letters Known	# Lowercase Letters Known	Total # Letters Known	# Letter Sounds Known	Placement Group 1, 2, or 3
Student Name						
First	Last					

Grouping Sheet (Pre-Alphabetic Phase)

STAGE 1: STUDENTS WHO CAN IDENTIFY 0–14 UPPER- AND LOWERCASE LETTERS.

STAGE 2: STUDENTS WHO CAN IDENTIFY 15–30 UPPER- AND LOWERCASE LETTERS.

STAGE 3: STUDENTS WHO CAN IDENTIFY 30 OR MORE UPPER- AND LOWERCASE LETTERS.

ABC Chart: Front (Pre-Alphabetic Phase)

ABC Chart: Back (Pre-Alphabetic Phase)

Letter Formation Language: Lowercase
(Pre-Alphabetic Phase)

Letter	Language Pathway
a	around and close, down, a
b	down, up and around, b
c	pull back and around, c
d	around, way up, down, d
e	out and around, e
f	pull back and down, cross, f
g	around and close, down, hook left, g
h	way down, up and a bump, h
i	down, dot, i
j	way down, hook left, dot, j
k	way down, kick in, out, k
l	way down, l
m	down, bump, bump, m
n	down, and a bump, n
o	around and close, o
p	way down, up, and around, p
q	around and close, way down, hook right, q
r	down, up and hook, r
s	around, slant, around, s
t	straight down, cross, t
u	down, around, down, u
v	in, out, v
w	in, out, in, out, w
x	criss cross, x
y	in, way down, y
z	across, slant, across, z

Letter Formation Language: Uppercase (Pre-Alphabetic Phase)

Letter	Language Pathway
A	down, down, across, A
B	down, up, around and around, B
C	pull back and around, C
D	down, up, around, D
E	down, out one, two, three, E
F	down, out one, two, F
G	pull back around, up, in, out, G
H	down, across, and down, H
I	across, down, across, I
J	across, down, hook left, J
K	down, kick in, out, K
L	down, across, L
M	down, up, in, out, down, M
N	down, up, slant, up, N
O	around and close, O
P	down, up, and around, P
Q	around and close, add a tail, Q
R	down, up, around, and a kick, R
S	around, slant, around S
T	across and down, T
U	down, around, up, U
V	in, out, V
W	in, out, in, out, W
X	criss cross, X
Y	in, out, down, Y
Z	across, slant, across, Z

Assessment to Transition to the Partial Alphabetic Phase

Directions for administering: Administer this assessment when students can complete the activities in the pre-alphabetic lesson plan with speed and automaticity. This will allow you to decide whether students are prepared to proceed to the partial alphabetic phase. Any scaffold in figure 1.4 (page 28) can be used in conjunction with this assessment.

You can also use this assessment to determine whether the pace of instruction should be increased, decreased, or remain the same, or if students need to be regrouped. Additional assessments for the pre-alphabetic phase can be found at **go.SolutionTree.com/literacy**.

The student should be able to score 80 to 90 percent correct for each task. The number correct expected is noted for each task.

Part 1: Letter-Sound Assessment (3 seconds or less)

Students should be able to identify at least 47 upper- and lowercase letters (approximately 90 percent).

Students should be able to identify at least 23 sounds (approximately 90 percent).

Part 2: Blending Compound Words, Syllables, Onsets and Rimes, and Phonemes (3 seconds or less)

Place a checkmark in the table cell if correct. The student must score 4 of 5 correct in each column. The first of each type (shaded) is an example that can be used along with the scaffolds in figure 1.4 (page 27). Visit **go.SolutionTree.com/literacy** for additional versions of this assessment.

Compound Words	Syllables	Onsets and Rimes	Phonemes
"What do you get when you combine. . .?"			
hair + tie = hairtie	win + dow = window	sh + op = shop	k + i + t = kit
snow + plow =	el + bow =	b + all =	b + i + t =
work + shop =	swim + ming =	f + ed =	g + a + b
in + side =	ride + er =	m + ilk =	m + u + t =
cell + phone =	jel + ly + fish =	ea + t =	s + o + p =
sun + shine =	pep + per + mint =	g + um =	m + e + n =
Total Correct =	Total Correct =	Total Correct =	Total Correct =

Part 3: Segmenting Compound Words, Syllables, Onsets and Rimes, and Phonemes (3 seconds or less)

Place a checkmark in the table cell if correct. The student must get 4 of 5 correct in each column. The first of each type (shaded) is an example.

Compound Words	Syllables	Onsets and Rimes	Phonemes
"What are the two words in the word — ?"	"What are the two or three syllables in the word — ?"	"What are the two parts in the word — ?"	"What are the three sounds in the word — ?"
shoestring = shoe + string	hungry = hun + gry	mit = m-it	lit = l + i + t
toothbrush =	minute =	tall = t-all	Sam =
horseshoe =	little =	bat = b-at	bug =
someday =	menu =	has = h-as	den =
stairway =	everything =	not = n-ot	hop =
sawdust =	anyway =	chin = ch-in	this =
Total Correct =	Total Correct =	Total Correct =	Total Correct =

Part 4: Isolate Initial and Final Sounds

Place a checkmark in the table cell if correct. The student must get 4 of 5 correct in each column. The first of each type (shaded) is an example.

Isolate Initial Sound	Isolate Final Sound
"What is the first sound you hear in the word — ?"	"What is the last sound you hear in the word — ?"
mug = /m/	cup = /p/
beg =	man =
sip =	sub =
gate =	wit =
light =	Ted =
hug =	bog =
Total Correct =	Total Correct =

Part 5: Concepts of Print

Place a checkmark in the Check if Correct column if correct. The student must score 10 of 13 correct.

Concept of Print	Teacher's Words	Student Action	Check if Correct
Holds book upright	"Show me how you hold a book you're going to read."	Holds book upright with front cover facing up.	
Front cover	"Show me the front cover."	Points to the front cover.	
Back cover	"Show me the back cover."	Turns the book over to the back cover.	
First word	"Show me the first word on this page."	Points to the first word on a page that you turn to.	
Last word	"Show me the last word on this page."	Points to the last word on a page that you turn to.	
Concept of a sentence	"Point to the words in a sentence."	Points to the words contained in a sentence.	
First letter	"Show me the first letter in this sentence."	Points to the first letter in a sentence on a page that you turn to.	
Last letter	"Show me the last letter in this sentence."	Points to the last letter in a sentence on that page.	
Concept of a word	"Show me a word on this page."	Points to a word on that page.	
Uppercase letter	"Show me an uppercase letter on this page."	Points to an uppercase letter on that page.	
Lowercase letter	"Show me a lowercase letter on this page."	Points to a lowercase letter on that page.	
Left to right directionality	"Show me how you move your finger across the page when you read."	Moves finger from left to right across the page.	
End punctuation	"Show me what comes at the end of a sentence."	Points to an end mark.	
			Total Correct =

Part 6: Handwriting (optional)

Make two copies of the Letter Formation Sheet online resource, which can be found at **go.SolutionTree.com/literacy**. Dictate each letter for the student to write—first the lowercase letters, then uppercase letters. Circle letters that need extra practice and integrate into small-group lessons.

Student Summary Score Sheet
(Pre-Alphabetic Phase)

Name _____ Date _____

Part 1: Letter-Sound Assessment

Uppercase letters: _____/26   Lowercase letters: _____/26   Sounds: _____/26

Part 2: Blending Compound Words, Syllables, Onsets and Rimes, and Phonemes

Compound words: _____/5   Syllables: _____/5

Onsets and rimes: _____/5   Phonemes: _____/5

Part 3: Segmenting Compound Words, Syllables, Onsets and Rimes, and Phonemes

Compound words: _____/5   Syllables: _____/5

Onsets and rimes: _____/5   Phonemes: _____/5

Part 4: Isolate Initial and Final Sounds

Initial sounds: _____/5   Final sounds: _____/5

Part 5: Concepts of print: _____/13

Part 6: Handwriting (optional):

Lowercase letter formation: _____/26   Uppercase letter formation: _____/26

_____

Total Score Parts 1–5: _____/141

80% = 113 (Student transitions to the partial alphabetic phase.)

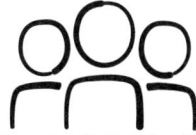

APPENDIX B

Teacher Resources for the Partial Alphabetic Phase

Lesson Plan Template
(Partial Alphabetic Phase)

Partial Alphabetic Phase			
Lesson 1			
Word Building (4–5 minutes)	Word List:	Level:	Scaffold:
High-Frequency Words (4–5 minutes)			
Complete Each Step:	Teach and map	Build	Write
Writing—Sentence Dictation (4–5 minutes)			

Teaching Focus:					
☐ Handwriting and letter formation	☐ Phonetic spelling	☐ High-frequency words	☐ Spacing	☐ Capitalization	☐ End punctuation

Notes for Next Lesson:

Lesson 2	
Text Title:	Phonics Skill:

Reading (8–9 minutes)

Give Overview and Introduce Phonics Skill or High-Frequency Words:

Strategies and Actions for Decoding (Check box when used during the lesson):

☐ Stretch / blend the letter sounds.	☐ Chunk the word at the onset and rime.
☐ Try this sound. . .	☐ Dictate or make word via sounds → letters.
☐ Have student blend sounds aurally, then read.	☐ Does that make sense?

Strategies and Actions for Fluency and Comprehension (Check box when used during the lesson):

☐ Frame 2-3 words for student to practice fluency.	☐ What did you read? Tell me about it.
☐ Read along and then repeat after me.	☐ What was the most important part?

Teaching Decoding (2–3 minutes)

Examples:

Discussing Text (2–3 minutes; use cards in appendix B, page 221)

Notes for Next Lesson:

Lesson 3			
Word Building (3–4 minutes)	Word List:	Level:	Scaffold:
Review High-Frequency Word (2–3 minutes)			
Complete Each Step:	Teach and map	Build	Write

Rereading (3–4 minutes)				
Reading Format:	☐ Independent read	☐ Echo read	☐ Choral read	☐ Partner read

Strategies and Actions for Fluency and Comprehension (Check box when used during the lesson):

☐ Frame 2–3 words for student to practice fluency.	☐ What did you read? Tell me about it.
☐ Read along and then repeat after me.	☐ What was the most important part?

Writing—Sentence Dictation (3–4 minutes)

Teaching Focus:

☐ Handwriting and letter formation	☐ Phonetic spelling	☐ High-frequency words	☐ Spacing	☐ Capitalization	☐ End punctuation

Notes for Next Lesson:

Anecdotal Notes
Lesson 1
Lesson 2
Lesson 3

Word Mat (Partial Alphabetic Phase)

a b c d e f g h i j k l m
n o p q r s t u v w x y z

Conversation Starter Comprehension Cards
(Partial Alphabetic Phase)

What if. . .	I wonder why. . .
I was surprised. . .	I thought. . .
It reminds me of. . .	I like the way. . .

Supplemental Word Lists (Partial Alphabetic Phase)

Word List 1			
Rime Unit	**Initial Letters to Be Substituted**	**Letters Needed**	**Words to Make**
Level C			
-ax	f, l, m, w	a, f, l, m, w, x	fax → lax → max → wax
-it	f, h, l, s	f, h, i, l, s, t	fit → hit → lit → sit
-ob	j, m, r, s	b, j, m, o, r, s	job → mob → rob → sob
Level D			
-og	f, h, j, l, n	f, g, h, j, l, n, o	fog → hog → jog → log → nog
-ad	f, h, l, m, r, s	a, d, f, h, l, m, r, s	fad → had → lad → mad → rad → sad
-at	f, h, l, r, s, v	a, f, h, l, r, s, t, v	fat → hat → lat → rat → sat → vat
-ed	f, J, l, N, r, w	d, e, f, j, l, n, r, w	fed → Jed → led → Ned → red → wed
-ap	l, m, n, r, s, y, z	a, l, m, n, p, r, s, y, z	lap → map → nap → rap → sap → yap → zap

Word List 2			
Unit	**Final Letters to Be Substituted**	**Letters Needed**	**Words to Make**
Level A			
ju-	g, t	g, j, t, u	jug → jut
me-	g, t	e, g, m, t	Meg → met
mi-	d, x	d, i, m, x	mid → mix
mu-	d, g	d, g, m, u	mud → mug
ne-	d, t	d, e, n, t	Ned → net
nu-	b, t	b, n, t, u	nub → nut
wa-	g, x	a, g, w, x	wag → wax
za-	g, p	a, g, p, z	zag → zap

Level B			
hi-	d, p, t	d, h, i, p, t	hid → hip → hit
ho-	g, p, t	g, h, o, p, t	hog → hop → hot
hu-	b, g, t	b, g, h, t, u	hub → hug → hut
je-	b, d, t	b, d, e, j, t	Jeb → Jed → jet
jo-	b, g, t	b, g, j, o, t	job → jog → jot
na-	b, g, p	a, b, g, n, p	nab → nag → nap
no-	d, g, t	d, g, n, o, t	nod → nog → not
ro-	b, d, t	b, d, o, r, t	rod → rob → rot
so-	b, d, p	b, d, o, p, s	sob → sod → sop
we-	b, d, t	b, e, d, t, w	web → wed → wet
Level C			
fa-	b, d, t, x	a, b, d, f, t, x	fab → fad → fat → fax
si-	d, p, t, x	d, i, p, s, t, x	Sid → sip → sit → six

Word List 3			
Initial Letter	**Medial Letters to Be Substituted**	**Letters Needed**	**Words to Make**
Level A			
h	a, i	a, d, h, i	had → hid
m	a, o	a, m, o, p	map → mop
m	a, i	a, i, m, x	max → mix
n	a, u	a, b, n, u	nab → nub
n	a, o	a, g, o, n	nag → nog
n	e, o	e, n, o, t	net → not
r	a, i	a, i, p, r	rap → rip
s	o, u	b, o, s, u	sob → sub
s	a, o	a, g, o, s	sag → sog
v	a, e	a, e, t, v	vat → vet
w	a, i	a, i, g, w	wag → wig
w	e, i	e, i, w, t	wet → wit
y	a, u	a, p, u, y	yap → yup
z	a, i	a, g, i, z	zig → zag

Level B			
f	a, i, o	a, f, i, o, x	fax → fix → fox
j	a, e, o	a, b, e, j, o	jab → Jeb → job
l	a, i, o	a, b, i, l, o	lab → lib → lob
l	a, i, o	a, i, l, o, p	lap → lip → lop
r	a, i, u	a, g, i, r, u	rag → rig → rug
r	a, o, u	a, o, r, t, u	rat → rot → rut
s	a, e, i	a, e, i, s, t	sat → set → sit
m	a, i, u	a, d, i, m, u	mad → mid → mud

Word List 4		
Letters Needed	**Starting Word**	**Substitute Initial, Medial, or Final Letter to Make the Next Word**
Level D		
a, b, d, g, j, l, o	jab	→ job → jog → log → lag → lad
a, d, e, g, l, m, u	mad	→ mud → mug → lug → leg → led
a, d, e, g, l, s, u	sud	→ sad → sag → lag → lug → leg
g, h, i, o, p, s, t, u	sop	→ sip → sit → hit → hut → hug
a, f, g, i, t, w, x	fat	→ fit → fig → wig → wag → wax
a, d, i, m, r, w, x	wax	→ max → mix → mid → rid → rad
b, d, e, o, r, s, u	red	→ rod → rob → sob → sub → sud
b, f, i, l, o, t, x	lit	→ lot → lox → box → fox → fix
a, b, d, f, i, l, x	fix	→ fax → fab → fib → lib → lid
a, d, i, p, s, t, z	zit	→ zip → zap → sap → sip → Sid
a, b, f, i, l, t, x	lib	→ fib → fit → fat → fax → fix
a, b, i, l, o, p, s, t	sap	→ sip → sit → lit → lot → lob
a, b, d, i, l, o, p, r	lob	→ lab → lap → rap → rip → rid
b, e, j, m, p, o, s, t	jet	→ jot → job → sob → mob → mop
a, g, f, h, i, n, p, o	fog	→ hog → hag → nag → nap → nip
a, b, d, e, n, o, r, t	rot	→ not → net → Ned → bed → bad
a, b, d, g, h, i, o, p	bad	→ had → hag → hog → hop → hip
a, d, e, h, i, s, t, v	vet	→ vat → sat → sad → had → hid
a, b, d, e, f, o, s, w	wed	→ fed → fad → fab → fob → sob
a, d, h, i, l, p, t, z	hit	→ zit → zip → zap → lap → lad
e, f, g, i, o, t, w, x	fox	→ fog → fig → fit → wit → wet
a, b, d, e, f, h, i, w	web	→ wed → fed → fad → had → hid

Decoding Assessment (Partial Alphabetic Phase)

Directions for administering: The word list contains 20 words, including a mix of nonsense words. Ask the student to read each word as you point to it. The student should be able to read each word in 2–3 seconds for the word to be considered read correctly. Use the teacher score sheet (page 226) to mark which words the student reads correctly. Add up the total number of words read correctly. If the student reads at least 16 words correctly, move the student to the full alphabetic phase. Stop the assessment if the student reads fewer than 15 words correctly.

- Mastery of the word list is reading 16 or more words correct, or 80 percent to 100 percent correct. As long as the student can maintain 80 percent decoding accuracy within 2–3 seconds for each word list, move to the decoding assessment for the full alphabetic phase (page 241) and follow the same assessment procedures. Or, when students can read 80 percent to 100 percent of the words correctly on the decoding assessment for the partial alphabetic phase, simply begin lessons in the full alphabetic phase.

- If the student reads 14–15 words correctly, or 70 percent to 75 percent, stop at this list and begin review lessons in the partial alphabetic phase.

- If the student reads 0–13 words correctly, or 65 percent or below, stop at this list and provide extensive instruction in the partial alphabetic phase.

Visit **go.SolutionTree.com/literacy** for additional word lists.

Teacher Score Sheet (Partial Alphabetic Phase)

Student Name _____ Date _____

CVC Word	Check if Correct
nof	
jek	
fix	
nap	
tuz	
cud	
pen	
kid	
zag	
ris	
del	
lex	
lob	
sov	
gob	
yes	
ham	
wit	
mut	
vac	
Total Correct	

Student Word List (Partial Alphabetic Phase)

CVC Word
nof
jek
fix
nap
tuz
cud
pen
kid
zag
ris
del
lex
lob
sov
gob
yes
ham
wit
mut
vac

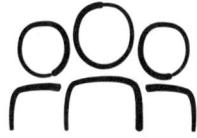

APPENDIX C

Teacher Resources for the Full Alphabetic Phase

Lesson Plan Template
(Full Alphabetic Phase)

Lesson 1		
Word Building (4–5 minutes)	Scaffold:	

Word List:	Phonics Skill:	Patterns:

Sight Words (4–5 minutes)			
Complete Each Step:	Teach and map	Build	Write

Writing—Sentence Dictation or Sentence Starter (4–5 minutes)

Teaching Focus:	☐ Handwriting	☐ Spacing	☐ Phonetic spelling	☐ Sight words
☐ Noun-verb agreement	☐ Sentence structure	☐ Possessives	☐ Irregular plural nouns	☐ Irregular verbs	☐ Past-, future-, present-tense verbs

Notes for Next Lesson:

Lesson 2

Text Title:	Phonics Skill:

Reading (8–9 minutes)
Give Overview and Introduce Phonics Skill or Sight Words:
Vocabulary:

Strategies and Actions for Decoding (Check box when used during the lesson):

☐ Stretch / blend the letter sounds.	☐ Dictate or make word via sounds → letters.
☐ Try this sound. . .	☐ You know this word. . . (write an analogy).
☐ Have student blend sounds aurally, then read.	☐ Does that make sense?
☐ Chunk the word or break it into syllables.	☐ Reread the sentence and tell me what it means.

Strategies and Actions for Fluency and Comprehension (Check box when used during the lesson):

☐ Swoop 3–4 words for student to practice fluency.	☐ What did you read? Tell me about it.
☐ Read along and then repeat after me.	☐ *What* happened to *who, where, when,* and *why*?

Teaching Decoding (2–3 minutes)	Skills:
Examples:	

Page 1 of 2

Discussing Text (2–3 minutes; use cards in appendix C, page 247)			
Notes for Next Lesson:			

Lesson 3			

Word Building (3–4 minutes)		Scaffold:	
Word List:	Phonics Skill:		Patterns:

Review Sight Words (3–4 minutes)			
Complete Each Step:	Teach and map	Build	Write

Rereading (3–4 minutes)

Reading Format:	☐ Independent read	☐ Echo read	☐ Choral read	☐ Partner read

Strategies and Actions for Fluency and Comprehension (Check box when used during the lesson):

☐ Swoop 3–4 words for student to practice fluency.	☐ Read along then repeat after me.
☐ Try to sound like you are talking.	☐ Were there any words or parts you didn't understand?
☐ Read to the punctuation before stopping.	☐ What did you read? Tell me about it.
☐ Make your voice go up for a question.	☐ What new information did you learn?
☐ Read it the way the character feels (exclamation).	☐ Why do you think. . .?

Writing—Sentence Dictation or Sentence Starter (3–4 minutes)

Teaching or Editing Focus:	☐ Handwriting	☐ Spacing	☐ Phonetic spelling	☐ Sight words
☐ Noun-verb agreement	☐ Sentence structure	☐ Possessives	☐ Irregular plural nouns	☐ Irregular verbs

☐ Past-, future-, present-tense verbs

Notes for Next Lesson:

Anecdotal Notes
Lesson 1
Lesson 2
Lesson 3

Page 2 of 2

Word Mat (Full Alphabetic Phase)

a b c d e f g h i j k l m
n o p q r s t u v w x y z

Supplemental Word Lists for Word Building (Full Alphabetic Phase)

Word List 1						
Phonics and Spelling Patterns: Digraphs						
ch	**sh**		**ck**			**th (unvoiced)**
chap	cash	rash	back	lock	sick	math
chat	dash	rush	buck	luck	sock	path
chin	dish	sash	chick	neck	suck	thud
chip	fish	sham	deck	pack	tack	with
chub	gash	shed	dock	peck	tick	
chug	gush	shim	hack	pick	tock	
rich	hush	ship	Jack	rack	tuck	
such	lush	shot	kick	rock	whack	
	mash	wish	lick	sack	wick	
	mush					

Word List 2					
Phonics and Spelling Patterns: Skill—Floss Rule					
ll			**ff**	**ss**	**zz**
all	fell	nill	buff	bass	fuzz
ball	fill	pill	duff	hiss	
bell	gull	sell	guff	kiss	
bill	hall	sill	muff	lass	
call	hill	tall	riff	mass	
chill	kill	tell		mess	
dill	lull	well		sass	
dull	mall	will			
fall	mill				

Word List 3									
Phonics and Spelling Patterns: Skill—Initial Consonant Blends									
bl	**br**	**cl**	**cr**	**dr**	**fl**	**fr**	**gl**	**gr**	**pl**
blam	Brad	clam	cram	drag	flab	frat	glad	grab	plat
bled	bran	clan	crop	drat	flag		glop	grass	plex
blip	brat	clap	crud	drib	flash		glug	grid	plod
blob		class		drip	flat			grim	plot
blot		clef			flax			grip	plum
bluff		clip			fled				plug
		clod			flesh				
		clot			flip				
					flog				
					flub				

pr	**sc**	**sk**	**sl**	**sn**	**sp**	**st**	**sw**	**tr**
prat	scab	skim	slag	sniff	spam	stag	swill	trap
prod		skin	slap	snub	spat	stat	Swiss	tress
		skit	slash		sped	stem		trill
		skull	slim		spin	stop		trod
			slit		spit	stub		
			slob		spud	stud		
			slosh			stun		
			slug					
			slum					

Word List 4

Phonics and Spelling Patterns: Skill—Final Consonant Blends

ft	lt	mp	nd	ng	
deft	cult	bump	band	bang	ping
gift	felt		bend	ding	pong
lift	hilt		fond	gang	rang
loft	jilt		hand	gong	ring
raft	melt		lend	hang	sing
shaft	silt		mend	hung	song
sift	tilt		pond	king	sung
soft			sand	lung	wing
			send	pang	

nk		nt		sk	st	
bank	mink	bent	punt	desk	best	lost
bonk	pink	bunt	rant	husk	bust	mast
bunk	punk	dent	rent	mush	cast	mist
dunk	rank	hint	runt	risk	chest	nest
funk	rink	hunt	sent	rusk	dust	pest
hunk	sank	lint	shunt	tusk	fast	rust
junk	sunk	mint	tent		fist	test
kink	tank	pant	vent		gust	vast
link	thank				jest	vest
	wink				just	west
					last	zest

Word List 5

Phonics and Spelling Patterns: Skill—Initial and Final Blends (Initial Blend Changes)

mp		nd	ng	nk		nt	st
clamp	clomp	spend	flung	blank	brink	plant	crust
cramp	crump		slung	clank	drink	scant	
stamp	grump			drank	stink	slant	
crimp	plump			flank	plonk	flint	
primp	slump			plank	plunk	print	
	stump			spank	spunk	stunt	
				stank	trunk		

Word List 6

Phonics and Spelling Patterns: Skill—Initial and Final Blends (Final Blend Changes)

bl	br	cl	cr	st	gr
blank	brand	clang	cramp	stamp	grand
bling	bring	clank	crump		
blink	brink	clink			

Word List 7

Phonics and Spelling Patterns: Initial and Final Consonant Clusters

scr	shr	spr	str	thr	-tch			-nch
scrimp	shrank	sprang	strap	thrash	batch	thatch	witch	bench
	shrunk	sprig	strength	thrill	catch	fetch	twitch	crunch
	shrug		strip	throng	hatch	sketch	botch	finch
			strum		latch	ditch	notch	lunch
			strut		match	hitch	splotch	munch
			strung		patch	pitch	hutch	pinch
					snatch	switch	clutch	punch
								ranch

Word List 8								
Phonics and Spelling Patterns: Skill—Silent _e_ Long Vowels, Soft _c_, _g_, -_dge_								
a		**i**		**o**	**u**	**c**	**g**	**-dge** (short vowels)
blade	graze	bride	spite	broke	use	place	binge	edge
blame	plane	crime	tribe	chose	cute	trace	bulge	budge
blaze	plate	drive	twice	close	dude	slice	cringe	dodge
brake	scale	glide	twine	drove	duke	spice	fringe	fudge
brave	shade	pride	whine	froze	fume	splice	range	hedge
crane	shake	prime	white	phone	fuse		singe	judge
crate	shame	prize	scribe	slope	June		plunge	ledge
craze	shape	shine	strife	smoke	lute			midge
drake	shave	slide	strike	spoke	muse			nudge
drape	skate	slime	stripe	stole	mute			bridge
flake	slate	smile	strive	stone	rude			grudge
flame	snake	spike	shrine	stove	rule			pledge
glade	spade			stroke	tube			sledge
glaze	stake				tune			trudge
grade	stale				brute			
grate	state				plume			
grave	whale				prune			

Word List 9			
Phonics and Spelling Patterns: Skill—Silent Letters			
kn	**mb**	**wr**	**qu**
knit	dumb	wrap	quip
knob		wren	quiz
knife		wrench	quill
		wrist	quake
		write	quell
		wrung	quench
			quick
			quite
			quote
			quiet
			squid

Word List 10						
Phonics and Spelling Patterns: Skill—Inflected Endings, Doubling, and *E*-Drop						
ed = /id/	ed = /d/	ed = /t/	Doubling With -*ed*	Doubling With -*ing*	*E*-Drop With -*ed*	*E*-Drop With -*ing*
acted	blamed	asked	batted	batting	biked	biking
crated	budged	basked	dotted	dropping	blazed	blaming
dusted	buzzed	chased	grinned	grabbing	chased	blazing
ended	cared	choked	patted	hugging	chimed	choking
lasted	changed	danced			piled	scraping
listed	craned	flaked			shaped	shaping
melted	cringed	hoped			smiled	shining
rented	dodged	jumped			stroked	smiling
stated	dredged	missed				
traded	grazed	shaped				
twisted	judged	sloped				
wanted	plunged	smoked				
	primed	stroked				
	rolled	walked				
	smiled					
	smudged					
	staged					
	wedged					
	whined					

Word List 11								
Phonics and Spelling Patterns: Skill—Common Long Vowels								
ay	**ai**		**ee**			**ea**		
gray	braid	paint	beech	preen	steel	beach	feast	speak
play	brain	plain	bleed	sheet	steep	beast	least	squeal
pray	chain	saint	cheese	sleek	street	breathe	leave	steal
splay	drain	stain	creek	sleet	sweep	cheat	peace	steam
stay	faint	waist	creep	speech	sweet	clean	peach	streak
	faith	praise	greet	speed	teeth	cream	please	stream
	frail	strait	kneel	spree	wheel	dream	reach	teach
	grain	straight		squeeze		ease	sneak	wheat
y	**iCC**	**oa**	**oCC**		**oo**		**ue**	
cry	bind	cloak	bold	host	bloom	school	cue	
dry	blind	coast	bolt	mold	broom	scoot	due	
fly	find	croak	both	most	gloom	shoot	blue	
fry	hind	float	cold	old				
sky	kind	roach	colt	poll				
try	rind	poach	fold					
why	wild	toast	folk					
	wind		gold					
			hold					

Decoding Assessment (Full Alphabetic Phase)

Directions for administering: Each word list contains 20 words, and some lists include a mix of nonsense words. Begin with word list 1. Ask the student to read each word as you point to it. The student should be able to read each word in 2–3 seconds for the word to be considered read correctly. Use the teacher score sheet (page 242) to mark which words the student reads correctly. Add up the total number of words read correctly for each list. If the student reads at least 16 words correctly, continue on to the next list. Stop at the list when the student reads fewer than 15 words correctly.

- Mastery of a word list is reading 16 or more words correct, or 80 percent to 100 percent correct. Move on to the next list and follow the same assessment procedures—as long as the student can maintain 80 percent decoding accuracy within 2–3 seconds for each word.

- If the student reads 14–15 words correctly, or 70 percent to 75 percent, stop at this list and begin review lessons with these phonics patterns.

- If the student reads 0–13 words correctly, or 65 percent or below, stop at this list and provide extensive instruction with this phonics pattern.

Visit **go.SolutionTree.com/literacy** for additional word lists.

Teacher Score Sheet (Full Alphabetic Phase)

Name _____ Date _____

Diagraphs, Floss Rule, ck	Check if Correct	Initial or Final Blends	Check if Correct	Initial and Final Blends	Check if Correct
when		blub		blink	
with		prom		slept	
mash		tret		draft	
buck		snip		slump	
miss		gled		stomp	
such		stag		prong	
that		glim		spent	
which		slug		gland	
fuzz		plod		swung	
this		flap		grant	
chop		bend		spunk	
fill		long		twist	
mass		bunk		blast	
shut		kept		frost	
cuff		cost		spend	
math		bang		flunk	
fizz		film		glint	
back		dust		frond	
thin		hint		dreft	
sick		blub		blink	
Total Correct		Total Correct		Total Correct	

Consonant Clusters / Trigraphs	Check if Correct	Long Vowel, Silent *e*, Soft *c*, *g*, *-dge*	Check if Correct	Inflected *-ed* and *-ing* Endings (After Silent *e*)	Check if Correct
scratch		stripe		crusted	
splint		glaze		thrushed	
shrank		flake		sliced	
strict		throne		snaking	
throb		fridge		grazing	
scrimp		rule		mixing	
thrust		grace		smelled	
strung		shine		stroking	
shrunk		note		clocked	
shrill		stage		spacing	
scruff		grime		stunning	
splotch		chase		thrilled	
sprung		prune		striking	
shrewd		sledge		blazing	
strum		strife		shrugged	
thrift		slope		pluming	
scrunch		place		stilted	
thrill		vote		shaving	
sprint		craze		flushed	
thrash		tube		flaking	
Total Correct		Total Correct		Total Correct	

Silent Consonants and Words With *qu*	Check if Correct	Contractions	Check if Correct	Common Long Vowels	Check if Correct
knot		I've		coach	
write		she's		grind	
quest		isn't		shook	
wreath		who's		squeal	
knit		wasn't		sleek	
wrap		let's		smooth	
quick		I'll		quaint	
knelt		we've		screen	
wrote		they're		spray	
wrath		don't		scold	
crumb		here's		stream	
plumb		you're		scoot	
wring		didn't		wheel	
knob		you've		spool	
quote		what's		throat	
knife		you'll		sweep	
thumb		he'll		breathe	
knock		that's		groan	
wreck		we'll		knead	
wren		can't		squeeze	
Total Correct		Total Correct		Total Correct	

Student Word List (Full Alphabetic Phase)

Diagraphs, Floss Rule, ck	Initial or Final Blends	Initial and Final Blends
when	blub	blink
with	prom	slept
mash	tret	draft
buck	snip	slump
miss	gled	stomp
such	stag	prong
that	glim	spent
which	slug	gland
fuzz	plod	swung
this	flap	grant
chop	bend	spunk
fill	long	twist
mass	bunk	blast
shut	kept	frost
cuff	cost	spend
math	bang	flunk
fizz	film	glint
back	dust	frond
thin	hint	dreft
sick	blub	blink

Consonant Clusters / Trigraphs	Long Vowel, Silent *e*, Soft *c*, *g*, *-dge*	Inflected *-ed* and *-ing* Endings
scratch	stripe	crusted
splint	glaze	thrushed
shrank	flake	sliced
strict	throne	snaking
throb	fridge	grazing
scrimp	rule	mixing
thrust	grace	smelled
strung	shine	stroking
shrunk	note	clocked
shrill	stage	spacing
scruff	grime	stunning
splotch	chase	thrilled
sprung	prune	striking
shrewd	sledge	blazing
strum	strife	shrugged
thrift	slope	pluming
scrunch	place	stilted
thrill	vote	shaving
sprint	craze	flushed
thrash	tube	flaking

Silent Consonants and Words With *qu*	Contractions	Common Long Vowels
knot	I've	coach
write	she's	grind
quest	isn't	shook
wreath	who's	squeal
knit	wasn't	sleek
wrap	let's	smooth
quick	I'll	quaint
knelt	we've	screen
wrote	they're	spray
wrath	don't	scold
crumb	here's	stream
plumb	you're	scoot
wring	didn't	wheel
knob	you've	spool
quote	what's	throat
knife	you'll	sweep
thumb	he'll	breathe
knock	that's	groan
wreck	we'll	knead
wren	can't	squeeze

Conversation Starter Comprehension Cards
(Full Alphabetic Phase)

What if. . .	I wonder why. . .
I was surprised. . .	I really can't understand. . .
I thought. . .	I think the author. . .
It reminds me of. . .	I like the way. . .
I never thought that. . .	I can't believe. . .

APPENDIX D

Teacher Resources for the Consolidated Alphabetic Phase

Lesson Plan Template
(Consolidated Alphabetic Phase)

Consolidated Alphabetic Phase			
Lesson 1			
Word Building (3–4 minutes)		Scaffold:	
Word List:	Skill:		Patterns:
Sight Words (2–3 minutes)			
Complete Each Step:	Teach and map	Build	Write .
Introduction, Preview Text, and Vocabulary (2–3 minutes)			
Text:			
Vocabulary:			
Graphic Organizer (5–6 minutes)			
Notes for Next Lesson:			
Lesson 2			
Discuss Graphic Organizers (3–4 minutes)			
Reading and Clarifying (5–6 minutes)			
Strategies and Actions for Decoding and Self-Monitoring:			

Strategies and Actions for Decoding and Self-Monitoring:

☐ Chunk the word or break it into syllables.

☐ Find the root or base word.

☐ Let's break it into parts.

☐ This word is pronounced _____. It means _____.

☐ Were there any words you didn't understand?

☐ Is there a context clue you can use?

☐ Reread the sentence and tell me what it means.

☐ Does that make sense?

Strategies and Actions for Fluency and Comprehension:

☐ Swoop or frame three- or four-word phrases for student to practice fluency.

☐ Read along and then repeat after me.

☐ Read to the _____ before stopping.

☐ Make your voice go up at the end for a question.

☐ Read it the way the character feels (exclamation).

☐ Try to sound like you're talking.

☐ Tell me about this paragraph, page [and so on].

☐ What is something new you learned? Tell me about it.

Teaching Vocabulary (4–5 minutes; teach context clues if needed)				

OR: Discussing Text (4–5 minutes)

☐ Paraphrasing	☐ Summarizing with vocabulary
☐ Paraphrasing with vocabulary	☐ Paragraph shrinking

Notes for Next Lesson:

Lesson 3

Plan for Writing (1 minute)	Writing Format:

Oral Rehearsal and Writing (10–12 minutes)

1. Rehearse orally.
2. Repeat sentence in phrases and write.
3. Reread to self-monitor.
4. Repeat process for each sentence.

Editing—Language Standards (1–2 minutes)

☐ Conventions	☐ Parts of speech	☐ Sentence structure	☐ Verb tenses
☐ Conjunctions	☐ Compound sentences	☐ Commas	☐ Quotation marks

Notes for Next Lesson:

Anecdotal Notes

Lesson 1

Lesson 2

Lesson 3

Word Mat
(Consolidated Alphabetic Phase)

a b c d e f g h i j k l m

n o p q r s t u v w x y z

Redesigning Small-Group Reading Instruction © 2025 Solution Tree Press • SolutionTree.com
Visit **go.SolutionTree.com/literacy** to download this free reproducible.

Supplemental Word Lists (Consolidated Alphabetic Phase)

Word List 1						
Long Vowel Phonics and Spelling Patterns						
Long *a*	**Short *e***		**Long *e***		**Long *i***	
ei	**ea**		**ie**		**igh**	
veil	dead	breast	brief	siege	sigh	sight
vein	head	breath	fiend	thief	fight	tight
reign	lead	tread	grief	yield	light	flight
weigh	read	stealth	niece	priest	night	fright
sleigh	meant	thread	piece		right	knight
freight	realm	threat				
	sweat	wealth				
	bread					

Long o			Long u	
ow			**ew**	
bow	flow	snow	dew	flew
low	glow	stow	new	knew
mow	grow	blown	blew	stew
sow	know	flown	brew	screw
own	show	shown	crew	threw
tow	slow	throw	drew	shrew
crow				

Word List 2						
R-Controlled Vowel Phonics and Spelling Patterns						
ar		**ar**	**or**		**/er/**	
		/or/			**er**	**ear**
barb	spark	warm	chord	scorn	fern	earl
barge	stark	warn	chore	shore	term	learn

carve	scarf		forge	short	nerve	yearn
large	smart		forth	snore	verse	
march	start		gorge	sport	swerve	
charm	gnarl		morph	store		
shark	starch		porch	swore		
			score	torch		

ir		ur		
bird	skirt	fur	lurk	lurch
firm	third	burr	spur	nurse
girl	thirst	purr	surf	purse
stir	twirl	burp	turf	spurt
whir	whirl	curb	turn	churn
birch	squirm	curl	blur	church
first	squirt	hurl	burst	
shirt				

Word List 3								
Vowel Diphthongs and *wa* Phonics and Spelling Patterns								
/oo/ Long o	/oi/		/ou/					
oo	oi		ou				ow	
hoof	oil	toil	out	count	round	stout	fowl	clown
soot	coil	void	foul	doubt	sound	couch	how	crown
took	coin	joint	loud	found	cloud	grouch	plow	drown
crook	foil	moist	couch	hound	proud	ground	down	frown
shook	loin	noise	mouth	mound	scout	sprout	town	prowl
	soil	spoil	south	mount	snout	shroud	brown	
			couch	pound	spout			
/ō/							/o/	
al	au		aw			wa		
balk	fault	taught	raw	yawn	crawl	swan	wasp	
halt	fraud	squad	dawn	straw	drawl	swap	watt	
salt	haunt	squall	fawn	claw	shawl	swat	swath	
chalk	sauce	squash	gnaw	draw	scrawl	wand	waltz	
scald	haunch	because	lawn	slaw	squawk	want	watch	
stalk	caught		pawn	thaw		wash	swatch	
waltz								

Word List 4					
Spelling Patterns With the Six Syllable Types					
Closed	Consonant and *-le*	Open	Vowel Combinations	Silent *e*	*R*-Controlled
cactus	bundle	bacon	beacon	cascade	bargain
candid	candle	basic	braided	combine	blurted
cotton	dazzle	begin	brighten	compose	burden
goblin	gentle	frozen	counted	confuse	carbon
index	hassle	hero	counting	donate	churning
mascot	juggle	human	employ	extreme	master
nutmeg	mantle	label	enjoy	frostbite	merging
plastic	needle	music	knowing	invade	pardon
puppet	shuffle	pilot	leaving	mistake	perfect
rocket	single	protest	loading	pancake	quirky
rustic	stumble	robot	lounging	remote	sister
splendid	swindle	rodent	pointed	sunrise	suburbs
subset	twinkle	silent	reason	sunstroke	survive
tinsel	uncle	veto	royal	tadpole	tardy
traffic	whiffle		slouching	umpire	thirty

Word List 5		
Words With Common Prefixes		
dis-	re-	un-
disburse	rebate	unblock
disclose	recede	unclip
discreet	redeem	unclog
disguise	reject	uncork
dislodge	remake	uncurl
dismount	rename	unhitch
dispatch	reprise	unhook
dispense	reside	unknown
displease	retain	unroll
dissolve	revere	unseal
distance	revert	unsnap
distinct	revive	unstick
distract	revolt	untuck
distress	revolve	untwist
district		unwrap

Word List 6			
Words With Common Suffixes			
-es	**-ed**	**-ing**	**-ly**
airwaves	attached	bleating	beastly
besides	behaved	bouncing	bristly
busses	deprived	briefing	deathly
closures	deserved	catching	earthly
features	detailed	dangling	ghastly
fractures	featured	haunting	ghostly
gestures	inclined	pleading	googly
glasses	informed	pleasing	grizzly
knives	inspired	plumbing	largely
mixtures	measured	sampling	newly
pastures	refined	squawking	nightly
scarves	reserved	tackling	oddly
squeezes	tattered	touching	shortly
shingles	traveled	wrapping	soundly
vultures	wretched	yearning	worldly

Context Clues Bookmark
(Consolidated Alphabetic Phase)

Context Clues Bookmark

Wondering what a word means?
Use context clues!

Definition: The meaning of the word is explained in the text.

Example: An example of the word is in a sentence.

Text feature: A text feature helps you understand what the word means.

Word parts: Use the base or root word, or prefix or suffix.

Synonym: A word with a similar meaning is used.

Antonym: A word with an opposite meaning is used.

Inference: Try to "read between the lines" and figure out what the author means.

Figurative language: Try to connect to the language the author uses.

Context Clues Bookmark

Wondering what a word means?
Use context clues!

Definition: The meaning of the word is explained in the text.

Example: An example of the word is in a sentence.

Text feature: A text feature helps you understand what the word means.

Word parts: Use the base or root word, or prefix or suffix.

Synonym: A word with a similar meaning is used.

Antonym: A word with an opposite meaning is used.

Inference: Try to "read between the lines" and figure out what the author means.

Figurative language: Try to connect to the language the author uses.

Decoding Assessment
(Consolidated Alphabetic Phase)

Directions for administering: Each word list contains 20 words. Begin with word list 1. Ask the student to read each word as you point to it. The student should be able to read each word in 2–3 seconds for the word to be considered read correctly. Use the teacher score sheet (page 260) to mark which words the student reads correctly. Add up the total number of words read correctly for each list. If the student reads at least 18 words correctly, continue on to the next list. Stop at the list when the student reads fewer than 17 words correctly.

- Mastery of a word list is reading 18 or more words correctly, or 90 percent to 100 percent correct. Move on to the next list and follow the same assessment procedures—as long as the student can maintain 90 percent decoding accuracy within 2–3 seconds for each word.

- If the student reads 16–17 words correctly, or 80 percent to 85 percent, stop at this list and begin review lessons with these phonics patterns.

- If the student reads 0–15 words correctly, or 75 percent or below, stop at this list and provide extensive instruction with this phonics pattern.

As students progress through the consolidated alphabetic phase, or if students in this phase are reading on grade level, use a Lexile measure to group students. Follow the guidelines in chapter 6 (page 149) for grouping students appropriately within 100 to 150 Lexile point bands.

Teacher Score Sheet
(Consolidated Alphabetic Phase)

Name _____ Date _____

R-Controlled Vowels ar, are, air	Check if Correct	*R*-Controlled Vowels er, ear, eer	Check if Correct	*R*-Controlled Vowels ir, ire	Check if Correct
scarf		earth		whirl	
flair		sneer		chirp	
carve		perch		squirm	
snare		earn		birch	
share		pearl		spire	
stair		spear		circle	
stark		nerve		first	
blare		learn		girls	
chair		beard		birth	
march		swerve		smirk	
charm		heard		shirt	
glare		search		wire	
harm		earl		tired	
square		steer		third	
shark		verse		siren	
stare		cheer		skirt	
starve		yearn		wired	
large		clear		thirst	
spare		stern		stir	
spark		swear		twirl	
Total Correct		Total Correct		Total Correct	

R-Controlled Vowels or, ore, oar	Check if Correct	*R*-Controlled Vowels ur, ure	Check if Correct
board		churn	
force		sure	
stork		purse	
soar		spurt	
sworn		surge	
scorch		blurt	
worn		pure	
chore		turf	
forge		curse	
torch		burke	
scorn		cure	
horn		purge	
boar		turn	
worn		burst	
thorn		spurn	
forth		nurse	
shore		curve	
short		scurf	
gorge		lurch	
spore		cured	
Total Correct		Total Correct	

Vowel Digraph Patterns oo, oi, oy	Check if Correct	Vowel Digraph Patterns eigh, ie, igh, short *e*, ea	Check if Correct	Vowel Digraph Patterns ow (long o), ew	Check if Correct
brook		yield		crow	
ploys		neigh		chewed	
hoof		thief		thrown	
foyer		breath		shrew	
crook		bright		knew	
joined		piece		blown	
hoist		sweat		stews	
royal		dread		shown	
wool		thigh		brew	
boiled		threat		flown	
coins		niece		chews	
nook		knight		owned	
shook		shield		screw	
point		plight		known	
coils		freight		newt	
stood		chief		stow	
spoil		slight		threw	
foist		wealth		growth	
broil		weigh		shrewd	
wood		rights		grows	
Total Correct		Total Correct		Total Correct	

Vowel Digraph Patterns ou, au	Check if Correct	Vowel Digraph Patterns ow, aw	Check if Correct	Vowel Digraph Patterns al, wa	Check if Correct
launch		squawk		chalk	
caught		drawn		swab	
grouch		clowns		waltz	
sauce		crawled		swatch	
couch		growls		wand	
scouts		drawer		false	
cause		scowl		watch	
sounds		shawl		malt	
mount		fowl		swamp	
taught		drown		scald	
doubt		sprawl		dwarf	
haunt		prowls		wasps	
rounds		yawns		swarm	
fraud		haul		halts	
shouts		gnaws		stalk	
mound		crowds		swath	
fault		brows		warped	
sprouts		drawl		swats	
gauze		vault		warts	
crouch		clawed		stall	
Total Correct		Total Correct		Total Correct	

Closed Syllables	Check if Correct	Consonant -le Syllables	Check if Correct	Open Syllables	Check if Correct
anklet		brittle		begin	
combat		chuckle		cubic	
complex		crumble		decide	
contract		dabble		donut	
dentist		drizzle		even	
distress		fizzle		focus	
fabric		gamble		hero	
happen		hobble		humid	
hundred		mingle		label	
inflict		peddle		music	
kindred		puzzle		photo	
mishap		ramble		protest	
muskrat		sample		redo	
pilgrim		shuttle		resist	
pumpkin		simple		restate	
subject		sniffle		rubric	
sudden		tattle		solo	
untwist		tingle		total	
windmill		truffle		virus	
within		whistle		zero	
Total Correct		Total Correct		Total Correct	

Vowel Combinations	Check if Correct	Silent e Syllables	Check if Correct	R-Controlled Syllables	Check if Correct
beaming		advice		border	
beetle		athlete		burger	
between		beware		curtain	
bouncing		combine		dirty	
contain		concrete		forest	
crayon		confuse		further	
crouched		costume		harbor	
drowning		debate		lantern	
explain		decide		market	
freedom		delete		normal	
freezing		describe		orbit	
grounded		empire		quicker	
haunted		explore		scarlet	
mounted		incline		shelter	
racoon		include		spirit	
rainbow		inhale		splendor	
reason		invite		splinter	
shouted		reptile		surprise	
tailspin		ringside		target	
treating		stockpile		thirsty	
unload		volume		turnip	
Total Correct		Total Correct		Total Correct	

Common Prefixes dis-	Check if Correct	Common Prefixes re-	Check if Correct	Common Prefixes un-	Check if Correct
discard		record		unable	
discount		reduce		undone	
discuss		refund		uneasy	
disdain		refuse		uneven	
disease		regard		unfair	
disjoin		regret		unfurl	
dislike		relate		unjust	
dismay		remain		unkind	
dismiss		remind		unless	
disown		remote		unlock	
disperse		remove		unpack	
displace		repair		unpaid	
display		repeat		unplug	
dispose		report		unreal	
dispute		reside		unrest	
dissent		resist		unsafe	
distant		result		unsaid	
distill		retail		unsure	
disturb		retire		untold	
		reward		unwell	
Total Correct		Total Correct		Total Correct	

Common Suffixes -es	Check if Correct	Common Suffixes -ed	Check if Correct	Common Suffixes -ing	Check if Correct	Common Suffixes -ly	Check if Correct
bedtimes		advised		smashing		barely	
blazes		blasted		stuffing		brightly	
changes		crested		stunning		clearly	
contrives		engaged		crackling		crawly	
cringes		figured		combing		crumbly	
cultures		flavored		pressing		kindly	
dentures		marbled		strapping		lightly	
mashes		natured		fledgling		monthly	
plunges		pointed		screening		mostly	
quizzes		refined		searching		nearly	
rambles		relaxed		rounding		neatly	
rattles		removed		flailing		promptly	
revives		rounded		sterling		quickly	
riches		sighted		clearing		rightly	
shelves		studied		dressing		slightly	
smashes		tangled		sounding		swiftly	
stages		uncured		shocking		timely	
strangles		unharmed		tickling		vastly	
textures		unmoved		twinkling		wobbly	
upsides		untamed		yapping		yearly	
Total Correct		Total Correct		Total Correct		Total Correct	

Student Word List
(Consolidated Alphabetic Phase)

R-Controlled Vowels ar, are, air	R-Controlled Vowels er, ear, eer	R-Controlled Vowels ir, ire
scarf	earth	whirl
flair	sneer	chirp
carve	perch	squirm
snare	earn	birch
share	pearl	spire
stair	spear	circle
stark	nerve	first
blare	learn	girls
chair	beard	birth
march	swerve	smirk
charm	heard	shirt
glare	search	wire
harm	earl	tired
square	steer	third
shark	verse	siren
stare	cheer	skirt
starve	yearn	wired
large	clear	thirst
spare	stern	stir
spark	swear	twirl

R-Controlled Vowels or, ore, oar	R-Controlled Vowels ur, ure
board	churn
force	sure
stork	purse
soar	spurt
sworn	surge
scorch	blurt
worn	pure
chore	turf
forge	curse
torch	burke
scorn	cure
horn	purge
boar	turn
worn	burst
thorn	spurn
forth	nurse
shore	curve
short	scurf
gorge	lurch
spore	cured

Vowel Digraph Patterns oo, oi, oy	Vowel Digraph Patterns eigh, ie, igh, short *e*, ea	Vowel Digraph Patterns ow (long o), ew
brook	yield	crow
ploys	neigh	chewed
hoof	thief	thrown
foyer	breath	shrew
crook	bright	knew
joined	piece	blown
hoist	sweat	stews
royal	dread	shown
wool	thigh	brew
boiled	threat	flown
coins	niece	chews
nook	knight	owned
shook	shield	screw
point	plight	known
coils	freight	newt
stood	chief	stow
spoil	slight	threw
foist	wealth	growth
broil	weigh	shrewd
wood	rights	grows

Vowel Digraph Patterns ou, au	Vowel Digraph Patterns ow, aw	Vowel Digraph Patterns al, wa
launch	squawk	chalk
caught	drawn	swab
grouch	clowns	waltz
sauce	crawled	swatch
couch	growls	wand
scouts	drawer	false
cause	scowl	watch
sounds	shawl	malt
mount	fowl	swamp
taught	drown	scald
doubt	sprawl	dwarf
haunt	prowls	wasps
rounds	yawns	swarm
fraud	haul	halts
shouts	gnaws	stalk
mound	crowds	swath
fault	brows	warped
sprouts	drawl	swats
gauze	vault	warts
crouch	clawed	stall

Closed Syllables	Consonant and -le Syllables	Open Syllables
anklet	brittle	begin
combat	chuckle	cubic
complex	crumble	decide
contract	dabble	donut
dentist	drizzle	even
distress	fizzle	focus
fabric	gamble	hero
happen	hobble	humid
hundred	mingle	label
inflict	peddle	music
kindred	puzzle	photo
mishap	ramble	protest
muskrat	sample	redo
pilgrim	shuttle	resist
pumpkin	simple	restate
subject	sniffle	rubric
sudden	tattle	solo
untwist	tingle	total
windmill	truffle	virus
within	whistle	zero

Vowel Combinations	Silent e Syllables	R-Controlled Syllables
beaming	advice	border
beetle	athlete	burger
between	beware	curtain
bouncing	combine	dirty
contain	concrete	forest
crayon	confuse	further
crouched	costume	harbor
drowning	debate	lantern
explain	decide	market
freedom	delete	normal
freezing	describe	orbit
grounded	empire	quicker
haunted	explore	scarlet
mounted	incline	shelter
racoon	include	spirit
rainbow	inhale	splendor
reason	invite	splinter
shouted	reptile	surprise
tailspin	ringside	target
treating	stockpile	thirsty
unload	volume	turnip

Common Prefixes dis-	Common Prefixes re-	Common Prefixes un-
discard	record	unable
discount	reduce	undone
discuss	refund	uneasy
disdain	refuse	uneven
disease	regard	unfair
disjoin	regret	unfurl
dislike	relate	unjust
dismay	remain	unkind
dismiss	remind	unless
disown	remote	unlock
disperse	remove	unpack
displace	repair	unpaid
display	repeat	unplug
dispose	report	unreal
dispute	reside	unrest
dissent	resist	unsafe
distant	result	unsaid
distill	retail	unsure
disturb	retire	untold
	reward	unwell

Common Suffixes -es	Common Suffixes -ed	Common Suffixes -ing	Common Suffixes -ly
bedtimes	advised	smashing	barely
blazes	blasted	stuffing	brightly
changes	crested	stunning	clearly
contrives	engaged	crackling	crawly
cringes	figured	combing	crumbly
cultures	flavored	pressing	kindly
dentures	marbled	strapping	lightly
mashes	natured	fledgling	monthly
plunges	pointed	screening	mostly
quizzes	refined	searching	nearly
rambles	relaxed	rounding	neatly
rattles	removed	flailing	promptly
revives	rounded	sterling	quickly
riches	sighted	clearing	rightly
shelves	studied	dressing	slightly
smashes	tangled	sounding	swiftly
stages	uncured	shocking	timely
strangles	unharmed	tickling	vastly
textures	unmoved	twinkling	wobbly
upsides	untamed	yapping	yearly

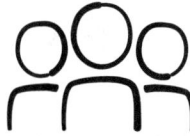

APPENDIX E

Teacher Resources for the Automatic Phase

Lesson Plan Template (Automatic Phase)

Automatic Phase		
Lesson 1		
Word Building (3–4 minutes)	Word List:	Text:
Skill:	Pattern:	**Literal Comprehension (6–7 minutes)**
Clarifying and Vocabulary (3–4 minutes)	Choose Strategy: ☐ Clarifying and understanding vocabulary ☐ Making connections ☐ Asking and answering questions ☐ Paraphrasing and retelling ☐ Using vocabulary to retell	
Notes for Next Lesson:		
Lesson 2		
Introduce Strategy (2–3 minutes):		
Discussing Text (4–5 minutes):		
Graphic Organizer (6–7 minutes)	Choose Inferential Comprehension Strategy:	
Sketch Graphic Organizer:	☐ Making inferences and drawing conclusions ☐ Text features and illustrations ☐ Main idea and details ☐ Compare and contrast ☐ Cause and effect	
	OR Choose Evaluate and Comprehension Strategy: ☐ Summarizing ☐ Evaluating author's points ☐ Point of view ☐ Theme ☐ Text structure	

Page 1 of 2

Lesson 3	
Provide a Prompt (1–2 minutes)	
Plan for Writing (3–4 minutes)	
Writing Type:	**Writing and Editing (8–10 minutes)**
Graphic Organizer	Edit for:
	☐ Oral rehearsal
	☐ Spelling
	☐ Conventions and grammar
	☐ Sentence construction and syntax
	☐ Punctuation, commas, quotation marks
	☐ Sentence variety and presentation of ideas
	☐ Sentence combining
	☐ Complex sentences
Notes for Next Lesson:	

Anecdotal Notes
Lesson 1
Lesson 2
Lesson 3

Word Mat (Automatic Phase)

Syllables and Word Parts

_____ _____ _____ _____ _____ _____

_____ _____ _____ _____ _____ _____

_____ _____ _____ _____ _____ _____

_____ _____ _____ _____ _____ _____

_____ _____ _____ _____ _____ _____

Dictation

_____ _____

_____ _____

_____ _____

_____ _____

Writing

_____

_____

_____

_____

_____

_____

_____

_____

Supplemental Word Lists (Automatic Phase)

ADDITIONAL WORD LISTS FOR PREFIXES

in- (in)	in-, (not)
incubator	inability
infielder	inaccurate
inpatient	incurable
intestine	ineptitude
intrusive	intermediary

ADDITIONAL WORD LISTS FOR SUFFIXES

-al (pertaining to, of the kind)	-ation (act or process of)	-ition (act or process of)	-ative (adjectival form of a noun)	-itive (adjectival form of a noun)
arrival	accusation	exposition	imperative	additive
federal	annotation	malposition	initiative	definitive
mineral	configuration	premonition	irritative	infinitive
ordinal	degradation	repetition	operative	intuitive
pivotal	resignation	supposition	preventative	repetitive

ADDITIONAL WORD LISTS FOR GREEK AND LATIN ROOTS

ann (yearly)	aqua (water)	bio (life)	chron (time)	cracy (type of)
annexed	aquaculture	biochemist	chronically	aristocracy
annotate	aqualungs	biofuel	chronicle	autocracy
annuals	aquanaut	biomarker	chronologic	bureaucracy
annuity	Aquarius	biosphere	chronology	democracy
annulate	aquatic	biotoxin	synchronize	technocracy

cycl (circle)	cent (one hundred)	con, co (with, joined)	col, com (with, joined)	contra, counter (against)
cyclical	bicentennial	coalesce	collate	contradict
cyclone	centennial	coexist	collude	counteract
dicyclic	iridescent	cohesive	compile	counterpart
epicycle	maleficent	condense	comply	counterplea
recycled	omnificent	converge	compromise	countersue

dys (bad, difficult)	dem (people)	geo (earth)	gon (angle)	hetero (different)
dysfunction	academic	geographic	flexagon	heterogeneous
dysgraphia	democratic	geology	heptagon	heterograft
dyslexic	demographic	geometric	perigon	heterolysis
dystopia	endemic	geomorphic	tetragon	heteroploidy
dystrophic	epidemic	geophysical	trigonous	heterotopic

homo (same)	ject (cast or throw)	jud (judge)	logy (study of)	lumin (light, shine)
homogenize	ejected	adjudicate	mythology	aluminum
homograft	injection	judiciary	methodology	illuminate
homograph	interject	judicious	meteorology	luminous
homologate	rejection	misjudgment	symbology	relumined
homophone	trajectory	prejudice	technology	voluminous

magn, mega (big)	mal (bad)	mech (machine)	metr, meter (measure)	mono (one)
magnanimous	malformation	mechanism	isometric	monocrat
magnify	malicious	aeromechanics	metrical	monogram
magnitude	malignant	biomechanics	odometer	monologue
magnitude	malnutrition	hydromechanics	optometry	monopoly
	malnutrition	electromechanics	speedometer	monoxide

mit, miss (send, let go)	migr (move)	min (less, smaller)	path (feeling, disease)	phobia (fear)
committed	emigrate	minified	empathize	acrophobia
mitigation	immigrate	minimal	pathogen	agoraphobia
omission	migration	minimize	pathology	claustrophobia
resubmit	remigrate	minished	sympathize	hydrophobia
transmission	transmigrate	minuend	telepathic	technophobia

phon (sound)	photo (light)	phys (nature)	psycho (mind)	quir, ques, quis (search, seek, ask)
diaphone	photocopy	biophysical	psychobabble	inquiry
dysphonic	photoemission	emphysema	psychology	inquisitive
megaphone	photograph	metaphysic	psychometric	prerequisite
symphony	photoreaction	nonphysical	psychopath	questionable
telephone	photoresist	physicist	psychosis	requirement

rupt (break)	scrib, script (write)	scop (look)	sent, sens (feel)	spect (look at, watch)
abruptly	description	kaleidoscope	dissention	circumspect
corruption	postscript	microscopic	insensitive	introspect
disruptive	prescriber	periscope	resentment	prospective
eruption	transcribe	telescopic	sensible	retrospect
interrupt	transcripts	thermoscope	sentimental	spectator

tain (hold)	tract (pull)	vid (see)	vis (see)
ascertain	abstraction	divider	provision
certainty	contracted	evidence	revisit
detainment	detractor	subdivide	subdivision
retainer	extraction	undivided	supervise
uncertain	retraction	vividly	televise

Clarifying Bookmark (Automatic Phase)

Clarifying Bookmark

Could you summarize what you read to a partner? If not, go back to what was tricky. . .

- I don't understand this part. . .
- I don't think this part means. . .
- What did this word mean in this sentence?
- Could you explain _____ to me?
- I think this part means _____ .
- Here's what I didn't understand about this part _____ .
- Did the author mean _____ ?

Clarifying Bookmark

Could you summarize what you read to a partner? If not, go back to what was tricky. . .

- I don't understand this part. . .
- I don't think this part means. . .
- What did this word mean in this sentence?
- Could you explain _____ to me?
- I think this part means _____ .
- Here's what I didn't understand about this part _____ .
- Did the author mean _____ ?

Clarifying Bookmark

Could you summarize what you read to a partner? If not, go back to what was tricky. . .

- I don't understand this part. . .
- I don't think this part means. . .
- What did this word mean in this sentence?
- Could you explain _____ to me?
- I think this part means _____ .
- Here's what I didn't understand about this part _____ .
- Did the author mean _____ ?

Making Connections Bookmark
(Automatic Phase)

Making Connections Bookmark

Text-Self

- What does this remind me of in my life?
- Is this similar to or different from something I've experienced?
- Has something like this ever happened to me?
- How does this relate to my life?

Text-Text

- How does this remind me of something else I've read?
- How is this text different from other books or articles I've read?
- How is this text similar to others that I've read?
- Have I read any other texts on a similar topic?

Text-World

- How does this remind me of something in the real world?
- How is this text similar to or different from things that happen or have happened in the real world?
- How did that part relate to the world around me?

Making Connections Bookmark

Text-Self

- What does this remind me of in my life?
- Is this similar to or different from something I've experienced?
- Has something like this ever happened to me?
- How does this relate to my life?

Text-Text

- How does this remind me of something else I've read?
- How is this text different from other books or articles I've read?
- How is this text similar to others that I've read?
- Have I read any other texts on a similar topic?

Text-World

- How does this remind me of something in the real world?
- How is this text similar to or different from things that happen or have happened in the real world?
- How did that part relate to the world around me?

Questioning Bookmark (Automatic Phase)

Questioning Bookmark

- How did. . .?
  or How does. . .?
- Why did. . .?
  or Why does. . .?
- What if. . .?
- When does. . .?
  or When can. . .?
- Do you think. . .?
- How are. . .?
- Where. . .?
- Who. . .?
- Why. . .?
- Doesn't. . .? or Didn't. . .?
- Can. . .? or Can't. . .?

Questioning Bookmark

- How did. . .?
  or How does. . .?
- Why did. . .?
  or Why does. . .?
- What if. . .?
- When does. . .?
  or When can. . .?
- Do you think. . .?
- How are. . .?
- Where. . .?
- Who. . .?
- Why. . .?
- Doesn't. . .? or Didn't. . .?
- Can. . .? or Can't. . .?

Questioning Bookmark

- How did. . .?
  or How does. . .?
- Why did. . .?
  or Why does. . .?
- What if. . .?
- When does. . .?
  or When can. . .?
- Do you think. . .?
- How are. . .?
- Where. . .?
- Who. . .?
- Why. . .?
- Doesn't. . .? or Didn't. . .?
- Can. . .? or Can't. . .?

Making Inferences Bookmark (Automatic Phase)

Making Inferences Bookmark

Example from
The Rough-Face Girl

Question
Why didn't the father give the stepsisters anything to dress up on?

Text Evidence
The stepsisters just walked over to the teepee to see the Invisible Being's sister.

Background Knowledge
Sometimes, parents worry about one of their kids more than any others.

Inference
The stepsisters think they are already pretty and they don't need anything else.

Use what you already know (background knowledge) and evidence from the text. Try to determine what the author wants you to figure out. This is also called "reading between the lines."

Making Inferences Bookmark

Example from
The Rough-Face Girl

Question
Why didn't the father give the stepsisters anything to dress up on?

Text Evidence
The stepsisters just walked over to the teepee to see the Invisible Being's sister.

Background Knowledge
Sometimes, parents worry about one of their kids more than any others.

Inference
The stepsisters think they are already pretty and they don't need anything else.

Use what you already know (background knowledge) and evidence from the text. Try to determine what the author wants you to figure out. This is also called "reading between the lines."

Text Features and Illustrations Bookmark
(Automatic Phase)

Text Features and Illustrations Bookmark

Explain to the other students in the group how the text illustrations and features help the reader better understand the text.

- How do the illustrations make you feel as a reader? Why?
- What mood do the illustrations create?
- How does the illustration or text feature match the text?
- How does the illustration or text feature support the words in the text?
- What extra information do the illustrations give you?
- What do the illustrations tell you about the characters, setting, problem, events, solution, main idea, and details?
- What is an inference you can make from the illustration or text feature?
- The text reads, "_____." How does the illustration contribute to or support the mood of the text?
- How does the text feature support the point the author makes about _____?

Text Features and Illustrations Bookmark

Explain to the other students in the group how the text illustrations and features help the reader better understand the text.

- How do the illustrations make you feel as a reader? Why?
- What mood do the illustrations create?
- How does the illustration or text feature match the text?
- How does the illustration or text feature support the words in the text?
- What extra information do the illustrations give you?
- What do the illustrations tell you about the characters, setting, problem, events, solution, main idea, and details?
- What is an inference you can make from the illustration or text feature?
- The text reads, "_____." How does the illustration contribute to or support the mood of the text?
- How does the text feature support the point the author makes about _____?

Summarizing Bookmark (Automatic Phase)

Summarizing Informational Text Bookmark

Text:

Author:

Author's Purpose:

Details: Key Words

Main Idea:

Text Structure:

Signal Words:

Summary:

Summarizing Literary Text Bookmark

Text:

Author:

Characters:

Setting:

Transitional and Signal Words for Summarizing Literary Text

first	then	next	after that
finally	in the end	as a result	at the beginning
as soon as	it started when	later on	soon after
before long	afterward	to begin with	ultimately
at this point	at that moment	by the end	at last

How Authors Support Their Points Bookmark (Automatic Phase)

How Authors Support Their Points Bookmark

Use these key words to find places in the text where the author makes a point or states their position.

for this reason	for instance	for example
in particular	such as	in other words
keeping in mind	for this purpose	therefore
like	as a result	if. . . then. . .
what needs to	in order to	surely
especially	should, would, or could	obviously
to illustrate	to this end	due to
most importantly	similarly	in particular
because of	it is clear	

Read on to find the details that contain the reasons why the author takes this position or makes this point.

How Authors Support Their Points Bookmark

Use these key words to find places in the text where the author makes a point or states their position.

for this reason	for instance	for example
in particular	such as	in other words
keeping in mind	for this purpose	therefore
like	as a result	if. . . then. . .
what needs to	in order to	surely
especially	should, would, or could	obviously
to illustrate	to this end	due to
most importantly	similarly	in particular
because of	it is clear	

Read on to find the details that contain the reasons why the author takes this position or makes this point.

Redesigning Small-Group Reading Instruction © 2025 Solution Tree Press • SolutionTree.com
Visit **go.SolutionTree.com/literacy** to download this free reproducible.

Point of View Bookmark (Automatic Phase)

Point of View Bookmark

First Person:

The main character tells the story.

Key words:

I, me, my, mine, we, us, our, ours

Second Person:

The narrator directly addresses the reader.

Key words:

you, your, yours, yourself

Third Person:

A narrator who is not a character in the story (an outsider) tells the story.

Key words:

he, she, him, her, his, hers, himself, herself, they, them, their

Third Person POV (Grades 3+)

Does the narrator know the thoughts of only one character? (Limited POV)

Does the narrator know the thoughts of every character? (Omniscient POV)

Point of View Bookmark

First Person:

The main character tells the story.

Key words:

I, me, my, mine, we, us, our, ours

Second Person:

The narrator directly addresses the reader.

Key words:

you, your, yours, yourself

Third Person:

A narrator who is not a character in the story (an outsider) tells the story.

Key words:

he, she, him, her, his, hers, himself, herself, they, them, their

Third Person POV (Grades 3+)

Does the narrator know the thoughts of only one character? (Limited POV)

Does the narrator know the thoughts of every character? (Omniscient POV)

Text Structure Bookmark (Automatic Phase)

Text Structure Bookmark

QUESTION AND ANSWER
Graphic Organizer

Signal Words

could be	may be	where
how	the best estimate	who
how many	what	why
it could be	when	you can conclude

COMPARE AND CONTRAST
Graphic Organizer

Signal Words

although	different from	in common
as opposed to	either. . . or. . .	likewise
as well as	even though	not only
but	however	similar to
compared with		yet

CAUSE AND EFFECT
Graphic Organizer

Signal Words

accordingly	due to	since
as a consequence	for this reason	so
as a result	if. . . then. . .	therefore
because	nevertheless	this led to

Text Structure Bookmark

DESCRIPTION (MAIN IDEA AND DETAILS)
Graphic Organizer

Signal Words

a number of	for example	is like
appears to be	for instance	looks like
as in. . .	in addition	such as
characteristics	including	to illustrate

SEQUENCE
Graphic Organizer

Signal Words

first, second, next, then, after that, finally	during	later
before	eventually	meanwhile
at last, lastly	first of all	not long after
in conclusion	following	previously
afterword	immediately	recently
at the same time as	in the first place	soon
	initially	when, whenever

PROBLEM AND SOLUTION
Graphic Organizer

Signal Words

a problem	since	one reason for
for this reason	so that	a solution
if. . . then. . .	because	this led to
in order to	led to	the question is
it involved	due to	

Common Themes (Automatic Phase)

Grades K–2			
acceptance	fairness	jealousy	perseverance
bravery	friendship	kindness	responsibility
compassion	greed	love	revenge
courage	honesty	loyalty	sportsmanship
cooperation	hope	peace	survival
Grades 3–4			
acceptance	culture	individuality	power
ambition	emotion	justice	pride
anger	family	life	regret
beauty	fear	loneliness	rights
challenge	freedom	loss	traditions
cowardice	heroism	possibilities	work
Grades 5–8			
abandonment	ethics	isolation	religion
alienation	faith	liberty	sacrifices
authority	fate	maturity	self-development
betrayal	free will	nationalism	spirituality
choices	grief	nature	success
coming of age	guilt	oppression	suffering
community	honor	prejudice	truth
conformity	identity	race	the journey
cruelty	illness	redemption	values
death	inequality	rejection	violence
duty	innocence	relationships	war

References and Resources

Al-Khasawneh, F. (2019). The impact of vocabulary knowledge on the reading comprehension of Saudi EFL learners. *Journal of Language and Education, 5*(3), 24–34.

Allington, R. L., & McGill-Franzen, A. M. (2021). Reading volume and reading achievement: A review of recent research. *Reading Research Quarterly, 56*(S1), S231–S238.

Almasi, J. F., & Yuan, D. (2023). Reading comprehension and the COVID-19 pandemic: What happened and what can we do about it? *The Reading Teacher, 77*(3), 383–391.

AM, M. A., Hadi, S., Istiyono, E., & Retnawati, H. (2023). Does differentiated instruction affect learning outcome? Systematic review and meta-analysis. *Journal of Pedagogical Research, 7*(5), 18–33.

Arciuli, J. (2017). The multi-component nature of statistical learning. *Philosophical Transactions of the Royal Society B: Biological Sciences, 372*(1711), Article 20160058.

Arciuli, J. (2018). Reading as statistical learning. *Language, Speech, and Hearing Services in Schools, 49*(3S), 634–643.

Benevides, M. (2015, April 23). *Extensive reading—How easy is easy?* [PowerPoint slides]. SlideShare. Accessed at www.slideshare.net/MarcosBenevides/how-easy-is-easy on May 23, 2024.

Benjamin, L. (2012). *Fly to the rescue!* Boston: Houghton-Mifflin.

Birch, R., Sharp, H., Miller, D., Ritchie, D., & Ledger, S. (2022). *A systematic literature review of decodable and levelled reading books for reading instruction in primary school contexts: An evaluation of quality research evidence.* Callaghan, New South Wales, Australia: The University of Newcastle, Australia. Accessed at www.newcastle.edu.au/__data/assets/pdf_file/0020/804611/Systematic-Literature -Review-UON-Decodable-and-Levelled-Books-PDF.pdf on May 23, 2024.

Brady, S. (2020). *A 2020 perspective on research findings on alphabetics (phoneme awareness and phonics): Implications for instruction (expanded version).* Accessed at www.thereadingleague.org/wp-content /uploads/2020/10/Brady-Expanded-Version-of-Alphabetics-TRLJ.pdf on May 23, 2024.

Bulat, J., Dubeck, M., Green, P., Harden, K., Henny, C., Mattos, M., et al. (2017, February). *What works in early grade literacy instruction* (Publication No. OP-0039-1702) [Occasional paper]. Research Triangle Park, NC: RTI Press. Accessed at https://dpjh8al9zd3a4.cloudfront.net/rti-press -publication/what-works-early-grade-literacy-instruction/fulltext.pdf on May 24, 2024.

Burden, P. R., & Byrd, D. M. (2019). *Methods for effective teaching: Meeting the needs of all students* (8th ed.). Hoboken, NJ: Pearson Education.

Cala, R. F. (2019). Integrating graphic organizers in lesson packages and its effect to students' levels of conceptual understanding. *International Journal of Secondary Education, 7*(4), 89–100.

Caravolas, M., Lervåg, A., Defior, S., Seidlová-Málková, G., & Hulme, C. (2013). Different patterns, but equivalent predictors, of growth in reading in consistent and inconsistent orthographies. *Psychological Science, 24*(8), 1398–1407.

Caravolas, M., Lervåg, A., Mikulajová, M., Defior, S., Seidlová-Málková, G., & Hulme, C. (2019). A cross-linguistic, longitudinal study of the foundations of decoding and reading comprehension ability. *Scientific Studies of Reading, 23*(5), 386–402.

Castles, A., Rastle, K., & Nation, K. (2018). Ending the reading wars: Reading acquisition from novice to expert. *Psychological Science in the Public Interest, 19*(1), 5–51.

Catts, H. W. (2021–2022, Winter). Rethinking how to promote reading comprehension. *American Educator, 45*(4), 26–33.

Celik, B. (2019). Developing writing skills through reading. *International Journal of Social Sciences and Educational Studies, 6*(1), 206–214.

Chall, J. S. (1983). *Stages of reading development.* New York: McGraw-Hill.

Clark, S. K. (2020). Examining the development of teacher self-efficacy beliefs to teach reading and to attend to issues of diversity in elementary schools. *Teacher Development, 24*(2), 127–142.

Connor, C. M., Morrison, F. J., Fishman, B., Crowe, E. C., Al Otaiba, S., & Schatschneider, C. (2013). A longitudinal cluster-randomized controlled study on the accumulating effects of individualized literacy instruction on students' reading from first through third grade. *Psychological Science, 24*(8), 1408–1419.

Conradi Smith, K., Amendum, S. J., & Williams, T. W. (2022). Maximizing small-group reading instruction. *The Reading Teacher, 76*(3), 348–356.

Conrad, N. J., Kennedy, K., Saoud, W., Scallion, L., & Hanusiak, L. (2019). Establishing word representations through reading and spelling: Comparing degree of orthographic learning. *Journal of Research in Reading, 42*(1), 162–177.

Council of Chief State School Officers. (2024a, February). *Science of reading legislation and implementation state scan.* Accessed at https://753a0706.flowpaper.com/SoRStateScan/#page=1 on August 23, 2024.

Council of Chief State School Officers. (2024b, March). *State-by-state scan: Science of reading legislation and implementation.* Accessed at https://app.powerbi.com/view?r=eyJrIjoiNDllZmU0ZGEtNTI2Y y00ZTNkLTg5ODctMzNlNGY3MjY0MTc3IiwidCI6IjIyNGZjMGYwLTg5OTQtNGZiYy1iM DAxLTgxZGFhNzFkMGEzMyIsImMiOjF9 on August 23, 2024.

Dehaene, S. (2013). Inside the letterbox: How literacy transforms the human brain. *Cerebrum, 7.*

Dessemontet, R. S., Martinet, C., de Chambrier, A.-F., Martini-Willemin, B.-M., & Audrin, C. (2019). A meta-analysis on the effectiveness of phonics instruction for teaching decoding skills to students with intellectual disability. *Educational Research Review, 26*, 52–70.

Dew, T. P., Swanto, S., & Pang, V. (2021). The effectiveness of reciprocal teaching as reading comprehension intervention: A systematic review. *Journal of Nusantara Studies, 6*(2), 156–184.

Diamond, L. (n.d.). *Small-group reading instruction and mastery learning: The missing practices for effective and equitable foundational skills instruction.* Alameda, CA: Center for the Collaborative

Classroom. Accessed at https://cdn.collaborativeclassroom.org/white-paper/small-group
-reading-instruction-and-mastery-learning.pdf on October 22, 2023.

DiGilio, A. (2022). *Daphne Dragon*. New York: Guided Readers.

Dijkstra, E. M., Walraven, A., Mooji, T., & Kirschner, P. A. (2016). Improving kindergarten
teachers' differentiation practices to better anticipate student differences. *Educational Studies*,
42(4), 357–377.

Dong, Y., Tang, Y., Chow, B. W.-Y., Wang, W., & Dong, W.-Y. (2020). Contribution of vocabulary
knowledge to reading comprehension among Chinese students: A meta-analysis. *Frontiers in
Psychology*, *11*, Article 525369.

Dubé, F., Dorval, C., & Bessette, L. (2013). Flexible grouping, explicit reading instruction in elementary
school. *Journal of Instructional Pedagogies*, *10*, 1–12.

Duke, N. K., & Cartwright, K. B. (2021). The science of reading progresses: Communicating advances
beyond the simple view of reading. *Reading Research Quarterly*, *56*(S1), S25–S44.

Duke, N. K., & Mesmer, H. A. E. (2018–2019, Winter). Phonics faux pas: Avoiding instructional
missteps in teaching letter-sound relationships. *American Educator*, *42*(4), 12–16.

Duke, N. K., Ward, A. E., & Pearson, P. D. (2021). The science of reading comprehension instruction.
The Reading Teacher, *74*(6), 663–672.

Ehri, L. C. (1995). Phases of development in learning to read words by sight. *Journal of Research in
Reading*, *18*(2), 116–125.

Ehri, L. C. (2005). Development of sight word reading: Phases and findings. In M. J. Snowling & C.
Hulme (Eds.), *The science of reading: A handbook* (pp. 135–154). Malden, MA: Blackwell.

Ehri, L. C. (2014). Orthographic mapping in the acquisition of sight word reading, spelling memory, and
vocabulary learning. *Scientific Studies of Reading*, *18*(1), 5–21.

Ehri, L. C. (2020). The science of learning to read words: A case for systematic phonics instruction.
Reading Research Quarterly, *55*(S1), S45–S60.

Ehri, L. C., & McCormick, S. (1998). Phases of word learning: Implications for instruction with delayed
and disabled readers. *Reading and Writing Quarterly*, *14*(2), 135–163. https://doi.org
/10.1080/1057356980140202

Ellefson, M. R., Treiman, R., & Kessler, B. (2009). Learning to label letters by sounds or names:
A comparison of England and the United States. *Journal of Experimental Child Psychology*,
102(3), 323–341.

Farrell, L., Hunter, M., & Osenga, T. (n.d.). *A new model for teaching high-frequency words*. Accessed
at www.readingrockets.org/topics/phonics-and-decoding/articles/new-model-teaching-high-
frequency-words on November 11, 2023.

Felts, S. (2019). Small group skills based instruction and reading fluency: A fourth grade classroom study.
Journal of Applied and Educational Research, *2*(1), Article 6.

Fisher, D., & Frey, N. (2013). *Engaging the adolescent learner: Gradual release of responsibility instructional
framework*. Newark, DE: International Reading Association. Accessed at https://keystoliteracy

.com/wp-content/uploads/2017/08/frey_douglas_and_nancy_frey-_gradual_release_of
_responsibility_intructional_framework.pdf on May 24, 2024.

Fisher, D., & Frey, N. (2021). *Better learning through structured teaching: A framework for the gradual release of responsibility* (3rd ed.). Arlington, VA: ASCD.

Foorman, B. R., Petscher, Y., & Herrera, S. (2018). Unique and common effects of decoding and language factors in predicting reading comprehension in grades 1–10. *Learning and Individual Differences, 63,* 12–23.

Foorman, B. R., Wu, Y.-C., Quinn, J. M., & Petscher, Y. (2020). How do latent decoding and language predict latent reading comprehension: Across two years in grades 5, 7, and 9? *Reading and Writing, 33*(9), 2281–2309.

Förster, N., Kawohl, E., & Souvignier, E. (2018). Short- and long-term effects of assessment-based differentiated reading instruction in general education on reading fluency and reading comprehension. *Learning and Instruction, 56,* 98–109.

Frey, N., Fisher, D., & Hattie, J. (2017). Surface, deep, and transfer? Considering the role of content literacy instructional strategies. *Journal of Adolescent and Adult Literacy, 60*(5), 567–575.

Fuchs, D., & Fuchs, L. S. (2005). Peer-assisted learning strategies: Promoting word recognition, fluency, and reading comprehension in young children. *The Journal of Special Education, 39*(1), 34–44.

Garden, P. D. (2022, October). Vocabulary instruction in the early grades. In K. Thomas, S. Landreth, A. Cummins, & C. Maynard (Eds.), *Texas Association for Literacy Education yearbook volume 9: TALE turns 10—A decade of literacy, service, and advocacy* (pp. 75–82). San Antonio: Texas Association for Literacy Education.

Georgiou, G. K., Papadopoulos, T. C., Fella, A., & Parrila, R. (2012). Rapid naming speed components and reading development in a consistent orthography. *Journal of Experimental Child Psychology, 112*(1), 1–17.

Georgiou, G. K., & Parrila, R. (2020). What mechanism underlies the rapid automatized naming-reading relation? *Journal of Experimental Child Psychology, 194,* Article 104840.

Georgiou, G. K., Parrila, R., Cui, Y., & Papadopoulos, T. C. (2013). Why is rapid automatized naming related to reading? *Journal of Experimental Child Psychology, 115*(1), 218–225.

Gersten, R., Newman-Gonchar, R., Haymond, K. S., & Dimino, J. (2017, April). *What is the evidence base to support reading interventions for improving student outcomes in grades 1–3?* (REL 2017–271) [Report]. Washington, DC: U.S. Department of Education. Accessed at https://files.eric.ed.gov/fulltext/ED573686.pdf on May 24, 2024.

Gilakjani, A. P., & Sabouri, N. B. (2016). How can students improve their reading comprehension skill? *Journal of Studies in Education, 6*(2), 229–240.

Goswami, U., & Bryant, P. (2016). *Phonological skills and learning to read* (Classic ed.). New York: Routledge.

Graham, S., & Santangelo, T. (2014). Does spelling instruction make students better spellers, readers, and writers? A meta-analytic review. *Reading and Writing, 27*(9), 1703–1743.

Hall, M. S., & Burns, M. K. (2018). Meta-analysis of targeted small-group reading interventions. *Journal of School Psychology, 66,* 54–66.

Hasbrouck, J., & Tindal, G. (2017). *An update to compiled ORF norms* (Technical Report No. 1702). Eugene, OR: Behavioral Research and Teaching. Accessed at https://files.eric.ed.gov/fulltext /ED605146.pdf on September 24, 2024.

Hedgcock, J. S., & Ferris, D. R. (2018). *Teaching readers of English: Students, texts, and contexts* (2nd ed.). New York: Routledge.

Henbest, V. S., & Apel, K. (2018). Orthographic fast-mapping across time in 5- and 6-year-old children. *Journal of Speech, Language, and Hearing Research, 61*(8), 2015–2027.

Henderson Megard, L. (n.d.). *Ricardo's dilemma* (D. Cockcroft, Illus.). Tucson, AZ: Learning A–Z.

Heubeck, E. (2023, September 15). *"I literally cried": Teachers describe their transition to science-based reading instruction.* Accessed at www.edweek.org/teaching-learning/i-literally-cried-teachers -describe-their-transition-to-science-based-reading-instruction/2023/09 on June 18, 2024.

Hoover, W. A., & Gough, P. B. (1990). The simple view of reading. *Reading and Writing, 2*(2), 127–160.

Hoover, W. A., & Tunmer, W. E. (2020). *The cognitive foundations of reading and its acquisition: A framework with applications connecting teaching and learning.* New York: Springer.

Hulme, C., Bowyer-Crane, C., Carroll, J. M., Duff, F. J., & Snowling, M. J. (2012). The causal role of phoneme awareness and letter-sound knowledge in learning to read: Combining intervention studies with mediation analyses. *Psychological Science, 23*(6), 572–577.

Hunter, M. (1982). *Mastery teaching.* Thousand Oaks, CA: Corwin Press.

Institute of Education Sciences. (2016, July). *Foundational skills to support reading for understanding in kindergarten through 3rd grade.* Washington, DC: Author. Accessed at https://ies.ed.gov/ncee /WWC/Docs/PracticeGuide/wwc_foundationalreading_040717.pdf on June 18, 2024.

James, K. H., Jao, R. J., & Berninger, V. (2016). The development of multileveled writing systems of the brain: Brain lessons for writing instruction. In C. A. MacArthur, S. Graham, & J. Fitzgerald (Eds.), *Handbook of writing research* (2nd ed., pp. 116–129). New York: Guilford Press.

Jefferson, R. E., Grant, C. E., & Sander, J. B. (2017). Effects of Tier 1 differentiation and reading intervention on reading fluency, comprehension, and high stakes measures. *Reading Psychology, 38*(1), 97–124.

Joseph, L. M., Alber-Morgan, S., Cullen, J., & Rouse, C. (2016). The effects of self-questioning on reading comprehension: A literature review. *Reading and Writing Quarterly, 32*(2), 152–173.

Jufrianto, M., Rahyuni, Gaffar, S., Akbal, F. A., Pratama, A. P., & Amir, A. S. (2023). Differentiated instruction in improving senior high school students' reading comprehension level. *Journal of Learning and Development Studies, 3*(2), 1–9.

Kang, E. Y., & Shin, M. (2019). The contributions of reading fluency and decoding to reading comprehension for struggling readers in fourth grade. *Reading and Writing Quarterly, 35*(3), 179–192.

Kidd, E. (2012). Implicit statistical learning is directly associated with the acquisition of syntax. *Developmental Psychology, 48*(1), 171–184.

Kidd, E., & Arciuli, J. (2016). Individual differences in statistical learning predict children's comprehension of syntax. *Child Development, 87*(1), 184–193.

Kilpatrick, D. A. (2015). *Essentials of assessing, preventing, and overcoming reading difficulties.* Hoboken, NJ: Wiley.

Kjeldsen, A.-C., Kärnä, A., Niemi, P., Olofsson, Å., & Witting, K. (2014). Gains from training in phonological awareness in kindergarten predict reading comprehension in grade 9. *Scientific Studies of Reading, 18*(6), 452–467.

Kubler, A. (1985). *Daphne dragon.* Auburn, ME: Child's Play.

Lawrence, J. F., Hagen, A. M., Hwang, J. K., Lin, G., & Lervåg, A. (2019). Academic vocabulary and reading comprehension: Exploring the relationships across measures of vocabulary knowledge. *Reading and Writing, 32*(2), 285–306.

LD Center. (2023, November 28). *Five research-based ways to teach vocabulary.* Accessed at https://texasldcenter.org/teachers-corner/five-research-based-ways-to-teach-vocabulary on September 19, 2024.

Lexile. (2018). *Lexile Framework for Reading* [Educator guide]. Accessed at https://lexile.com/wp-content/uploads/2018/09/Lexile-Educator-Guide-MM0066W.pdf on September 19, 2024.

Martinez, D., Georgiou, G. K., Inoue, T., Falcón, A., & Parrila, R. (2021). How does rapid automatized naming influence orthographic knowledge? *Journal of Experimental Child Psychology, 204,* Article 105064.

Martin, R. (1992). *The rough-face girl* (D. Shannon, Illus.). New York: Putnam.

McKeown, M. G. (2019). Effective vocabulary instruction fosters knowing words, using words, and understanding how words work. *Language, Speech, and Hearing Services in Schools, 50*(4), 466–476.

McMaster, K. L., & Fuchs, D. (2016). Classwide intervention using peer-assisted learning strategies. In S. R. Jimerson, M. K. Burns, & A. M. VanDerHeyden (Eds.), *Handbook of response to intervention: The science and practice of multi-tiered systems of support* (2nd ed., pp. 253–268). New York: Springer.

Melby-Lervåg, M., Lyster, S.-A. H., & Hulme, C. (2012). Phonological skills and their role in learning to read: A meta-analytic review. *Psychological Bulletin, 138*(2), 322–352.

Meriyati, M., Sumianto, S., Nusraningrum, D., Cheriani, C., Guilin, X., & Jiao, D. (2023). Optimizing the use of differentiated instruction strategies to accommodate diverse student needs. *Journal International Inspire Education Technology, 2*(2), 79–89.

MetaMetrics. (n.d.). *About Lexile measures for reading.* Accessed at https://metametricsinc.com/education-companies/lexile-for-reading-and-writing/about-lexile-for-reading on January 13, 2024.

Moats, L. C. (2020). *Speech to print: Language essentials for teachers* (3rd ed.). Baltimore: Brookes.

Moll, K., Ramus, F., Bartling, J., Bruder, J., Kunze, S., Neuhoff, N., et al. (2014). Cognitive mechanisms underlying reading and spelling development in five European orthographies. *Learning and Instruction, 29,* 65–77.

National Council on Teacher Quality. (2024, January). *State of the states 2024: Five policy actions to strengthen implementation of the science of reading.* Accessed at www.nctq.org/dmsView/Print-Ready_SOTS_2024_Five_policy_actions_for_reading on September 10, 2024.

National Reading Panel. (2000). *Teaching children to read: An evidence-based assessment of the scientific research literature on reading and its implications for reading instruction—Reports of the subgroups.* Accessed at www.nichd.nih.gov/sites/default/files/publications/pubs/nrp/Documents/report.pdf on May 24, 2024.

Nation, K. (2017, July 23). *Reading comprehension and vocabulary: What's the connection?* [Blog post]. Accessed at https://readoxford.org/reading-comprehension-and-vocabulary-whats-the-connection on May 28, 2024.

Nation, K. (2019). Children's reading difficulties, language, and reflections on the simple view of reading. *Australian Journal of Learning Difficulties, 24*(1), 47–73.

Neitzel, A. J., Lake, C., Pellegrini, M., & Slavin, R. E. (2022). A synthesis of quantitative research on programs for struggling readers in elementary schools. *Reading Research Quarterly, 57*(1), 149–179.

NWEA Connection. (2022, January 7). *How are Lexile scores computed?* Accessed at https://connection.nwea.org/s/article/How-are-Lexile-scores-computed?language=en_US on May 28, 2024.

Ogle, D. M. (1986). K-W-L: A teaching model that develops active reading of expository text. *The Reading Teacher, 39*(6), 564–570.

O'Reilly, T., Wang, Z., & Sabatini, J. (2019). How much knowledge is too little? When a lack of knowledge becomes a barrier to comprehension. *Psychological Science, 30*(9), 1344–1351.

Palincsar, A., & Brown, A. L. (1984). Reciprocal teaching of comprehension-fostering and comprehension-monitoring activities. *Cognition and Instruction, 1*(2), 117–175.

Parsons, S. A., Vaughn, M., Scales, R. Q., Gallagher, M. A., Parsons, A. W., Davis, S. G., et al. (2018). Teachers' instructional adaptations: A research synthesis. *Review of Educational Research, 88*(2), 205–242.

Poetry Foundation. (n.d.). *Little boy blue.* Accessed at www.poetryfoundation.org/poems/46972/little-boy-blue-56d2271bef1fa on September 13, 2024.

Poulsen, M., Protopapas, A., & Juul, H. (2023). How RAN stimulus type and repetition affect RAN's relation with decoding efficiency and reading comprehension. *Reading and Writing, 37*(1), 89–102.

Pritchard, S. C., Coltheart, M., Marinus, E., & Castles, A. (2018). A computational model of the self-teaching hypothesis based on the dual-route cascaded model of reading. *Cognitive Science, 42*(3), 722–770.

Proepper, E. (2016). *Scaffolded silent reading: More effective than sustained silent reading?* [Master's thesis, University of Wisconsin–Superior]. Minds@UW. Accessed at https://minds.wisconsin.edu/bitstream/handle/1793/75617/Proepper_ScaffoldedSilentReading.pdf?sequence=1&isAllowed=y on March 6, 2025.

Protopapas, A., Altani, A., & Georgiou, G. K. (2013). Development of serial processing in reading and rapid naming. *Journal of Experimental Child Psychology, 116*(4), 914–929.

Puzio, K., Colby, G. T., & Algeo-Nichols, D. (2020). Differentiated literacy instruction: Boondoggle or best practice? *Review of Educational Research, 90*(4), 459–498.

Ramirez-Avila, M. R., & Barreiro, J. P. (2021). The effect of summarizing narrative texts to improve reading comprehension. *Journal of Foreign Language Teaching and Learning, 6*(2), 94–110.

Reading Rockets. (n.d.). *K–5 whole-group literacy instruction: Sample schedule and activities.* Accessed at www.readingrockets.org/classroom/instructional-routines-and-grouping/k-5-whole-group on September 11, 2024.

Retelsdorf, J., Schwartz, K., & Asbrock, F. (2015). "Michael can't read!" Teachers' gender stereotypes and boys' reading self-concept. *Journal of Educational Psychology, 107*(1), 186–194.

Reutzel, D. R., & Cooter, R. B. (2023). *Teaching children to read: The teacher makes the difference* (9th ed.). Hoboken, NJ: Pearson.

Roberts, T. A., Vadasy, P. F., & Sanders, E. A. (2018). Preschoolers' alphabet learning: Letter name and sound instruction, cognitive processes, and English proficiency. *Early Childhood Research Quarterly, 44*, 257–274.

Rogde, K., Hagen, Å. M., Melby-Lervåg, M., & Lervåg, A. (2019). The effect of linguistic comprehension instruction on generalized language and reading comprehension skills: A systematic review. *Campbell Systematic Reviews, 15*(4), Article e1059.

Röthlisberger, M., Zangger, C., & Juska-Bacher, B. (2023). Matthew effect in vocabulary and reading: A comparison of good and average readers in grade 1 to grade 3. *International Journal of Educational Research Open, 5*, Article 100278.

Ruotsalainen, J., Pakarinen, E., Poikkeus, A.-M., & Lerkkanen, M.-K. (2022). Literacy instruction in first grade: Classroom-level associations between reading skills and literacy instruction activities. *Journal of Research in Reading, 45*(1), 83–99.

Savage, R., Georgiou, G., Parrila, R., & Maiorino, K. (2018). Preventative reading interventions teaching direct mapping of graphemes in texts and set-for-variability aid at-risk learners. *Scientific Studies of Reading, 22*(3), 225–247.

Scarborough, H. S. (2001). Connecting early language and literacy to later reading (dis)abilities: Evidence, theory, and practice. In S. B. Neuman & D. K. Dickinson (Eds.), *Handbook of early literacy research* (Vol. 1, pp. 97–110). New York: Guilford Press.

Schmitt, N., Jiang, X., & Grabe, W. (2011). The percentage of words known in a text and reading comprehension. *The Modern Language Journal, 95*(1), 26–43.

Sedita, J. (2005). Effective vocabulary instruction. *Insights on Learning Disabilities, 2*(1), 33–45.

Seidenberg, M. (2017). *Language at the speed of sight: How we read, why so many can't, and what can be done about it.* New York: Basic Books.

Shanahan, T. (2015, October 18). *To Lexile or not to Lexile, that is the question* [Blog post]. Accessed at www.shanahanonliteracy.com/blog/to-lexile-or-not-to-lexile-that-is-the-question on May 28, 2024.

Shanahan, T. (2016, March 14). *Putting on your underwear first: Why instructional sequence doesn't always matter* [Blog post]. Accessed at www.shanahanonliteracy.com/blog/putting-on-your-underwear -first-why-instructional-sequence-doesnt-always-matter on May 28, 2024.

Shanahan, T. (2020, September 12). *Seatwork that makes sense for reading* [Blog post]. Accessed at www .shanahanonliteracy.com/blog/seatwork-that-makes-sense-for-reading on May 28, 2024.

Shanahan, T. (2021a, February 6). *Letter names or sounds first?. . .you might be surprised by the answer* [Blog post]. Accessed at www.shanahanonliteracy.com/blog/letter-names-or-sounds-first-you-might-be-surprised-by-the-answer on May 28, 2024.

Shanahan, T. (2021b, March 13). *On eating elephants and teaching syllabication* [Blog post]. Accessed at www.shanahanonliteracy.com/blog/on-eating-elephants-and-teaching-syllabication on May 28, 2024.

Shanahan, T. (2022, June 4). *Print-to-speech or speech-to-print? That is the question* [Blog post]. Accessed at www.shanahanonliteracy.com/blog/print-to-speech-or-speech-to-print-that-is-the-question on October 30, 2023.

Shanahan, T. (2023, December 2). *Why main idea is not the main idea—or, how to teach reading comprehension* [Blog post]. Accessed at www.shanahanonliteracy.com/blog/why-main-idea-is-not-the-main-idea-or-how-best-to-teach-reading-comprehension on May 28, 2024.

Share, D. L. (2004). Knowing letter names and learning sounds: A causal connection. *Journal of Experimental Child Psychology, 88*(3), 213–233.

Share, D. L. (2011). On the role of phonology in reading acquisition: The self-teaching hypothesis. In S. A. Brady, D. Braze, & C. A. Fowler (Eds.), *Explaining individual differences in reading: Theory and evidence* (pp. 45–68). New York: Psychology Press.

Sinambela, E., Manik, S., & Pangaribuan, R. E. (2015). Improving students' reading comprehension achievement by using K-W-L strategy. *English Linguistics Research, 4*(3), 13–29.

Socol, A. R. (2024, January 17). *The literacy crisis in the U.S. is deeply concerning—and totally preventable* [Blog post]. Accessed at https://edtrust.org/the-equity-line/the-literacy-crisis-in-the-u-s-is-deeply-concerning-and-totally-preventable on May 28, 2024.

Sparks, R. L., Patton, J., & Murdoch, A. (2014). Early reading success and its relationship to reading achievement and reading volume: Replication of "10 years later." *Reading and Writing, 27*(1), 189–211.

Spear-Swerling, L. (2019). Here's why schools should use structured literacy. *The Examiner, 8*(2).

Spencer, M., Kaschak, M. P., Jones, J. L., & Lonigan, C. J. (2015). Statistical learning is related to early literacy-related skills. *Reading and Writing, 28*(4), 467–490.

Steacy, L. M., Wade-Woolley, L., Rueckl, J. G., Pugh, K., Elliott, J. D., & Compton, D. L. (2019). The role of set for variability in irregular word reading: Word and child predictors in typically developing readers and students at-risk for reading disabilities. *Scientific Studies of Reading, 23*(6), 523–532.

Stockard, J., Wood, T. W., Coughlin, C., & Rasplica Khoury, C. (2018). The effectiveness of direct instruction curricula: A meta-analysis of a half century of research. *Review of Educational Research, 88*(4), 479–507.

Suggate, S. P. (2016). A meta-analysis of the long-term effects of phonemic awareness, phonics, fluency, and reading comprehension interventions. *Journal of Learning Disabilities, 49*(1), 77–96.

Treiman, R. (2018). What research tells us about reading instruction. *Psychological Science in the Public Interest, 19*(1), 1–4.

Treiman, R., Pennington, B. F., Shriberg, L. D., & Boada, R. (2008). Which children benefit from letter names in learning letter sounds? *Cognition, 106*(3), 1322–1338.

Treiman, R., Sotak, L., & Bowman, M. (2001). The roles of letter names and letter sounds in connecting print and speech. *Memory and Cognition, 29*(6), 860–873.

Valiandes, S. (2015). Evaluating the impact of differentiated instruction on literacy and reading in mixed ability classrooms: Quality and equity dimensions of education effectiveness. *Studies in Educational Evaluation, 45*, 17–26.

Vaughn, M., Parsons, S. A., & Massey, D. (2020). Aligning the science of reading with adaptive teaching. *Reading Research Quarterly, 55*(S1), S299–S306.

Walpole, S., & McKenna, M. C. (2017). *How to plan differentiated reading instruction: Resources for grades K–3* (2nd ed.). New York: Guilford Press.

Wanzek, J., Petscher, Y., Al Otaiba, S., Rivas, B. K., Jones, F. G., Kent, S. C., et al. (2017). Effects of a year long supplemental reading intervention for students with reading difficulties in fourth grade. *Journal of Educational Psychology, 109*(8), 1103–1119.

Wanzek, J., Wood, C., & Schatschneider, C. (2023). Teacher vocabulary use and student language and literacy achievement. *Journal of Speech, Language, and Hearing Research, 66*(9), 3574–3587.

Wasowicz, J. (2021). A speech-to-print approach to teaching reading. *LDA Bulletin, 53*(2), 10–18.

Wolff, U. (2014). RAN as a predictor of reading skills, and vice versa: Results from a randomised reading intervention. *Annals of Dyslexia, 64*(2), 151–165.

Young, T. T. (2023). Redesigning for equity and achievement: Non-leveled guided reading instruction. *Reading and Writing Quarterly, 39*(1), 54–71.

Index

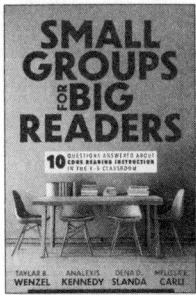

Small Groups for Big Readers
Taylar B. Wenzel, Analexis Kennedy, Dena D. Slanda, and Melissa R. Carli

The authors advocate for small-group reading instruction as an effective way for teachers to help all students grow as skilled, developing readers. Through small-group instruction, K–5 teachers can better identify individual student learning interests, needs, and goals.

BKG189

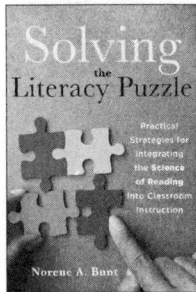

Solving the Literacy Puzzle
Norene A. Bunt

Using graphic organizers, assessments, and reflection questions, educators can unpack five core components of literacy instruction within the science of reading framework. This comprehensive guide prepares teachers to confidently implement effective literacy instruction in their classrooms.

BKG158

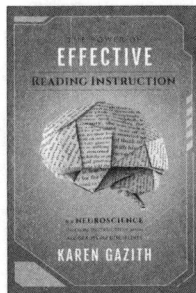

The Power of Effective Reading Instruction
Karen Gazith

Through research-supported tools and strategies, this book explores how children learn to read and how neuroscience should inform reading practices in schools. K–12 educators will find resources and reproducible tools to effectively implement reading instruction and interventions, no matter the subject taught.

BKG104

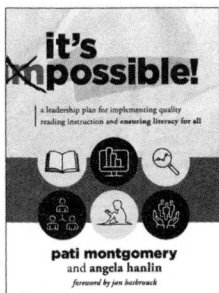

It's Possible!
Pati Montgomery and Angela Hanlin

Based on research regarding how to improve outcomes for students and highly effective schools, leaders, including principals, now have a reliable guide to ensure universal literacy instruction while supporting their teachers and increasing reading proficiency for all students.

BKG161

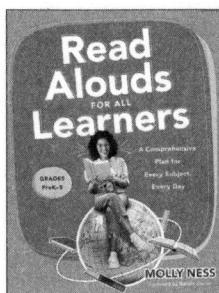

Read Alouds for All Learners
Molly Ness
Foreword By: Natalie Wexler

In *Read Alouds for All Learners: A Comprehensive Plan for Every Subject, Every Day, Grades PreK–8*, Molly Ness provides a compelling case for the integration, or reintegration, of the read aloud in schools and a step-by-step resource for preK–8 educators in classrooms.

BKG116